SHARKS

SHARKS

CONSULTANT EDITOR

John D. Stevens

Checkmark Books™

An imprint of Facts On File, Inc.

Published in the United States by
Checkmark Books
An imprint of Facts On File, Inc.
11 Penn Plaza, New York, NY 10001

Conceived and produced by Weldon Owen Pty Limited
59 Victoria Street, McMahons Point, NSW 2060, Australia
A member of the Weldon Owen Group of Companies
Sydney ¶ San Francisco

First published in 1987
Second edition 1999
Copyright © Weldon Owen Pty Limited 1999

Publisher: Sheena Coupe
Associate Publisher: Lynn Humphries
Editorial Assistant: Sarah Anderson
Index: Garry Cousins
Art Director: Sue Burk
Designer: Kylie Mulquin
Maps: Lorenzo Lucia, Greg Campbell
Production Manager: Caroline Webber
Production Assistant: Kylie Lawson
Vice President International Sales: Stuart Laurence

Checkmark Books
An imprint of Facts On File, Inc.
11 Penn Plaza
New York NY 10001

ISBN 0-8160-3990-9

A catalog record of this book is available from Facts On File.

Checkmark Books are available at special discounts when purchased in bulk quantities for
businesses, associations, institutions or sales promotions. Please call our Special Sales
Department in New York at (212) 967-8800 or (800) 322-8755

You can find Facts On File on the World Wide Web at http.//www.factsonfile.com

Printed by Kyodo Printing Co. (Singapore) Pte Ltd
Printed in Singapore

10 9 8 7 6 5 4 3 2 1

A WELDON OWEN PRODUCTION

FRONT COVER: A Caribbean reef shark cruises above the coral of its tropical habitat.

Photo by Doug Perrine/ Auscape

PAGE 1: The sand tiger is a large, heavy-bodied shark that inhabits both the seafloor and
surface waters.

PAGES 2–3: A shark rests under a ledge at the Burma Banks in the Andaman Sea.

Photo by Doug Perrine/ Auscape

PAGES 4–5: A shark with its yolk still attached illustrates one of the efficient reproductive
methods developed by these sophisticated fishes.

PAGES 6–7: The graceful pelagic blue shark lives and hunts in the open ocean and is
rarely encountered close to land.

PAGES 10–11: A diver revives a "drowning" shark, captured as part of a scientific research
program, by forcing water through its gills.

BACK COVER: A Port Jackson shark rests on the seafloor. This sedentary species is
harmless unless accidentally disturbed or handled.

Photo by Kelvin Aitken/ Ocean Earth Images

Jeff Rotman

CONSULTANT EDITOR

Dr. John D. Stevens
Principal Research Scientist,
CSIRO Marine Research, Hobart, Tasmania, Australia

CONTRIBUTORS

Dr. George H. Burgess
Senior Biologist in Ichthyology and Director of the International Shark Attack File,
Florida Museum of Natural History, University of Florida, U.S.A.

Dr. Leonard J. V. Compagno
Curator of Fishes, Head of Shark Research Center, Division of Life Sciences,
South African Museum, Cape Town, South Africa

Carson Creagh B.Sc.
Editor and natural history writer, Sydney, New South Wales, Australia

Kevin Deacon
Photographer and marine naturalist, Sydney, New South Wales, Australia

Dr. Guido Dingerkus
Director, Natural History Consultants, Goshen, New York, U.S.A.

Richard Ellis M.A.
Marine artist and author, New York, U.S.A.

Dr. Edward S. Hodgson
Professor Emeritus and Chairman of Biology, Tufts University, Medford, Massachusetts, U.S.A.

Roland Hughes B.Sc.
Former editor, *Australian Natural History*, Sydney, New South Wales, Australia

Dr. C. Scott Johnson
Research Scientist, Biological Services Branch, Naval Ocean Systems Center, San Diego,
California, U.S.A.

Chadwick S. Macfie B.Sc.
Research Assistant, Florida Museum of Natural History, University of Florida, U.S.A.

Dr. John G. Maisey
Curator and Research Chair, Department of Vertebrate Paleontology,
American Museum of Natural History, New York, U.S.A.

Richard Martin
Director, ReefQuest Expeditions, Vancouver, Canada

Dr. Arthur A. Myrberg Jr.
Professor of Marine Science, Rosenstiel School of Marine and Atmospheric Science,
University of Miami, Florida, U.S.A.

A.M. Olsen M.Sc.
Former Chief Fisheries Officer, Department of Agriculture and Fisheries,
Adelaide, South Australia, Australia

Larry J. Paul B.Sc. (Hons)
Fisheries Scientist, National Institute of Water and Atmospheric Research, Wellington,
New Zealand

Marty Snyderman
Marine photographer, cinematographer and author, San Diego, California, U.S.A.

Dr. John D. Stevens
Principal Research Scientist, CSIRO Marine Research,
Hobart, Tasmania, Australia

Dr. Leighton R. Taylor Jr.
Author and biologist, California, U.S.A.

Valerie Taylor
Marine photographer and author, Sydney, New South Wales, Australia

Dr. Timothy C. Tricas
Associate Professor, Department of Biological Sciences, Florida Institute of Technology, U.S.A.

John West
Coordinator of the Australian Shark Attack File and Operations Manager, Life Sciences,
Taronga Zoo, Sydney, Australia

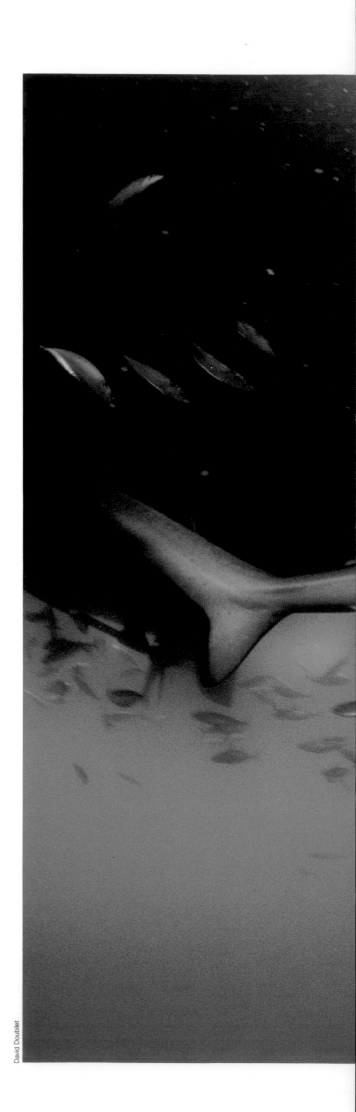

David Doubilet

CONTENTS

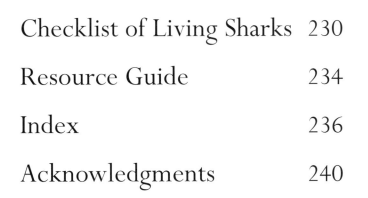

MYTH AND REALITY

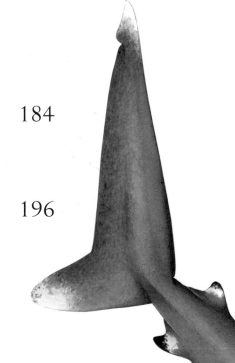

INTRODUCTION

Sharks have occasionally exacted a terrible price from humans who have trespassed on their territory. No better understood than the medium they inhabit, these animals have inspired a complex mythology that reflects the mixture of fear and fascination with which people have always regarded them. The superstition behind this mythology pervades the popular media's often morbid fascination with shark attacks. Attitudes deeply ingrained in the human psyche still persist, despite the detailed and painstaking research of recent years which has thrown new light on the biology and behavior of sharks and dispelled a great deal of mystique surrounding them.

Written by some of the world's leading experts on the subject, and global in its scope, this fully revised edition of **Sharks** presents a balanced and comprehensive survey of sharks, their habits and habitats. Its subject matter is wide, ranging from the evolution, biology and behavior of sharks, to an examination of their commercial use and place in the ecological system. There are chapters on the kinds of sharks and their distribution, and others surveying the cause and incidence of shark attacks in the waters of the United States, Australia, New Zealand, the Pacific and South Africa. Those who work with sharks or whose studies have thrown new light on these creatures write about their experiences and conclusions. Myth and reality confront each other as the latest research findings are presented along with an examination of the shark's peculiar role in myth-making, both historic and contemporary. There is new material on conservation and endangered species, and practical information on the increasingly popular activity of diving with and observing sharks in their natural habitat.

This enlightening and informative text is supported by revealing and often spectacular photographs, illustrations, maps and diagrams culled from the collections of the world's pre-eminent marine photographers or created especially for this publication.

John D. Stevens
CONSULTANT EDITOR

Jeff Rotman

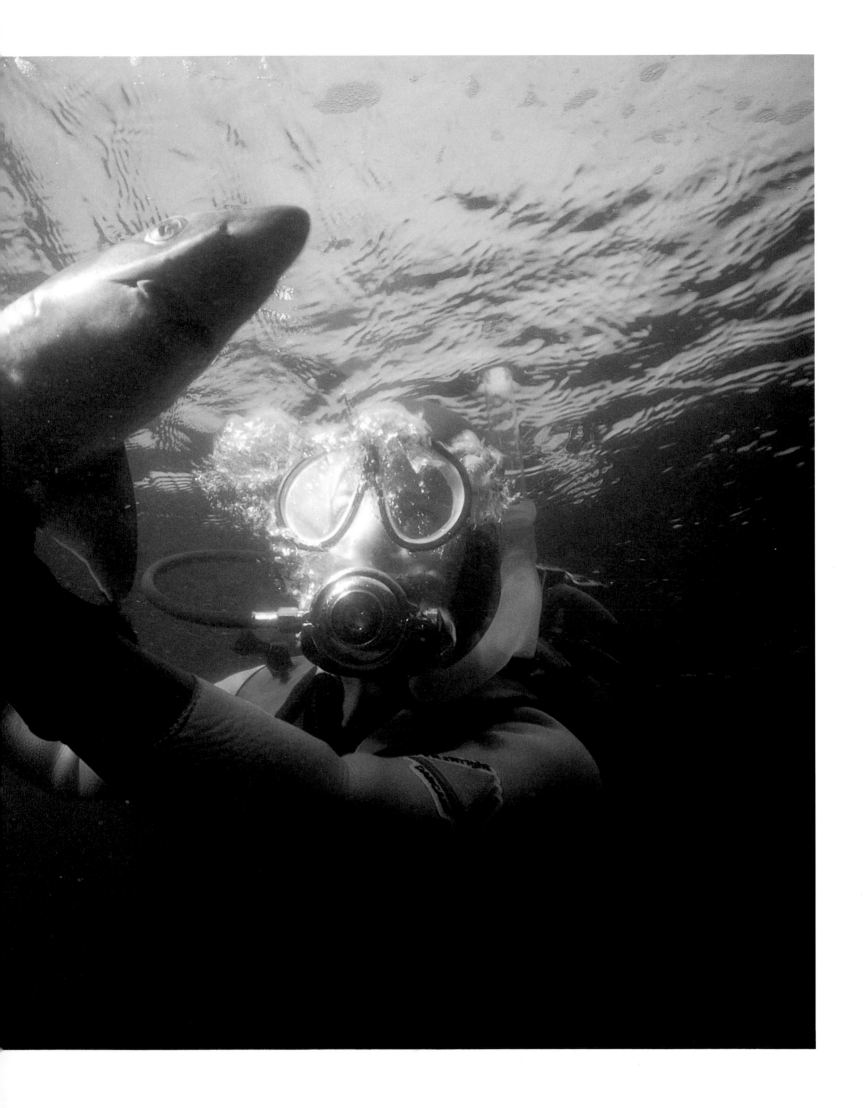

Ron & Valerie Taylor

ABOVE: Today's sharks are products of more than 450 million years of unparalleled evolutionary success.

THE SHARK

THE ORIGIN OF THE SHARK

JOHN G. MAISEY

T*he fossil record of sharks is three times as long as that of the dinosaurs. It extends back through the pages of earth history more than a hundred times as far as that of humans. This pedigree represents more than 450 million years of independent evolution. There were sharks in the oceans of the prehistoric world long before the first backboned animals crawled onto land, before the first insects took to the air, even before many plants had effectively colonized the continents. If we could be transported to that distant time, sharks would be one of the few familiar sights in a world of unfamiliar organisms.*

Familiar, but somehow different. Not the sinister profile of the great white, the streamlined hydrofoil of the hammerhead or the serrated teeth of the tiger shark. No modern sharks would be recognizable. The most ancient fossil assigned by paleontologists to a still-living group of sharks is approximately 180 million years old—certainly a respectable ancestry—but the majority of modern groups can be traced back a "mere" 100 million years.

For the most part, the shark fossil record is fragmentary. Usually all we find is their teeth, sometimes in great abundance. The oldest recognized shark fossils are microscopic scales (skin denticles) about 450 million years old. Curiously, no fossil shark teeth older than about 400 million years have been discovered, leading some scientists to suggest that the first sharks had not evolved teeth.

BELOW: A hybodont shark from the Pennsylvanian rocks of Kansas. This is one of the earliest complete examples of this group and shows that very little evolutionary change took place between 350 and 100 million years ago.

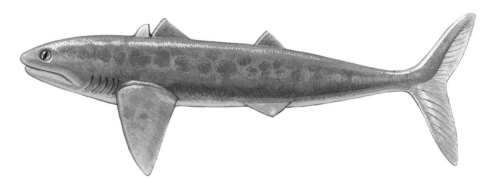

FOSSIL EVIDENCE

In exceptional cases, pieces of the internal skeleton and even complete fossil sharks have been discovered. Such finds are subjected to the most detailed investigation in order to extract the maximum scientific information. To understand why the fossil record should be so biased it is worthwhile considering some aspects of the anatomy of sharks.

Unlike a bony fish, whose head is usually sheathed by large bones and whose body is clad in big bony scales, the skin of a shark is covered from nose to tail—except around the eyes, corners of the mouth, cloaca and gills—by a fine shagreen of minute denticles. As the shark ages these denticles are periodically shed and replaced or augmented by new ones; they do not grow larger. In many ancient sharks, however, the denticles grew incrementally before they were shed. Although fossil shark denticles are abundant, they are usually overlooked, except by micropaleontologists. On the other hand, virtually every paleontologist, amateur as well as professional, has found fossil shark teeth.

Estimates suggest that over the span of just a few years a shark may grow, utilize and then discard tens of thousands of teeth. Since this prodigious output has been a characteristic of sharks for much of their history, it is small wonder that shark teeth are probably the world's most common vertebrate fossils. Besides being produced over the ages in unimaginable quantities, shark teeth are solid and resilient objects, easily prone to fossilization. The inorganic material in shark teeth is the mineral apatite (calcium phosphate), the same as in bone. Vast quantities of phosphate are therefore metabolized by sharks during their lifetimes.

Instead of internal bones, the shark has a cartilaginous skeleton, with a superficial bonelike layer broken up into thousands of isolated apatite prisms, each no larger than one of the denticles that cover the skin. When a shark dies, the decomposing skeleton rapidly disintegrates and the apatite prisms scatter. Fossil sharks have been preserved only where the bottom sediments have permitted rapid burial and there has been little disturbance by currents or scavengers.

PALEOZOIC AND LATER SHARKS

Among the most ancient and primitive sharks is *Cladoselache*, about 375 million years old, found within Paleozoic strata of Ohio, Kentucky and Tennessee. These rocks were once the soft muds that formed the floor of a shallow ocean extending over much of North America. *Cladoselache* was of unexceptional size—it was only about a meter long—with long, slender jaws and stiff triangular fins supported by elongate bars of cartilage. Its teeth had several pointed cusps that were often worn down and blunted,

evidently by prolonged use. *Cladoselache* probably did not replace its teeth as frequently as modern sharks. Its tail (caudal fin) was similar in shape to those of fast-swimming mako and white sharks. Some *Cladoselache* specimens contain whole fishes swallowed tail first. This suggests that *Cladoselache* had great speed and agility, a characteristic that no doubt helped it to avoid being eaten by the giant armored fishes (arthrodires) that were more than 6 meters long and shared the oceans with it.

We are only just beginning to understand the diversity achieved by other Paleozoic sharks. New discoveries in the United States, Europe and Australia reveal that some were armored by bladelike spines projecting from the dorsal fins. In others, only the males possessed these structures, which sometimes curved grotesquely over the head. Yet others had great spirals of serrated teeth, like slowly growing circular-saw blades, wedged under the chin. Around 350 million years ago some sharks began evolving into bizarre creatures from which the living chimaeroids (rabbitfishes) are descended.

Following this great period of shark radiation there seems to have been prolonged evolutionary stasis. From about 300 to 150 million years ago most fossil sharks can be assigned to just two

ABOVE: The long-extinct *Cladoselache* shares many characteristics with modern sharks. It was probably a swift and powerful predator.

BELOW: This gigantic xenacanth shark, almost 2 meters long, swam in the lakes and rivers of western Europe some 250 million years ago. It is so finely preserved that its sex (male) can be determined from the structure of its pelvic fin.

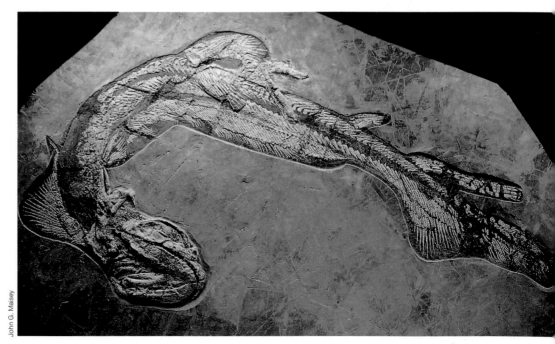

John G. Maisey

RIGHT: One of the oldest known "modern" sharks is *Palaeospinax*, from the Lower Jurassic (approximately 180 million years ago) of Europe. It has well-formed vertebrae and its teeth, scales and skeleton reveal many other advanced features.

John G. Maisey

BELOW: This photograph allows a comparison of fossil teeth from *Carcharodon megalodon* with a tooth from a present-day great white.

groups. One of these (called xenacanths) was almost exclusively confined to freshwater environments. In spite of this, between its origin (approximately 450 million years ago) and its extinction (about 220 million years ago) it achieved worldwide distribution. From such an ecologically specialized group, xenacanths achieved a remarkable longevity.

The other group (called hybodonts) appeared some 320 million years ago and was predominant in oceans and freshwater habitats throughout the age of dinosaurs, during the Triassic and Jurassic periods. The hybodonts were gradually ousted by modern forms toward the end of that era and finally become extinct at the same time as the last dinosaurs. Dinosaur and hybodont fossils occur together in Upper Cretaceous strata of Wyoming.

THE "MODERN" PERIOD

What is the earliest geological record of modern sharks? Fossil mako and mackerel shark teeth occur approximately 100 million years ago, and teeth of primitive carcharhinids are recorded soon after. The oldest white shark teeth date from 60 to 65 million years ago.

Early in white shark evolution there are at least two lineages: one with coarsely serrated teeth that probably gave rise to the modern great whites, and another with finely serrated teeth and a tendency to attain gigantic size. This group reached maximum development worldwide during the Miocene (approximately 10–25 million years ago) and includes the gargantuan *Carcharodon megalodon*, whose teeth exceed 18 centimeters in height and whose body length may have exceeded 12 meters.

What factors contributed to the rise of the large predatory sharks like the great white? It may be significant that their first appearance coincides with the extinction of dinosaurs and the widespread diversification of mammals. We know that some early mammalian groups evolved into aquatic forms around that time. Certainly, wherever we find fossil teeth of the big sharks we also get an abundance of marine mammal bones, and these bones frequently show signs of having been chewed on by sharks. One scenario, then, would link later shark evolution with the rise of marine mammals, some 60 million years ago.

Ron & Valerie Taylor

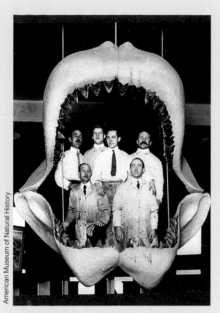

ABOVE: The grand-daddy of them all, Professor Bashford Dean's reconstruction of *Carcharodon megalodon* in New York's Museum of Natural History. Modern calculations suggest it is considerably oversized.

ABOVE: Another *bête ancienne*, this time hanging from the ceiling of the Natural History Museum in Brussels, with a string of vertebrae for good measure.

RECONSTRUCTING AN ANCIENT MONSTER
CARCHARODON MEGALODON

In 1982 John Maisey was invited to oversee the construction of a new restoration of the jaws of *Carcharodon megalodon* for the Smithsonian Institution in Washington, DC. It had been known for years that the original reconstruction by Professor Bashford Dean (in the American Museum of Natural History, New York) was grossly oversized and technically inaccurate. Since Dean's model several other, more or less fanciful, attempts had been made to reproduce the jaws of the ancient monster. The opportunity for a more authentic restoration stemmed from the discovery of a partial set of Miocene teeth in a North Carolina phosphate quarry by Pete Harmatuk, an avid amateur collector. When more data about an individual fossil white shark came to light, it was possible to make accurate comparisons with modern great whites and to come up with a more reasonable restoration.

The Smithsonian's version went on public display in October 1985. To the great disappointment of some people, the jaws in the new restoration are only two-thirds the size of those in Professor Dean's version.

BELOW: Shark jaws, fanciful and otherwise. The version at left, bearing an uncanny resemblance to a set of dentures, hangs in a Massachusetts college. The teeth have been simply graded according to size and are inserted back-to-front. The concrete choppers in the center delight a visitor to Florida Marineland. The jaws below are the 1985 restoration now hanging in the Smithsonian Institution in Washington, DC.

ABOVE: The sand tiger is also known as the gray nurse or spotted raggedtooth shark.

Kevin Deacon/Auscape

WHAT'S IN A NAME?

CARSON CREAGH

Requiem or whaler . . . gray nurse or sand tiger? The confusing variety of common names we use for sharks (and, indeed, for all animals) can mean that two people may be talking about the same animal and not know it. *Carcharias taurus*—the sand tiger, according to the International Commission on Zoological Nomenclature—is known as the gray nurse in Australia. In North America and New Zealand, it is referred to as the sand tiger; in South Africa it is the spotted raggedtooth shark.

The variety of names given to this species seems to stem from its appearance and from media coverage of shark attacks. It is a fierce-looking shark, with long, protruding teeth and the yellow eyes we would like to associate with the terror of the oceans. In fact, as shark expert Dr. Leonard Compagno has recorded, it is relatively inoffensive and unaggressive unless provoked. Its unwarranted reputation as a maneater seems to be due to no more than its name: "gray nurse" looks much more stirring in a newspaper headline than "whaler," which is the Australian common name for members of the family Carcharhinidae, to which most of the sharks known to be responsible for attacks on humans belong.

How much more stirring, though, is "requiem," with its funereal associations, than "whaler"? Perhaps if Australians had adopted "requiem" instead of "whaler" to describe sharks that are truly dangerous, the inoffensive gray nurse would not have been killed in such numbers by divers. No doubt they felt they were ridding the waters of danger but, as Compagno says, theirs was a "crude and barbaric sport, analogous to shooting domestic cattle with a pistol." The decline in numbers that resulted from such "sport" has, fortunately, been halted and the gray nurse is now a protected species in Australia.

It seems that dangerous sharks attract the greatest number of common names. *Carcharodon carcharias*, the great white shark, is also known as the white pointer, the white shark, the great blue shark, or, dramatically, as white death. The shortfin mako *Isurus oxyrinchus* is sometimes called the blue pointer; a name that causes confusion with the blue shark *Prionace glauca* and the great white—or blue—shark.

The value of scientific names is therefore to remove much of this confusion: a single, internationally recognized name that not only defines a particular species but helps to place it in a standardized taxonomic position. Taxonomy (from the Greek words *tasso*, to arrange, and *nomia*, distribution) refers to the classification of organisms within related groups of various sizes. Sharks belong to the phylum Chordata, the subphylum Vertebrata, the class Chondricthyes, one of eight orders, 29 families, around 99 genera and approximately 350 species.

The cautious "around" 99 genera and "approximately" 350 species are indications of the dynamic nature of taxonomy: new species, and new discoveries about familiar species, keep the classification of all organisms in a state of flux. In 1984, Dr. Leonard Compagno noted that four species of shark—the Australian school shark, the commercially important soupfin

Ron & Valerie Taylor

ABOVE: The great white shark's alternative common name—white death—was conferred in recognition of its awesome power.

shark, the north Atlantic tope and the South American vitamin shark—are all, in fact, members of the single species *Galeorhinus galeus*. The value of his discovery lies in increasing our knowledge of shark distribution and populations; knowledge that will help scientists monitor populations and fishing pressures and develop a greater understanding of the processes of shark evolution.

School sharks grow to a length of around one and a half meters. Another species, almost 10 times as long, has also been the subject of changes and not a little confusion in its scientific name. The whale shark, at nearly 14 meters the world's largest fish, has seen considerable variation in the spelling of its scientific name: from *Rhiniodon typus* to *Rhinodon*, *Rhincodon* and *Rhineodon*. The International Commission on Zoological Nomenclature decides which scientific name is most valid, usually on the basis of priority (which name was used first), and has given *Rhincodon typus* official status. The variety in this case is all the more confusing because each of the names means roughly the same thing: literally "nose-tooth."

Marty Snyderman

ABOVE: The whale shark may be unique as the world's largest fish, but its zoological history has seen a number of variations in its scientific name.

KINDS OF SHARKS

Leonard J. V. Compagno

Sharks are usually divided into eight main groups, or orders, based on common features including body and snout shape, number of gill openings, position of mouth, and the presence or absence of an anal fin and dorsal fin spines. These eight orders are further divided into 34 families and more than 350 species. On the following pages, the living sharks are reviewed by order and family in a broad phylogenetic or evolutionary order. The sharks are not drawn to size.

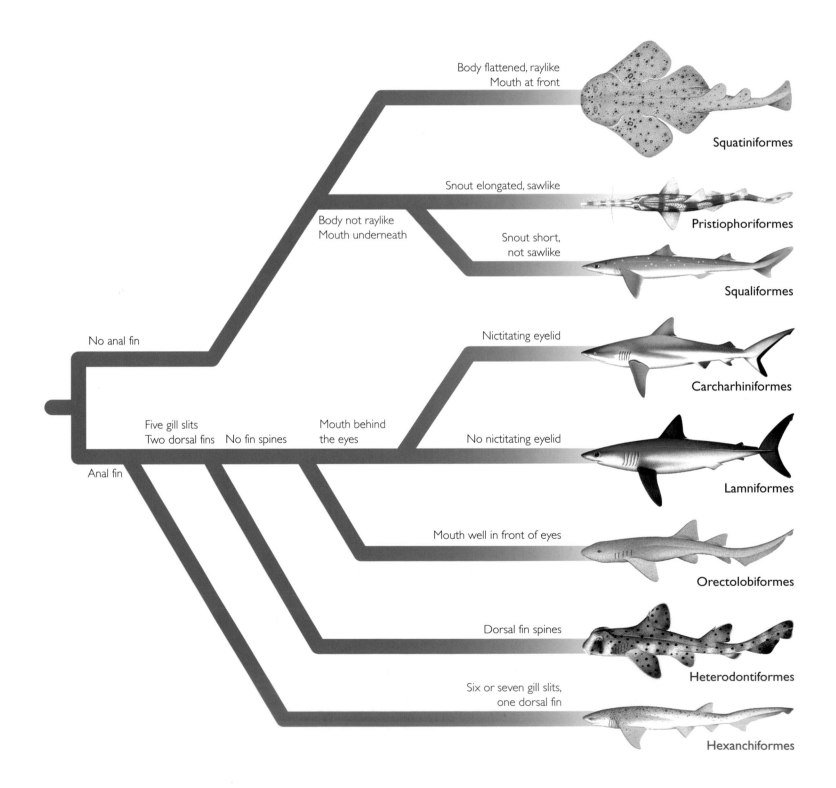

Body flattened, raylike
Mouth at front

Squatiniformes

Snout elongated, sawlike

Pristiophoriformes

Snout short, not sawlike

Squaliformes

Body not raylike
Mouth underneath

Nictitating eyelid

Carcharhiniformes

No nictitating eyelid

Lamniformes

No anal fin

Five gill slits
Two dorsal fins   No fin spines   Mouth behind the eyes

Mouth well in front of eyes

Orectolobiformes

Anal fin

Dorsal fin spines

Heterodontiformes

Six or seven gill slits, one dorsal fin

Hexanchiformes

1 ORDER HEXANCHIFORMES:
SIXGILL, SEVENGILL AND FRILLED SHARKS

Sharks with a single spineless dorsal fin, six or seven pairs of gill openings and an anal fin. This small group contains two families and at least five species, is worldwide in distribution and occurs mostly in deep water. Members of this group are ovoviviparous livebearers (the young hatch from eggs within the body).

Frilled shark
*Chlamydoselachus
anguineus*

Family Chlamydoselachidae
Frilled Sharks

SPECIES *Chlamydoselachus anguineus*, frilled shark.
APPEARANCE This slender, almost eel-like shark is unmistakable. It has a fierce-looking snakelike head with a terminal mouth, small tricuspid teeth in both jaws, six pairs of gill openings with large frilly margins and low fins.
SIZE Maximum length 1.9 meters.
HABITAT Usually on or near the bottom on outer continental and island shelves and upper slopes at depths between 120 and

1,280 meters, but occasionally inshore or at the surface.
DISTRIBUTION Scattered marine localities worldwide. This may include at least two species.
REPRODUCTION Litters of eight to 12 young and a gestation period of up to two years.
DIET Eats deepwater fishes, small sharks and bottom-dwelling and oceanic squids.

Broadnose sevengill shark
Notorynchus cepedianus

Family Hexanchidae
Six and Sevengill Sharks

NUMBER OF SPECIES Four.
APPEARANCE Heavy-bodied sharks with high fins and subterminal mouths behind long snouts. The upper teeth have high narrow cusps suitable for impaling prey; the lower, cutting teeth are like broad toothcombs. Two of the species have six pairs of gill openings; the other two have seven pairs.
SIZE The dwarf of the group, the sharpnose sevengill, does not exceed 1.4 meters; the largest, the giant bluntnose sixgill, grows to almost 5 meters.
HABITAT The two sixgills and the sharpnose sevengills occur

mostly in deeper water on outer shelves and upper slopes from 90 to 1,875 meters; the spotted sevengill favors continental shelves and breeds in shallow bays.
DISTRIBUTION Wideranging in coastal and offshore waters of all cold temperate to tropical seas. None is oceanic.
REPRODUCTION Large litters of between nine and 108 young.
DIET Relatively large prey: bony fishes, other sharks, rays, chimaeras, marine mammals, squid, crabs, shrimps and carrion. The bluntnose sixgill and broadnose sevengill are indiscriminate feeders on all kinds of carrion as well as live prey.

2 ORDER SQUALIFORMES: DOGFISH SHARKS

Sharks with two dorsal fins (often with fin spines), no anal fin, cylindrical bodies, short mouths and snouts. Many have powerful cutting teeth in both jaws. In some species these are in the lower jaw only and the upper teeth serve to hold the food.

This large and varied group contains seven families and more than 94 species. It is found in all oceans, sometimes at depths of 6,000 meters. All species are ovoviviparous livebearers.

Bramble shark
Echinorhinus brucus

Family Echinorhinidae
Bramble Sharks

SPECIES *Echinorhinus brucus*, bramble shark; *Echinorhinus cookei*, prickly shark.
APPEARANCE Large sharks with stout, cylindrical bodies, small spiracles, broadly arched mouths with smooth lips. They have no dorsal fin spines; the first dorsal fin is over the pelvic fins. The bramble shark has large, heavy platelike denticles; the prickly shark has small conical denticles.
SIZE The bramble shark reaches a length of 3.1 meters, and the prickly shark grows to about 4 meters.

HABITAT Both species are primarily deepwater slope dwellers. They range down to 900 meters but occur on the shelves in water as shallow as 11 meters.
DISTRIBUTION The bramble shark ranges widely in temperate and tropical seas. At present the prickly shark is known only as a Pacific Ocean dweller.
REPRODUCTION Litters of between 15 and 24 young.
DIET Both species eat a variety of bottom prey.

Piked dogfish
Squalus acanthias

Families Squalidae, Centrophoridae, Etmopteridae, Somniosidae and Dalatiidae
Dogfish Sharks

NUMBER OF SPECIES Formerly placed in a single family but now divided into five families: Squalidae, spurdog; Centrophoridae, gulper dogfish; Etmopteridae, lanternsharks; Somniosidae, sleeper sharks; and Dalatiidae, kitefin sharks.
APPEARANCE This diverse group ranges from very small to gigantic. They have stout to slender cylindrical, or somewhat compressed bodies, small to large spiracles, mouths that vary from broadly arched to transverse, and the first dorsal fin in front of the pelvic fins.

SIZE Some lantern and kitefin sharks are mature between 15 and 20 centimeters; many reach between 30 and 90 centimeters. The Greenland and Pacific sleeper sharks grow to 6–7 meters.
HABITAT Most dogfish sharks are found on or near the bottom on the temperate to tropical continental and insular slopes.
DISTRIBUTION Different species are found in all seas.
REPRODUCTION Litters range in size from one or two to more than 20.
DIET These sharks feed on a variety of prey.

Family Oxynotidae
Roughsharks

NUMBER OF SPECIES Five.
APPEARANCE Small, bizarre-looking sharks with high compressed bodies, rough skin, small to large spiracles, transverse mouths with lip papillae, strong dorsal fin spines and the first dorsal well in front of the pelvic fins.
SIZE Most grow to less than 1 meter long. One species sometimes reaches 1.5 meters.
HABITAT Upper continental and insular slopes and outer shelves at depths of between 40 and 720 meters.
DISTRIBUTION The family has a wide, though not uniform, distribution in temperate and tropical seas.
REPRODUCTION Litters contains seven or eight young.
DIET Bottom invertebrates and small fishes.

Prickly dogfish
Oxynotus bruniensis

3 ORDER PRISTIOPHORIFORMES: SAWSHARKS

Sawsharks are a minor group of harmless bottom sharks that resemble small sawfishes. The saw snouts are probably used to disable prey. The order comprises a single family with five or more species. All are ovoviviparous livebearers.

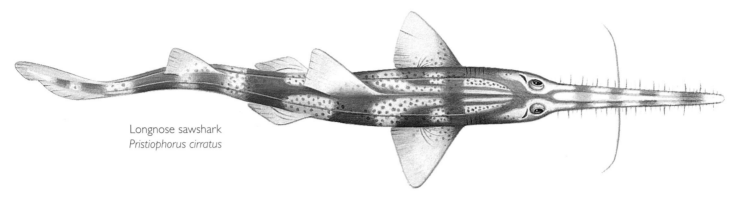

Longnose sawshark
Pristiophorus cirratus

Family Pristiophoridae
Sawsharks

NUMBER OF SPECIES Five described.
APPEARANCE Sawsharks have long, flat bladelike snouts, edged with slender, needle-sharp lateral teeth and a pair of long barbels in front of the nostrils. They have two dorsal fins and no anal fin, short transverse mouths and small cuspidate holding teeth in both jaws.
SIZE Between 1 and 1.6 meters long.
HABITAT Sawsharks occur at moderate depths on the shelves and upper slopes, on mud, sand and gravel bottoms. The Bahamas sawshark ranges down to a depth of 915 meters.
DISTRIBUTION Different species occur in the western Pacific, the western North Atlantic, the southeastern Atlantic and the western Indian Ocean.
REPRODUCTION Litters contain between five and 12 young.
DIET Small fishes, crustaceans and squid.

4 ORDER SQUATINIFORMES: ANGELSHARKS

This highly distinctive group of sharks comprises a single family of at least 15 species. All these species are ovoviviparous livebearers.

Family Squatinidae
Angelsharks

NUMBER OF SPECIES At least 15 described.
APPEARANCE Angelsharks are raylike fishes with mottled dorsal surfaces. Their large pectoral fins extend forward over the ventrally directed gills but are not, as they are in batoids, attached to the head. There are two dorsal fins and no anal fin. A short terminal mouth is armed with small impaling teeth and the caudal fin has a lower lobe longer than the upper.
SIZE The largest reach a length of 2.4 meters; most species do not exceed 1.5 meters.
HABITAT Shallow to moderate depths on the continental shelves and upper slopes from intertidal to depths of 1,390 meters. Often found half-buried on sandy or muddy bottoms during the daytime.
DISTRIBUTION Broadly distributed in cool temperate to tropical waters in most seas except the central Pacific Ocean and most of the Indian Ocean.
REPRODUCTION Litters contain between 10 and 20 or more young.
DIET Mostly small fishes, crustaceans, squid and octopuses, bivalves and sea-snails.

Pacific angelshark
Squatina californica

5 ORDER HETERODONTIFORMES: BULLHEAD SHARKS

These are the only living sharks that combine fin spines on their two dorsal fins and an anal fin. They comprise a single family that contains eight described species.

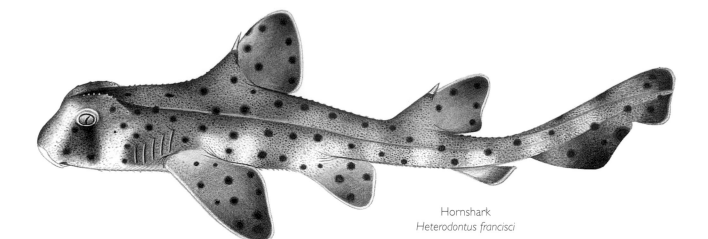

Hornshark
Heterodontus francisci

Family Heterodontidae
Bullhead Sharks

NUMBER OF SPECIES At least eight.

APPEARANCE Bullhead sharks have big, thick heads with a broad crest over each eye. They have very short, piglike snouts and short, nearly transverse mouths. Grooves connect the mouth and the nostrils. Their jaws characteristically have enlarged, flattened crushing teeth in the rear and small cusped holding teeth at the front.

SIZE Adults grow to between 55 and 165 centimeters long.

HABITAT Shallow to moderately deep continental and insular waters at depths from intertidal to at least 275 meters.

DISTRIBUTION Warm temperate to tropical waters in the western Indian and the western and eastern Pacific oceans.

REPRODUCTION Bullhead sharks are oviparous. They lay eggs enclosed in conical eggcases with screwlike flanges and sometimes terminal tendrils and deposit them in nest sites among rocks in late winter or spring. These hatch out after seven to 12 months. The young may take 10 or more years to mature.

DIET Mostly invertebrates: they crush sea-urchins, sea-stars, crabs, shrimps, barnacles, marine worms, sea-snails and other hard prey with their rear teeth. They also catch small fishes.

Port Jackson shark
Heterodontus portusjacksoni

6 ORDER ORECTOLOBIFORMES: CARPETSHARKS

This small but diverse group of seven families and at least 31 species of warm water sharks have piglike snouts and short mouths that in most species are connected to the nostrils by grooves. There is an anal fin but, unlike the bullhead sharks, no fin spines on the two dorsal fins. Carpetsharks have uniquely formed barbels at the inside edges of the nostrils.

All are warm temperate or tropical sharks of shallow to moderate depths. Their distribution centers on the tropics of the western Pacific, especially Australia, and the Indian Ocean, though some species range more widely.

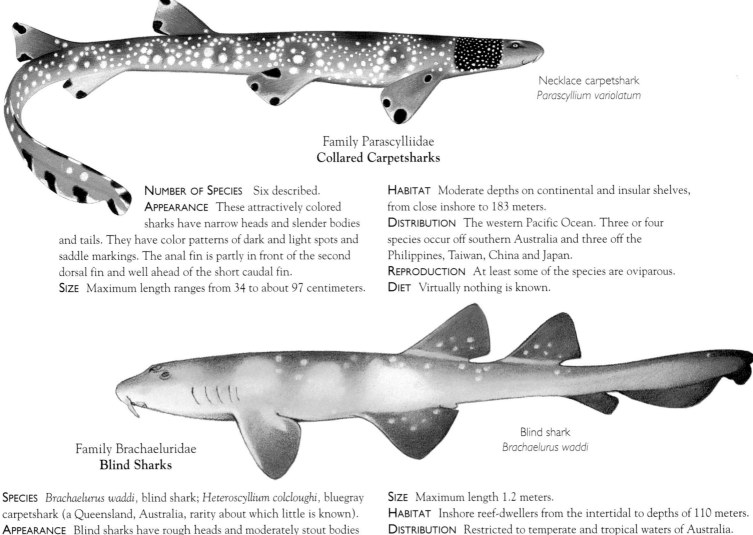

Necklace carpetshark
Parascyllium variolatum

Family Parascylliidae
Collared Carpetsharks

NUMBER OF SPECIES Six described.
APPEARANCE These attractively colored sharks have narrow heads and slender bodies and tails. They have color patterns of dark and light spots and saddle markings. The anal fin is partly in front of the second dorsal fin and well ahead of the short caudal fin.
SIZE Maximum length ranges from 34 to about 97 centimeters.

HABITAT Moderate depths on continental and insular shelves, from close inshore to 183 meters.
DISTRIBUTION The western Pacific Ocean. Three or four species occur off southern Australia and three off the Philippines, Taiwan, China and Japan.
REPRODUCTION At least some of the species are oviparous.
DIET Virtually nothing is known.

Blind shark
Brachaelurus waddi

Family Brachaeluridae
Blind Sharks

SPECIES *Brachaelurus waddi*, blind shark; *Heteroscyllium colcloughi*, bluegray carpetshark (a Queensland, Australia, rarity about which little is known).
APPEARANCE Blind sharks have rough heads and moderately stout bodies and tails. The anal fin is behind the second dorsal fin and just in front of the short caudal fin. They have small light spots or dark blotches but no elaborate color pattern.

SIZE Maximum length 1.2 meters.
HABITAT Inshore reef-dwellers from the intertidal to depths of 110 meters.
DISTRIBUTION Restricted to temperate and tropical waters of Australia.
REPRODUCTION Ovoviviparous, with seven or eight young per litter.
DIET Small fishes, crabs, shrimps, cuttlefish and sea anemones.

Family Orectolobidae
Wobbegongs

NUMBER OF SPECIES Six described (at least one undescribed).
APPEARANCE Large, flattened, broad-bodied sharks with short tails. Their cryptic coloration of spots, blotches, lines and saddles and the unique lobes of skin on the sides of the head combine to camouflage them on the sea bottom.
SIZE They reach a maximum length of 3.6 meters. Most, however, are smaller.
HABITAT On rocky and coral reefs and on the sandy bottom, from the intertidal to a depth of at least 110 meters.
DISTRIBUTION Mostly off Australia and Papua New Guinea. Two species also occur off Japan and one species is confined to the western north Pacific.
REPRODUCTION Ovoviviparous, with large litters of 20 or more young.
DIET Bottom fishes, octopuses, crabs and lobsters.

Ornate wobbegong
Orectolobus ornatus

6 ORDER ORECTOLOBIFORMES: CARPETSHARKS (CONTINUED)

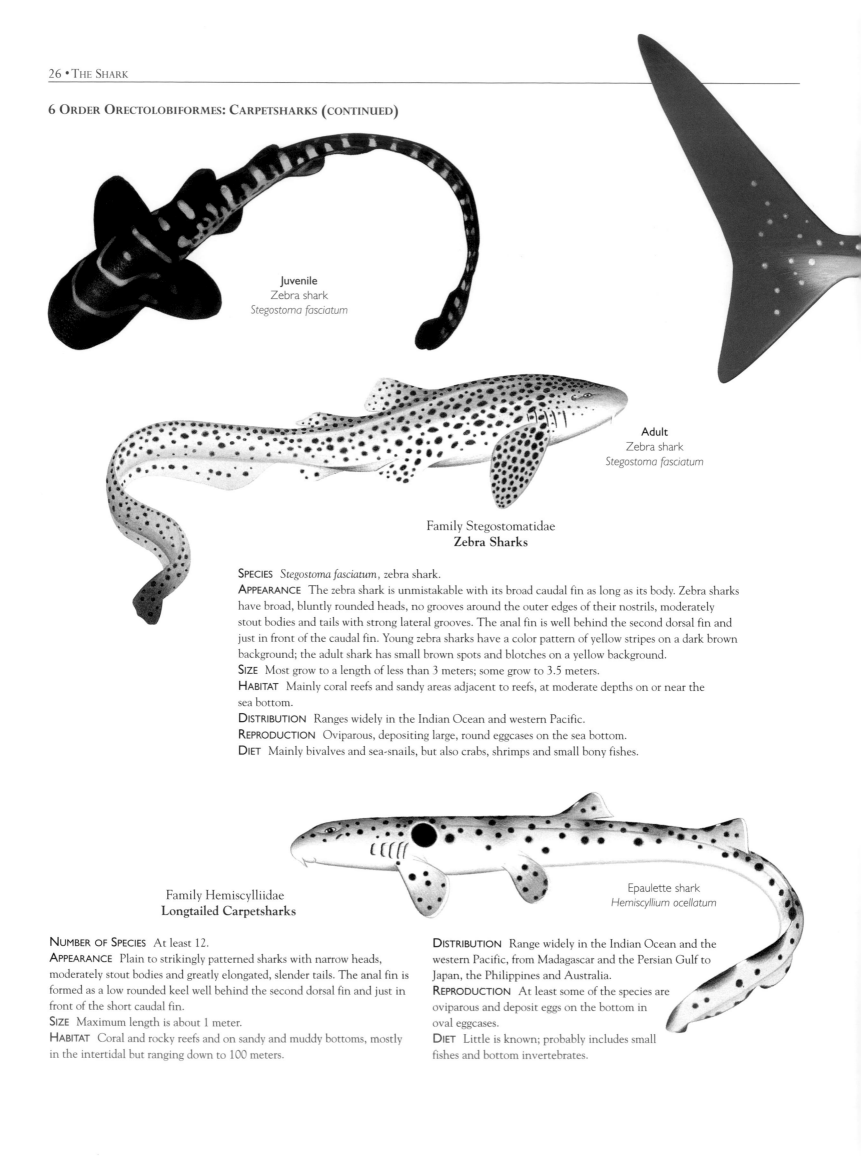

Juvenile
Zebra shark
Stegostoma fasciatum

Adult
Zebra shark
Stegostoma fasciatum

Family Stegostomatidae
Zebra Sharks

SPECIES *Stegostoma fasciatum*, zebra shark.
APPEARANCE The zebra shark is unmistakable with its broad caudal fin as long as its body. Zebra sharks have broad, bluntly rounded heads, no grooves around the outer edges of their nostrils, moderately stout bodies and tails with strong lateral grooves. The anal fin is well behind the second dorsal fin and just in front of the caudal fin. Young zebra sharks have a color pattern of yellow stripes on a dark brown background; the adult shark has small brown spots and blotches on a yellow background.
SIZE Most grow to a length of less than 3 meters; some grow to 3.5 meters.
HABITAT Mainly coral reefs and sandy areas adjacent to reefs, at moderate depths on or near the sea bottom.
DISTRIBUTION Ranges widely in the Indian Ocean and western Pacific.
REPRODUCTION Oviparous, depositing large, round eggcases on the sea bottom.
DIET Mainly bivalves and sea-snails, but also crabs, shrimps and small bony fishes.

Family Hemiscylliidae
Longtailed Carpetsharks

Epaulette shark
Hemiscyllium ocellatum

NUMBER OF SPECIES At least 12.
APPEARANCE Plain to strikingly patterned sharks with narrow heads, moderately stout bodies and greatly elongated, slender tails. The anal fin is formed as a low rounded keel well behind the second dorsal fin and just in front of the short caudal fin.
SIZE Maximum length is about 1 meter.
HABITAT Coral and rocky reefs and on sandy and muddy bottoms, mostly in the intertidal but ranging down to 100 meters.

DISTRIBUTION Range widely in the Indian Ocean and the western Pacific, from Madagascar and the Persian Gulf to Japan, the Philippines and Australia.
REPRODUCTION At least some of the species are oviparous and deposit eggs on the bottom in oval eggcases.
DIET Little is known; probably includes small fishes and bottom invertebrates.

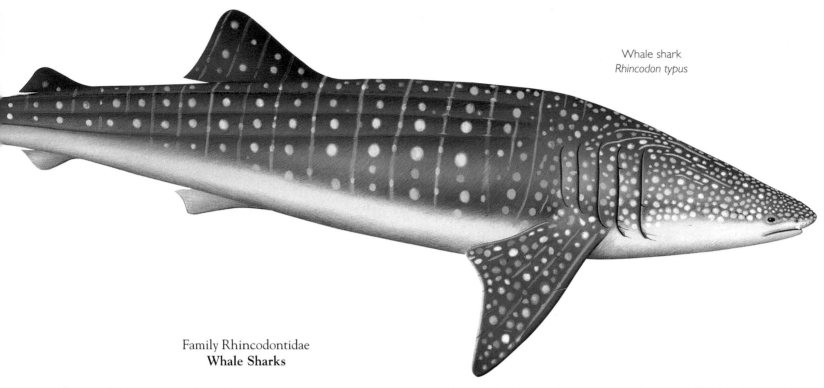

Whale shark
Rhincodon typus

Family Rhincodontidae
Whale Sharks

SPECIES *Rhincodon typus*, whale shark.
APPEARANCE This very distinctive shark has a broad flat head, truncated snout, terminal mouth and tiny teeth. It has huge gill openings, lateral ridges on the trunk and tail and a huge crescent caudal fin with a long lower lobe. Light spots and vertical horizontal lines against a dark background create a unique checkerboard color pattern.
SIZE Huge specimens, possibly 18 meters long, have been sighted. The largest accurately measured was 12.1 meters long.

HABITAT Usually near the surface, close inshore and far from land in the great ocean basins.
DISTRIBUTION All warm temperate and tropical seas.
REPRODUCTION Ovoviviparous. Previously thought to lay eggs on the substrate, but recently found to be live-bearing, with huge litters of up to 300 young.
DIET A filter-feeder that can ingest a wide variety of food organisms, from one-celled algae and minute crustaceans to mackerel and small tuna.

Family Ginglymostomatidae
Nurse Sharks

NUMBER OF SPECIES Three.
APPEARANCE These sharks vary from small to large. They have broad heads, no grooves around the outer edges of their nostrils and moderately stout bodies and tails. The anal fin is slightly behind the second dorsal fin and just in front of the short caudal fin. There is no color pattern but at most there are scattered dark spots and obscure saddles in young sharks.
SIZE The short-tail nurse shark reaches a length of only 75 centimeters; the other species exceed 3 meters.
HABITAT Off sandy beaches, mud and sand flats, and from the intertidal on reefs to depths of at least 70 meters.
DISTRIBUTION In all warm seas, including the eastern Pacific, the eastern and western Atlantic and the Indian Ocean.

REPRODUCTION At least one species, the nurse shark, is ovoviviparous and produces litters of 20 to 30 young. The tawny nurse shark has been variously reported as ovoviviparous or oviparous but was recently shown to be ovoviviparous with large fetuses that are uterine cannibals and eat unfertilized eggs.
DIET Small fishes, crabs, lobsters, shrimps, octopuses, squid, bivalves, sea-snails, sea-urchins and corals.

Nurse shark
Ginglymostoma cirratum

7 ORDER LAMNIFORMES: MACKEREL SHARKS

The mackerel sharks, with seven families and 15 or 16 species, are found in all seas except for high arctic and antarctic latitudes. Most of them have elongated snouts, long mouths that reach behind the eyes, an anal fin and two spineless dorsal fins.

They range from the intertidal to depths of more than 1,200 meters, and from the surfline to the great ocean basins. They share with some other sharks a form of ovoviviparous reproduction—uterine cannibalism—in which embryo sharks feed on their younger siblings and fertilized eggs for a protracted period before birth.

Sand tiger
Carcharias taurus

Family Odontaspididae
Sand Tiger Sharks

NUMBER OF SPECIES Three or four.
APPEARANCE These large, heavy-bodied sharks have fairly long, flattened or conical, pointed snouts, small to fairly large eyes, protrusible jaws with large, slender-cusped teeth. The gill openings are short and there are precaudal pits but no lateral caudal keels.
SIZE All species are large and reach a maximum length of between 3 and 3.6 meters.
HABITAT These sharks are associated with continental or

insular landmasses; none is oceanic. They reach depths of 190 to 1,200 meters. They occur both at the bottom and near the surface.
DISTRIBUTION Found in all warm temperate and tropical seas, though distribution of individual species may be patchy.
REPRODUCTION Only known in the gray nurse shark, which has two young per litter.
DIET Bony fishes, small sharks and rays, cephalopods and large crustaceans.

Basking shark
Cetorhinus maximus

Family Cetorhinidae
Basking Sharks

SPECIES *Cetorhinus maximus*, basking shark.
APPEARANCE A gigantic, heavy-bodied, spindle-shaped shark with minute eyes, a moderately long hooked or conical snout, a large mouth with only slightly protrusible jaws and minute hooked teeth. It has enormous gill openings that virtually encircle the head, precaudal pits and strong caudal keels, and a short, nearly symmetrical, crescent-shaped caudal fin with a long ventral lobe.
SIZE Second only to the whale shark in size. Individuals between 12.2 and

15.2 meters long have been reported, but most do not exceed 9.8 meters.
HABITAT Most abundant in cold temperate coastal continental waters. In shelf waters basking sharks occur well offshore but range right up to the surfline and into enclosed bays.
DISTRIBUTION The north and south Atlantic and Pacific oceans.
REPRODUCTION Uncertain, but presumably ovoviviparous.
DIET A filter-feeder that traps minute planktonic crustaceans, principally copepods, on rows of unique gillraker denticles.

Goblin shark
Mitsukurina owstoni

Family Mitsukurinidae
Goblin Sharks

SPECIES *Mitsukurina owstoni*, goblin shark.
APPEARANCE Perhaps remarkable for being the ugliest of living sharks, the goblin shark has a long, flat daggerlike snout, tiny eyes, a soft flabby body, long protrusible jaws with large, slender, needlelike teeth, and a long low caudal fin without a ventral lobe or precaudal pits.
SIZE Reaches a length of about 3.6 meters.
HABITAT This sluggish bottom-dwelling shark occurs mainly on the continental shelves and outer slopes in depths down to at least 725 meters. Occasionally it is found close inshore.
DISTRIBUTION Its distribution is spotty but spans most oceans, including the western and eastern Atlantic and the western Pacific Ocean.
REPRODUCTION Poorly known.
DIET Probably includes small soft-bodied prey, including fishes, shrimps and squids.

Crocodile shark
Pseudocarcharias kamoharai

Family Pseudocarchariidae
Crocodile Sharks

SPECIES *Pseudocarcharias kamoharai*, crocodile shark.
APPEARANCE It is named for its prominent, long, narrow-cusped teeth. The crocodile shark is a small, spindle-shaped oceanic shark with huge eyes, a long, conical, pointed spout, protrusible jaws and fairly long gill openings. It has precaudal pits, low lateral caudal keels and a short asymmetrical caudal fin with a moderately long ventral lobe.
SIZE Maximum length about 1.1 meters.
HABITAT Mainly in the open ocean and off continental waters.
DISTRIBUTION A spotty distribution in the eastern Atlantic, western Indian Ocean, western north Pacific, the central Pacific and the eastern Pacific.
REPRODUCTION Four young per litter.
DIET Midwater bony fishes, squid and crustaceans.

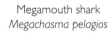

Megamouth shark
Megachasma pelagios

Family Megachasmidae
Megamouth Sharks

SPECIES *Megachasma pelagios*, megamouth shark.
APPEARANCE A large heavy-bodied, flabby, cylindrical oceanic shark with small eyes, short, bluntly rounded snout, huge mouth and protrusible jaws with very small, and numerous, hook-shaped teeth. It has short gill openings, precaudal pits but no caudal keels, and a long asymmetrical caudal fin with a moderately long ventral lobe.
SIZE Adults 4.4 to 5.4 meters long.
HABITAT Specimens have been caught offshore in the open ocean at seven to 166 meters depth in water 824 to 4,600 meters deep. They also occur inshore on continental shelves and have been washed alive onto beaches.
DISTRIBUTION Probably circumtropical, but spottily known from the Pacific, eastern Indian Ocean and central Atlantic.
REPRODUCTION Probably ovoviviparous and with uterine cannibalism, as with many other lamnoids.
DIET The megamouth is a filter-feeder on small euphausiid shrimp, copepods and pelagic jellyfish.

7 ORDER LAMNIFORMES: MACKEREL SHARKS (CONTINUED)

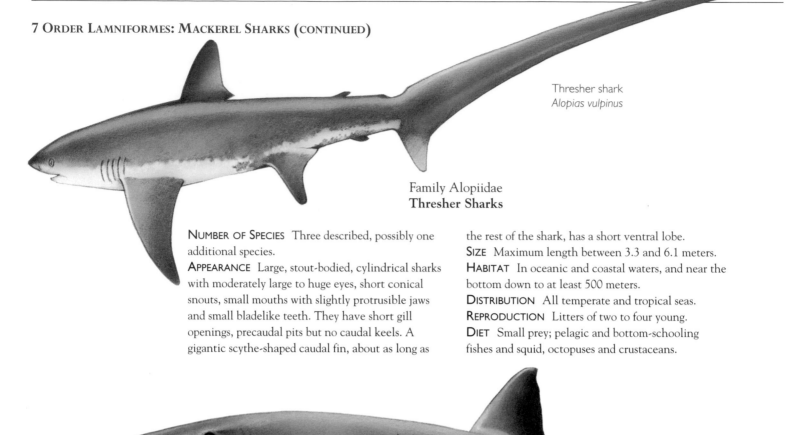

Thresher shark
Alopias vulpinus

Family Alopiidae
Thresher Sharks

NUMBER OF SPECIES Three described, possibly one additional species.
APPEARANCE Large, stout-bodied, cylindrical sharks with moderately large to huge eyes, short conical snouts, small mouths with slightly protrusible jaws and small bladelike teeth. They have short gill openings, precaudal pits but no caudal keels. A gigantic scythe-shaped caudal fin, about as long as the rest of the shark, has a short ventral lobe.
SIZE Maximum length between 3.3 and 6.1 meters.
HABITAT In oceanic and coastal waters, and near the bottom down to at least 500 meters.
DISTRIBUTION All temperate and tropical seas.
REPRODUCTION Litters of two to four young.
DIET Small prey; pelagic and bottom-schooling fishes and squid, octopuses and crustaceans.

Great white shark
Carcharodon carcharias

Family Lamnidae
Mackerel Sharks

NUMBER OF SPECIES Five.
APPEARANCE Large, heavy-bodied, spindle-shaped sharks with small to moderately large eyes, long conical snouts, large mouths and only slightly protrusible jaws with large cuspidate or bladelike teeth. The large gill openings do not encircle the head. They have precaudal pits and strong caudal keels. A short, nearly symmetrical, crescent-shaped caudal fin has a long ventral lobe.
SIZE The smallest of the group (porbeagle and salmon sharks) reach between 3 and 3.7 meters; the largest, the great white, reaches about 6 meters in length.

HABITAT Oceanic and coastal water, from the surface, intertidal, surfline and enclosed bays down to depths of 1,280 meters.
DISTRIBUTION Found in all cold temperate to tropical seas.
REPRODUCTION Litters of between two and 16 young.
DIET Small to large bony fishes, squid, other sharks and, in the case of the great white, also sea turtles, seabirds, seals, sea lions, porpoises, dolphins and carrion from dead whales and other mammals.

Shortfin mako
Isurus oxyrinchus

8 ORDER CARCHARHINIFORMES: GROUNDSHARKS

This group dominates the world's shark fauna, with approximately 215 described species and many additional species to be described. They swim in the tropics, are very common in temperate continental waters, share habitats with squaloids and other groups in deep benthic waters. Some species, such as the blue, silky and oceanic whitetip sharks, form the bulk of the oceanic sharks. The group is varied in a gradient from the most primitive small, inactive, small-toothed catsharks, through the intermediate houndsharks and weasel sharks to the large, powerful requiem sharks and hammerheads, which dominate warm seas. Most of the potentially dangerous species occur in this group.

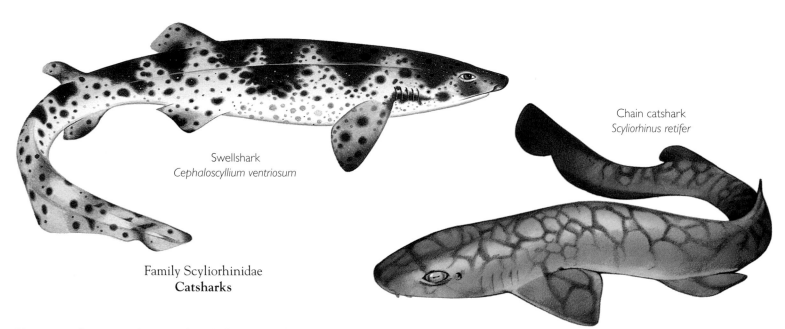

Swellshark
Cephaloscyllium ventriosum

Chain catshark
Scyliorhinus retifer

Family Scyliorhinidae
Catsharks

NUMBER OF SPECIES At least 106 described species and many more undescribed. It is by far the largest family of sharks.

APPEARANCE Small sharks with elongated, catlike eyes and large spiracles. The first dorsal fin is over or behind the pelvic fins, there are no precaudal pits and the caudal fin has no strong ventral lobe. Many of the shelf species have colorful and variegated patterns of spots, blotches, saddles, stripes and reticulations, but those found in deeper water often lack them, and range from uniform whitish or pinkish to jet black.

SIZE The largest catsharks reach a length of about 1.6 meters; most are smaller—less than 80 centimeters long—and some dwarf species do not exceed 28–30 centimeters.

HABITAT The majority of catshark species are deepwater slope sharks. None is oceanic and most occur on or near the bottom, though some deepwater slope species range well above the substrate. Catsharks occur in coastal marine waters, from the intertidal to the outer shelf.

DISTRIBUTION Catsharks have a vast geographic range in tropical to cold temperate and boreal waters in all oceans, except the Southern.

REPRODUCTION Most are oviparous and lay elongated, flattened egg cases with tendrils at their corners. A few are ovoviviparous and produce litters of from two to 10 young.

DIET Catsharks feed primarily on invertebrates.

Graceful catshark
Proscyllium habereri

Family Proscylliidae
Finback Catsharks

NUMBER OF SPECIES About five.

APPEARANCE This family of small, plain or brightly patterned sharks is very similar to the true catsharks (Scyliohinidae), but its members have their first dorsal fins positioned in front of the pelvic fins. They also have elongated, catlike eyes, comblike rear teeth, no precaudal pits and no strong ventral caudal lobe.

SIZE The pygmy ribbontail catshark matures at between 15 and 18 centimeters and is one of the smallest living sharks, but other species are mature at 28 to 65 centimeters long.

HABITAT Outer shelves and upper slopes at depths of 50 to 715 meters.

DISTRIBUTION A scattered distribution in the western north Atlantic and Indo-West Pacific.

REPRODUCTION All species are ovoviviparous livebearers, except the graceful catshark, which is oviparous.

DIET Small bony fishes, crustaceans, cephalopods and bivalves.

8 ORDER CARCHARHINIFORMES: GROUNDSHARKS (CONTINUED)

False catshark
Pseudotriakis microdon
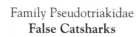

Family Pseudotriakidae
False Catsharks

SPECIES Two described species. This family includes the false catshark, *Pseudotriakis microdon*, the giant of the group; the slender houndshark *Gollum attenuata*; and an undescribed dwarf species.

APPEARANCE False catsharks are plain dark-colored sharks with large first dorsal fins on the back in front of the pelvic fins, flat heads with grooves in front of the catlike eyes, large spiracles, a large mouth, very numerous small teeth, no precaudal pits and a caudal fin without a strong ventral lobe.

SIZE Adults are between 56 and 295 centimeters long.

HABITAT Continental and insular slopes at depths of between 200 and 1,500 meters. Sometimes occurs inshore.

DISTRIBUTION Ranges widely in the north Atlantic; also occurs in the western Indian Ocean and in the western and central Pacific.

REPRODUCTION Ovoviviparous with a litter of two to four fetuses; fetuses of two species are uterine cannibals and eat unfertilized eggs.

DIET Probably feeds on a variety of deepwater bottom fishes and invertebrates.

Barbeled houndshark
Leptocharias smithii

Family Leptochariidae
Barbeled Houndsharks

SPECIES *Leptocharias smithii*, barbeled houndshark.

APPEARANCE Closely resembles the true houndsharks and the finback catsharks, but differs from both in its longer labial furrows and in combining nearly circular eyes, minute spiracles and nostrils with barbels. Its tail lacks precaudal pits and its caudal fin lacks a strong ventral lobe.

SIZE Adults are up to 82 centimeters long.

HABITAT Common at depths from 10 to 75 meters, especially off river mouths. It favors muddy bottoms.

DISTRIBUTION The West African tropics, from Mauritania to Angola; may range north off Morocco and into the Mediterranean.

REPRODUCTION Viviparous (placental livebearers) with a unique globular yolk-sac placenta; litters of seven young.

DIET Crustaceans, octopuses, sponges and small bony fishes.

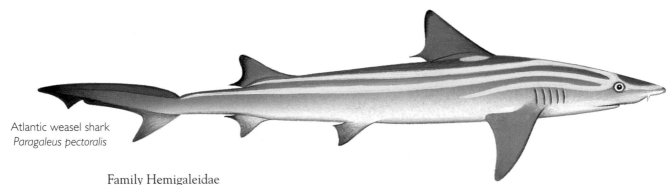

Atlantic weasel shark
Paragaleus pectoralis

Family Hemigaleidae
Weasel Sharks

NUMBER OF SPECIES Seven described.

APPEARANCE Small to moderately large sharks that are very similar to the requiem sharks. They have nearly circular eyes, small spiracles and nostrils without barbels. The first dorsal fin is in front of the pelvic fins and there are precaudal pits. The caudal fin has a strong ventral lobe.

SIZE Most do not exceed 1.4 meters in length. One species, the snaggletooth shark, reaches 2.4 meters.

HABITAT Inshore sharks, occurring in shelf waters at modest depths, from the intertidal to about 100 meters.

DISTRIBUTION Except for one species in the eastern Atlantic, weasel sharks are characteristic of the Indo-West Pacific, from South Africa and the Red Sea to Japan and Australia.

REPRODUCTION All are viviparous, giving birth to between one and 14 young per litter.

DIET Bony fishes, small sharks and rays, crustaceans, cephalopods and other invertebrates.

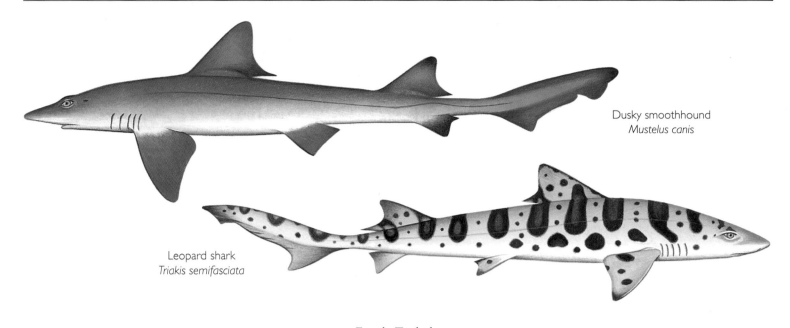

Dusky smoothhound
Mustelus canis

Leopard shark
Triakis semifasciata

Family Triakidae
Houndsharks

NUMBER OF SPECIES About 37 described species but with several others undescribed.

APPEARANCE Small to moderately large sharks with elongated to nearly circular eyes, large to minute spiracles, and nostrils with anterior flaps usually not formed as barbels. The first dorsal fin is in front of the pelvic fins, there are no precaudal pits and the caudal fin sometimes has a strong ventral lobe.

SIZE A few species reach a length of 2 meters, but most do not exceed 1.2 meters; some reach maturity at less than 30 centimeters.

HABITAT Most occur on the continental and insular shelves.

A few species are deepwater slope dwellers, and range to below 2,000 meters; none is oceanic. Houndsharks occur mostly on mud, sand and rock bottoms, commonly in enclosed bays, but at least one species occurs on coral reefs.

DISTRIBUTION Found in all tropical and temperate seas.

REPRODUCTION All are livebearers. Slightly more than half the species are viviparous; the rest are ovoviviparous. One to 52 pups per litter.

DIET Most feed on bottom-dwelling invertebrates, particularly crustaceans; some feed heavily on bony fishes and a few specialize on cephalopods. None regularly eats carrion.

Family Sphyrnidae
Hammerhead Sharks

NUMBER OF SPECIES Eight.

APPEARANCE Hammerheads are unmistakable; when viewed from above or below their expanded and flattened heads have the shape of a hammer or a mallet. They have circular, widely spaced eyes, and lack spiracles and barbels on the nostrils. The first dorsal fin is in front of the pelvic fins. They have precaudal pits and the caudal fin has a strong ventral lobe.

SIZE Five of the species are small and do not exceed 1.5 meters in length. The other three reach lengths of between 3 and more than 5 meters.

HABITAT Confined to coastal and offshore continental and insular waters, from the intertidal and surface down to at least 275 meters.

DISTRIBUTION Warm temperate and tropical seas.

REPRODUCTION All are viviparous livebearers, with litters of between four and 37 young.

DIET Bony fishes, other sharks, batoids, squids, octopuses and cuttlefish, crustaceans and sea-snails.

Great hammerhead
Sphyrna mokarran

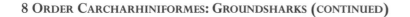

8 ORDER CARCHARHINIFORMES: GROUNDSHARKS (CONTINUED)

Blue shark
Prionace glauca

Family Carcharhinidae
Requiem sharks

NUMBER OF SPECIES 49

APPEARANCE Small to large sharks with circular or nearly circular eyes, usually without spiracles or barbels. The first dorsal fin is in front of the pelvic fins, there are precaudal pits and the caudal fin has a strong ventral lobe.

SIZE Many species are large and grow to more than 2 or 3 meters long. Some of the small species do not exceed 70 centimeters. The tiger shark reaches a length of 5.5, possibly 7.4, meters.

HABITAT A very wide habitat range: from estuaries and the intertidal to the open ocean; from muddy bays and hypersaline estuaries to coral and rocky reefs; and in freshwater rivers and lakes. None is a specialist deepwater bottom dweller but at least two species range down to 400–600 meters and

three species are truly oceanic.

DISTRIBUTION Extremely wide. Found in all tropical and temperate seas. This group dominates the tropical shark fauna in the diversity of species and often in number of individuals.

REPRODUCTION All species are viviparous except the tiger shark, which is ovoviviparous. Litters vary from one to 135, though most are between two and 20 young.

DIET Requiem sharks are among the most important large marine predators and take a broad spectrum of prey: bony fishes, sharks and rays, cephalopods, sea-snails, crustaceans, carrion, even sea-turtles, sea-snakes, seabirds and large marine mammals.

Bull shark
Carcharhinus leucas

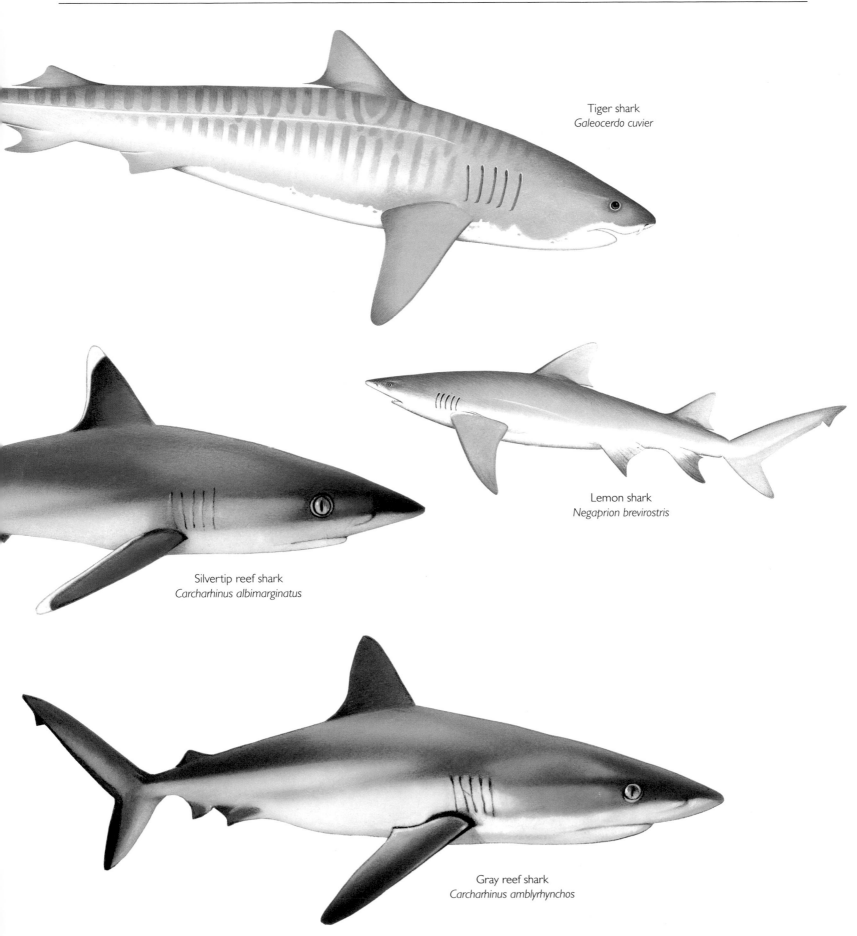

Tiger shark
Galeocerdo cuvier

Lemon shark
Negaprion brevirostris

Silvertip reef shark
Carcharhinus albimarginatus

Gray reef shark
Carcharhinus amblyrhynchos

RIGHT: Sophisticated adaptations for different lifestyles. A lemon shark *Negaprion brevirostris*, a common predator in tropical America, swims over a partially concealed stingray. The lemon shark is fast-swimming and active, hunting fish, shellfish, seabirds and small rays, while the stingray eats mollusks and crustaceans.

ABOVE: One of the many myths concerning sharks and their relatives is that they must "swim or die" since they lack swim bladders and rely on movement to force water through their gills. The myth is exploded by the success of bottom-dwelling sharks and rays, like this guitarfish, which spends most of its time partially buried in sand on the seafloor.

SHARKS AND THEIR RELATIVES

LEONARD J.V. COMPAGNO

Sharks belong to a major group, class Chondrichthyes. The other members of this group are their close relatives and derivatives—the rays, or batoids—and more distant relatives—the chimaeras and elephantfishes (Holocephali). All have mouths and nostrils on the underside of the head, ampullae of Lorenzini in the head, teeth in conspicuous rows or in fused tooth plates, scales in the form of dermal denticles, paired and unpaired fins that are supported only by cartilaginous radials and ceratotrichia (horny, cartilaginous rods). They all have simplified, cartilaginous skeletons without bone. The males have claspers and the females are fertilized internally and produce large eggs.

The approximately 600 species of batoids or rays are essentially highly modified "flat" or "winged" sharks that are most closely related to the sawsharks (Pristiophoridae). They include the sawfishes, guitarfishes, skates, torpedo rays, stingrays, butterfly rays, eagle rays, cownosed rays and mantas. They differ from other sharklike fishes in having their pectoral fins expanded forward and fused to the sides of their heads over the gill openings, so that their gill openings are on the underside of their heads. They have short, flat bodies and long tails. Some species have long, sharklike caudal and dorsal fins; other species lack them altogether. The pectoral fins supplement or replace the caudal fin as a means of propulsion.

The chimaeras, or ratfishes, are compressed cartilaginous fishes with only four gill openings that are covered with a soft gill cover or operculum without bony plates. These small, harmless, often silvery fishes differ from sharks in a number of ways: their upper jaws are fused to the braincase; the jaws are not supported by the hyoid arch; they have largely naked skins without denticles; and their rodentlike teeth consist simply of three pairs of ever-growing tooth plates. They have simplified guts and their stomachs merge with their valvular intestines. As well as pelvic claspers, a male chimaera has an unpaired frontal clasper or tenaculum on the forehead and paired prepelvic claspers or tenacula in front of the pelvic fins.

Lynn Cropp/Auscape

Jean-Paul Ferrero/Auscape

ABOVE: The manta or devilfish is one of the most spectacular members of the order Batoidea, which includes the rays, skates, guitarfishes and electric rays. Unlike most batoids, however, it is pelagic (an open-ocean dweller) and a filter feeder on plankton and small fish. Mantas grow to nearly 7 meters wide and can weigh almost 1,400 kilograms.

LEFT: The common Australian stingray or stingaree *Urolophus mucosus*, first collected by Joseph Banks in 1770, is often found in water less than 10 centimeters deep in bays and estuaries. Its caudal spine can inflict painful wounds, and fishermen or others walking in shallow water are advised to shuffle their feet to avoid being "stung."

SHARK BIOLOGY

JOHN D. STEVENS

*S*harks arose some 450 million years ago and have remained virtually unchanged for the past 70 million years. They are still a dominant group. Admittedly, they live in an environment that is fairly resistant to fluctuations and have been subject to limited interference from humans, but considering the geological time scale they have spanned, sharks appear to be exceptionally successful. Their success is due to the original "building blocks" they inherited from their primitive ancestors, but sharks demonstrate some fascinating adaptations to a variety of ecological niches and to the constraints of a demanding environment—adaptations that have enabled them to become the most important predators in the sea.

Sharks almost certainly evolved from the placoderms, a group of primitive jawed fishes. Placoderms experimented with different jaw and fin designs; the variety of these in this group is surprising. By contrast, even early sharks were fairly conservative in design and had already settled on a predatory existence similar to many of the modern forms.

BELOW: A shark's body form is closely related to its way of life. The "typical" shark, represented by the requiem family, has a streamlined body and highly efficient system of movement. Mackerel sharks are conico-cylindrical and stouter than the requiem sharks. In contrast, the angelshark is adapted to its sluggish bottom-dwelling existence.

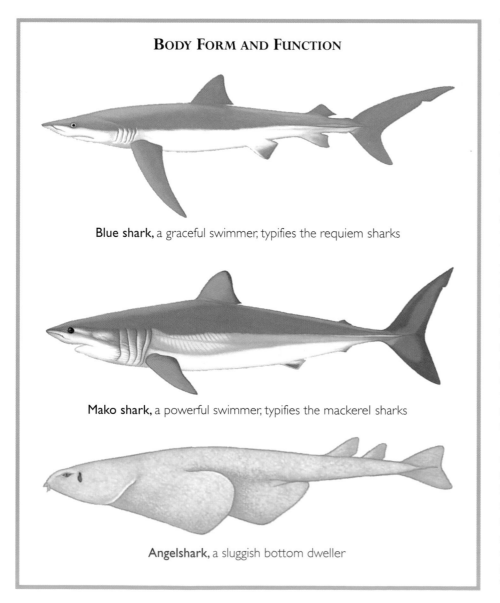

BODY FORM AND FUNCTION

Blue shark, a graceful swimmer, typifies the requiem sharks

Mako shark, a powerful swimmer, typifies the mackerel sharks

Angelshark, a sluggish bottom dweller

THE TYPICAL SHARK

If asked to draw a typical shark, most of us would sketch something like the top diagram on the left, which is best represented by the requiem genus *Carcharhinus*. An active predatory lifestyle in a demanding medium 800 times denser than air requires an efficient locomotory system. While a swimmer can be forgiven for not appreciating the finer points of an approaching shark, its superb grace is indisputable.

The body form of sharks is related to their way of life. Our typical shark has a streamlined slender body, a longish snout and pectoral fins, a tail fin with the upper lobe longer than the lower lobe and a thickish caudal tail stem. The forward part of the shark's body is flattened to reduce drag during rapid turning and to allow lateral movement during normal swimming. The elevated middle sections induce more drag, acting as a fulcrum when the shark turns. These sharks swim with a slightly sinuous eel-like motion, their muscles sending transverse waves down the body. Since the amplitude of these waves reaches a peak near the tail, this section is also flattened to reduce drag while providing lift to the tail.

In general, sharks control their position in the water by balancing opposing forces generated during forward motion. The longer upper tail lobe drives the shark down through the water, and this is counteracted by lift generated from the pectoral fins and the flattened ventral surfaces of the head region. Buoyancy control with minimal expenditure of energy is important in maintaining an animal's position in the water. While bony fishes developed gas bladders, sharks

Ron & Valerie Taylor

solved this problem by acquiring large, oily livers and reducing the density of body tissues. One of the most important developments was the replacement of bone with cartilage, which is a lighter and more elastic framework.

The less dense the body of a shark, the less lift is required to maintain its position in the water. The difference in the density of various species is related to their way of life: typical sharks, which tend to be active pelagic and midwater swimmers, are less dense than bottom-living forms. The blue shark *Prionace glauca* and piked dogfish *Squalus acanthias* weigh in water only 2.5 percent and 2.7 percent of what they weigh in air, compared with 5.5 percent for the bottom-living angelshark *Squatina squatina*.

It would seem logical for fast-swimming species to reduce their density even further so that they could reduce the area of the fins needed to provide lift, thus minimizing drag. However, there would be no real advantage in being neutrally buoyant because the fins need to be a certain size for adequate maneuverability. Reduction in density can be accomplished instead by developing a large, oily liver containing oil of low specific gravity. In the blue shark, for example, the liver can account for up to 20 percent of the body weight. The other major tissues that contribute to an overall

reduction in density are the white muscles, skeletal tissues and skin. Blue sharks also have a low-density "jelly" in the snout.

The skin of sharks consists of dermal denticles (actually modified teeth), which give the skin its sandpaper texture. Each denticle consists of a basal plate or root, a pedicel and a crown that caps the pedicel and may expand outward from it. At first sight it is curious that sharks have a rough skin, as this might appear to increase drag due to friction. However, it has been suggested that the alignment of the denticles channels the water, resulting in a flow that acts to reduce friction. The arrangement of the denticles may also make sharks hydrodynamically "quiet," which would be an advantage in stalking prey. The denticles of faster pelagic sharks are smaller and lighter than those of the more sluggish benthic or bottom-living species.

A shark's fins provide lift, braking and turning power, acceleration and tracking, and prevent pitch, roll and yaw. It has been postulated that the typical body form of sharks is an adaptation for cruising, a requirement of their predatory way of life. In the typical shark, the placement of the pectoral and dorsal fins probably results in poor acceleration, but the spacing between them is critical in interacting with the water flow to increase efficiency and thrust.

ABOVE: While requiem sharks epitomize the "typical" shark in terms of body form, the great white is, to many people, the archetypal shark, superbly evolved for cruising.

RIGHT: A shark's skin is covered with a sort of flexible armor—thousands of small, scalelike denticles composed of a flattened basal plate and a backward-facing spine. In bullhead sharks the denticles have lost the spines and resemble hexagonal columns; in the prickly dogfish *Oxynotis bruiensis* the skin is so rough that it can cause painful abrasions.

BELOW: It was once believed that sharks are less efficient than bony fishes because they lack a gas-filled swim bladder. However, sharks can move up and down in the water column more easily than bony fishes since they obtain close to neutral buoyancy through oily livers that are not affected by variations in pressure due to depth.

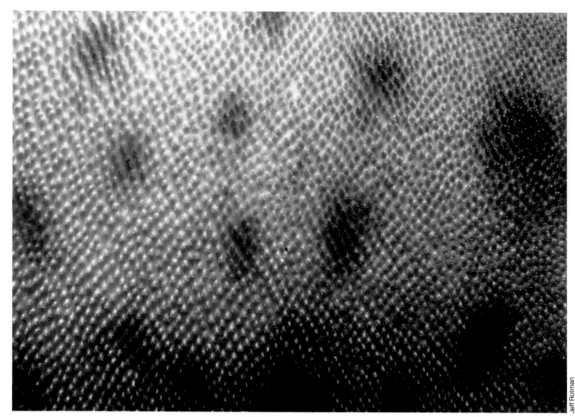

Jeff Rotman

Marty Snyderman

Sharks have two main types of muscles, red and white. In the typical shark, the red muscle lies in a thin layer just under the skin and outside the white muscle. It has a good blood supply and uses aerobic oxidation of fat as its energy source. Red muscle functions in sustained slow swimming and in a typical shark, such as the blue shark, comprises around 11 percent of the total muscle. White muscle has a poor blood supply, functions by the anaerobic breakdown of glycogen and is only used during fast sprint swimming. Because white muscle operates anaerobically, sharks cannot sustain high sprint speeds and quickly become exhausted.

Cruising speeds of typical sharks have been calculated in various ways. A 2-meter bull shark *Carcharhinus leucas* was observed swimming at around 2.5 kilometers per hour over a measured distance. Telemetry studies on blue sharks indicated speeds of 1.3 kilometers per hour during the day and 2.8 kilometers per hour at night, when the sharks were more active. Maximum speed generally decreases with length and the smaller piked dogfish cruises at around 1 kilometer per hour.

Sprint speeds are less well known, but in one questionable series of experiments a 60-centimeter-long blue shark reputedly maintained its position in a current equivalent to 38 kilometers per hour and in short bursts attained 69 kilometers per hour. A blacktip reef shark *Carcharhinus melanopterus* hooked on rod and line achieved bursts of 29 kilometers per hour and a similar speed was estimated for an

A VARIETY OF SHARK TAILS

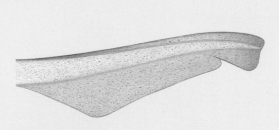

TIGER SHARK

The tiger shark's tail is strongly epicercal (the upper lobe is longer and heavier than the lower lobe). This species moves by swinging its body from side to side, and the large upper lobe delivers the maximum amount of power for slow cruising or sudden bursts of speed in pursuit of prey. The tiger shark's varied diet means that it must be able to twist and turn rapidly when hunting turtles, fish, stingrays and other sharks.

NURSE SHARK

Common in shallow waters on the tropical coasts of America and Africa, the nurse shark *Ginglymostoma cirratum* is a nocturnal species that spends daylight hours resting on the bottom or in caves and crevices: its prey consists mainly of invertebrates such as crabs, lobsters, sea urchins and octopuses. The nurse shark swims with an eel-like motion, using broad sweeps of its elongated tail to propel it slowly in search of food.

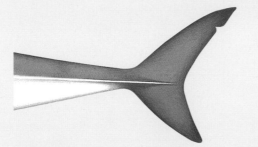

PORBEAGLE

The porbeagle *Lamna nasus* is a heavily built pelagic shark related to the mako and great white and is a voracious feeder on school fishes such as mackerel and herring. Porbeagles use their tails for propulsion rather than swinging their bodies from side to side; the large lower lobe of the tail fin provides greater speed after fast-moving prey, and lateral "keels" at the base of the tail may reduce drag for efficient hunting.

THRESHER SHARK

Thresher sharks are found in tropical and temperate oceans around the world and are active hunters of fish and squid, which they are believed to herd, then stun, with the powerful and incredibly elongated upper lobe of their tails. All three species are active and strong-swimming sharks; the development of a tail that is almost as long as the rest of the body has not been at the expense of speed or predatory efficiency.

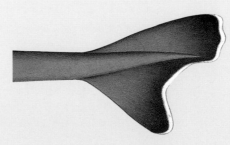

OCEANIC WHITETIP

The oceanic whitetip *Carcharhinus longimanus* is a large and stocky species usually found far offshore. Although it is generally slow moving, it is capable of short bursts of speed, aided by the propulsion of its powerful tail.

COOKIECUTTER

The cookiecutter shark *Isistius brasiliensis* hunts squid and crustaceans, but will also attach itself to marlin, tuna, dolphins—even the little-known megamouth shark. Its tail has broad upper and lower lobes of almost the same size.

David Doubilet

Al Giddings/Ocean Images

ABOVE: The main thrust of shark evolution has been toward a highly efficient predatory lifestyle, epitomized by the great white shark. When it finds prey, the great white tears away chunks of flesh with its powerful jaws and daggerlike teeth.

RIGHT: *Carcharodon carcharias*, the great white shark, is almost perfectly hydrodynamic. Its stiff, tunalike body allows it to cruise for long periods at a relatively low speed until it encounters one of the many animals it includes in its diet.

individual of the same species chased by a boat in shallow water. In general, typical sharks (pelagic, midwater and near-bottom feeders) are better designed for sprinting than sustained cruising.

MACKEREL SHARKS

Body form and locomotion are related to way of life, and having looked at a typical shark we can examine the ways in which species have become specialized. Over and above size differences, around 40 percent of species differ significantly from the typical shark body plan.

One family, the Lamnidae or mackerel sharks, which contains the great white shark *Carcharodon carcharias*, shortfin mako *Isurus oxyrinchus* and porbeagle *Lamna nasus*, has become highly specialized for a pelagic existence. The mako is probably the fastest and most active shark and is renowned as a sportfish, often repeatedly leaping clear of the water when hooked—and for a mako to jump clear of the water it must have a starting velocity of at least 35 kilometers per hour.

The body form of the mackerel sharks is conico-cylindrical, with the maximum width occurring well forward on the body. They are stouter than the typical shark and most closely conform to a perfect hydrodynamic shape. They have a bluntly pointed snout, thin caudal tail stem and a tailfin whose lobes are about equal in length. The tail has a high ratio of height to length, which produces maximum thrust with minimum drag and provides almost all of the propulsion; these sharks swim with a particularly rigid action.

One of the major adaptations of the mackerel sharks is a high body temperature and the ability to maintain temperatures 5–11° Celsius above

ambient water temperature. The effect of this is to make the muscles operate more effectively. In a unique experiment conducted off New York, a 4.6-meter white shark was tracked for three and a half days while its depth, muscle temperature and the water temperature were recorded by acoustic telemetry. The shark swam at an average speed of 3.2 kilometers per hour and stayed mainly in the thermocline (the boundary between warm and cold water) where it kept its muscle temperature at 3–5° Celsius above ambient temperature.

Mackerel sharks have larger amounts of red muscle which, in contrast with other species, is sited deep in the body close to the vertebral column. The red muscle is connected to the circulatory system by a complicated capillary network that acts as a heat exchange to reduce heat loss.

Mackerel sharks are well adapted for maintaining high cruising speeds and parallel many of the adaptations shown by tuna, which have a similar lifestyle among the bony fishes. Mackerel sharks' bodies tend to be slightly denser than those of the typical sharks: the porbeagle, for example, has a density of about 3.2 percent in water and has a relatively smaller pectoral and caudal fin area. But because their cruising speed is significantly higher, mackerel sharks are able to develop sufficient lift with a heavier body and smaller fins.

BOTTOM-DWELLING SHARKS

Another group of sharks adapted to a fairly sluggish existence, feeding on or near the bottom in shallow water, include the carpetsharks (Orectolobiformes) and catsharks (Scyliorhinidae). They are characterized by a large head, tapering body and weak, thin tail. They swim with a pronounced eel-like motion,

ABOVE: Bottom-dwelling sharks such as this ornate wobbegong *Orectolobus ornatus* lie in wait for suitable prey—octopuses, crabs, lobsters and bony fish—which they grasp with their sharp, fanglike teeth. Most wobbegongs have tassels, called dermal lobes, that help to break up their outline against a sandy or rocky bottom.

LEFT: Some of the smaller reef sharks rest in caves or beneath coral outcrops during the day. They are often cleaned by shrimps or cleaner fish at such times and their respiration and heart rates slow down considerably.

Bay Picture Library

David Doubilet

ABOVE: The giant basking shark *Cetorhinus maximus* is a filter feeder like the whale and megamouth sharks and obtains plankton simply by swimming along with its mouth open. Its gill slits are so large that they almost encircle the head.

Brian Pitkin/Seaphot

4.7 percent and around 8 percent red muscle. Since drag is not a major consideration, these sharks tend to have larger fins that give them greater maneuverability on the bottom. Many species do, however, need to be able to accelerate rapidly to catch their prey, which they do with the help of larger, more posteriorly placed median fins, such as those of the nurse shark *Ginglymostoma cirratum*.

Some species of sharks, notably the dogfish sharks (Squaliformes), the frilled shark *Chlamydoselachus anguineus* and the goblin shark *Mitsukurina owstoni* have invaded the deep sea. Many of these species have large livers (around 25 percent of body weight) that contain up to 90 percent oil, much of which is of low specific gravity. One of these low specific gravity compounds, squalene, is extracted commercially from shark livers and used as a base in the cosmetics industry.

Many of the deep-sea sharks either have a low body density or are neutrally buoyant. Food is scarce in the deep sea and these species probably need to be more active than their shallow-water counterparts. Because the density of liver oil varies little with water depth, these sharks can rise quickly toward the surface after prey more easily than can bony fish, which have gas bladders for buoyancy.

with the motive force provided by the whole rear end of the body, not just the tail. The front of the body swings in a wide arc with the pivot point near the first dorsal fin, which is situated well back on the body.

Because they spend much of their time on or near the bottom, buoyancy is not so important; neither is it necessary to have large amounts of red muscle for continuous cruising. This is illustrated by the smallspotted catshark *Scyliorhinus canicula* which has a density of

OUTSIDE THE MOLD

The two largest sharks, the whale shark *Rhincodon typus* and basking shark *Cetorhinus maximus*, feed on plankton by cruising at 3 to 5 kilometers per hour, filtering water through their gill slits. The basking shark has a large liver containing

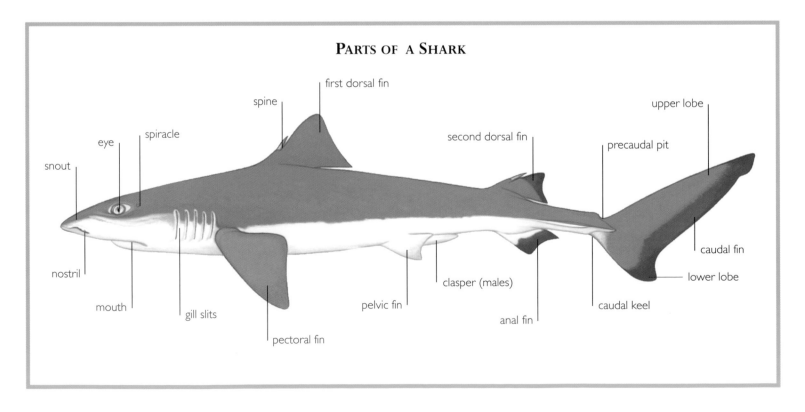

PARTS OF A SHARK

snout
eye
spiracle
spine
first dorsal fin
second dorsal fin
upper lobe
precaudal pit
caudal fin
lower lobe
nostril
mouth
gill slits
pectoral fin
pelvic fin
clasper (males)
anal fin
caudal keel

Al Giddings/Ocean Images

LEFT AND BELOW: Even more bizarre than the thresher sharks, hammerheads, family Sphyrnidae, have evolved winglike structures that are thought to aid their maneuverability. The location of the eyes at the end of the "wings" gives them superior binocular vision and the expanded nasal area and increased numbers of electroreceptors increase olfactory and bioelectrical sensitivity.

squalene and is close to neutral buoyancy; it can thus travel slowly, using its small pectoral fins to provide lift. The biology of the whale shark has not been closely studied, but it, too, is probably also close to neutral buoyancy. The basking shark and, to a lesser extent, the whale shark are similar in body form to the mackerel sharks and though slow, are powerful swimmers, as fishermen who hunt them for their liver oil can attest.

In contrast, the third planktivorous shark, the recently discovered megamouth *Megachasma pelagios*, appears to be a weak swimmer with its soft, flabby body and fins. It is a deep-swimming shark; its density is reduced by extremely poor calcification, soft, loose skin, and flabby connective tissue and muscles. This reduction of body tissues and weak swimming ability are probably responses to a nutrient-poor environment.

Extremes of body form are shown by the hammerheads *Sphyrna* spp., threshers *Alopias* spp., angelsharks *Squatina* spp. and the frilled shark. One function of the bizarre head of hammerheads is to act as a "wing," providing extra lift at the front of the shark that enables it to bank quickly and make rapid vertical movements. The dorso-ventrally flattened head induces minimal drag during turning.

The scalloped *Sphyrna lewini* and smooth hammerhead *Sphyrna zygaena* feed extensively on squid, which are jet-propelled and extremely maneuverable. The "hammer" enables these sharks to catch their fast and agile prey, but it has been taken beyond mere hydrodynamic considerations in the winghead shark *Eusphyra blochii* whose head width is 40 to 50 percent of its body length.

The thresher sharks, which have an upper tail lobe up to 50 percent of their body length, are especially interesting. Apart from their tails, their streamlined bodies are much like those of the mackerel sharks; they also have the same elevated

Warren Williams/Seaphot

body temperature and the associated internal red muscle and heat-exchange system—features unique to threshers and mackerel sharks. They are powerful swimmers, as demonstrated by their ability to jump clear of the water. The thresher's tail seems totally out of place in a powerful swimmer, yet does not seem to be a hindrance.

The angelsharks have become dorso-ventrally flattened like the rays, and are an extreme case of specialization for bottom-dwelling. Buoyancy is not important; they are, along with some of the rays, among the most dense of elasmobranchs. The angelshark has a density of 5.5 percent; its liver contributes little buoyancy and its muscle and skeleton are relatively dense. The swimming mechanisms of the angelshark have not been investigated, but it presumably moves by creating vertical waves along the flattened pectoral fins, as rays do.

The frilled shark is an example of extreme elongation. Its deepsea habits are poorly known,

but its long, eel-like body may be an adaptation to life on a rocky sea bottom, where this species may hunt for prey hidden in crevices. The frilled shark's jaws can be protruded so it can feed on large prey, rather as a snake does; the long body provides less resistance in the water should the shark be dragged along by its prey.

BREATHING AND BLOOD

Swimming at cruising speeds, like other aerobic activities, depends on the efficiency with which the respiratory and vascular systems supply oxygen. Oxygen is extracted from the water by the gills, from where it is transferred to the blood. The circulatory system then delivers oxygenated blood to the tissues and organs.

Shark gills consist of a series of cartilaginous arches from which extend two alternating rows of elongated gill filaments. Thin, platelike secondary lamellae extend at right angles to the filaments. Blood flows across these lamellae in the opposite direction to the flow of water—an arrangement that makes the uptake of oxygen and dumping of carbon dioxide more efficient. The gills open to the outside through slits—usually five, sometimes six or seven. It is not known why some species have a greater number of gill slits, but those that do are generally more primitive sharks. Water enters mainly through the mouth, passes over the gills and leaves through the gill slits.

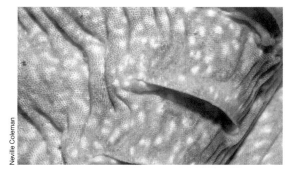

Neville Coleman

Some species— mainly sluggish bottom-living forms such as the catsharks and wobbegongs—pump water over the gills by rhythmically contracting muscles that open and close the valves at the entrance and exit of the system. Other species employ ram-jet ventilation, which uses the forward motion of the shark to move water backward over the gills. The highly active mackerel sharks, for example, rely entirely on ram-jet ventilation and must keep swimming to breathe. Between these extremes species such as the sand tiger *Carcharias taurus* and the piked dogfish are able to switch from respiratory pumping when at rests to ram-jet ventilation at cruising speeds, thereby saving energy.

In the bony fishes, the gills of the highly active species (such as tuna) that employ ram-jet ventilation are generally strengthened and fused. However, the majority of both highly active and less active sharks have considerably strengthened

LEFT: Active pelagic or open-ocean sharks often employ ram-jet respiration, relying on forward movement to force water through their gills. Relatively sluggish benthic sharks have more muscular gills that supply oxygen while the animal is resting on the bottom.

FACING PAGE The sand tiger spends much of its time cruising slowly at a variety of depths.

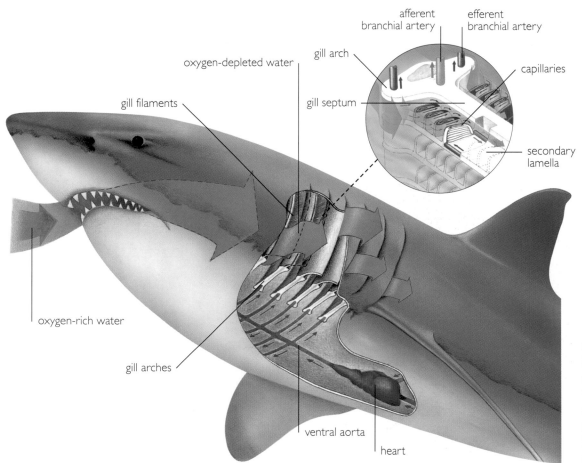

LEFT How a shark breathes. The illustration shows the heart, gill arches and direction of water flow. Water enters the mouth, passes over the gills and out through the gill slits. The cutaway diagram shows how the water flows in a counter-direction to the blood.

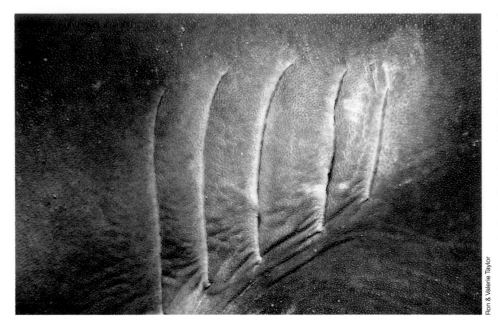

ABOVE: The Port Jackson shark *Heterodontus portusjacksoni* has been observed pumping water into its gills through the first gill slit and out through the others, enabling the shark to chew its food mainly mollusks and sea urchins without having to take water in through the mouth and risking food being lost through the gill slits.

Jaw Attachment

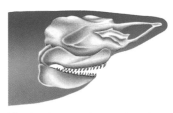

The jaw is normally positioned below the skull.

The jaw remains close to the skull as the mouth opens.

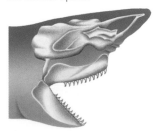

The upper jaw detaches from the skull to enable powerful forward thrust.

gills suited to their cruising or intermittent cruising lifestyles. Ancestral sharks may have had similarly strengthened gills; such a preadaptation to a swift oceanic lifestyle could have expedited the evolution of the active mackerel sharks. Not surprisngly, mackerel sharks have larger gill areas than other species, although the gill area of the active blue shark is similar to those of sluggish or bottom-living species. Ram-jet ventilation may allow the gill area to be smaller than if the species relies solely on pump ventilation.

The oxygen-carrying capacity of blood is a function of the number of red blood cells and the amount of hemoglobin in these cells. Typical requiem sharks have a hematocrit (percentage of red cells to total blood volume) of 20 to 25 percent and a hemoglobin content of around six grams per hundred milliliters. These values are much the same in hammerheads, but are lower in deepwater species. In contrast, mackerel sharks have much higher hematocrits (33 to 39 percent) and hemoglobin contents (14 grams per hundred milliliters) that are close to those found in mammals, birds and warm-bodied tuna. High hemoglobin levels in both mackerel sharks and tuna are probably needed to maintain elevated body temperatures.

More active species of mammals have larger hearts than less active ones. However, the hearts of most sharks weigh much the same in proportion to their body weight, irrespective of their habits. For example, the hearts of both the relatively active requiem sharks and the sluggish bottom-living smallspotted catshark are 0.1 percent of body weight. Only the mackerel sharks have relatively large hearts, ranging from around about 0.2 percent of body weight in the mako and white shark to 0.3 and 0.4 percent in the porbeagle and salmon shark *Lamna ditropis*. The heavier heart of the mackerel sharks is associated with their elevated body temperature: the extra

weight comes from the unusually thick, muscular ventricle, which has a relatively much smaller volume than in other pelagic species.

SHARKS' JAWS

Energy for activities such as swimming must ultimately come from food, and sharks owe much of their success to the efficiency and diversity of their feeding mechanisms.

The jaws of ancestral sharks seem to have been derived from a modification of the first gill arch. In the most primitive of known sharks, the cladodonts, the mouth was terminal (at the front of the head) rather than ventral (underslung) and the long jaws consisted of a single upper and lower jaw cartilage. The upper jaw was bound tightly to the cranium by ligaments which allowed little independent movement, and was braced from behind (like the lower jaw) by the cartilages of the second gill arch. Cladodont sharks were probably active pelagic predators, but their long jaws and pointed teeth were an adaptation to seizing and tearing prey rather than to cutting or sawing as in modern forms. Among living species the jaw of the frilled shark still fairly closely resembles the primitive jaw.

In the hybodont sharks that succeeded the cladodonts the jaw shortened, allowing the bite to be more powerful, and the teeth became modified for both cutting and crushing, which enabled hybodonts to exploit such prey as mollusks and other invertebrates. Similar species still exist today in the Port Jackson sharks, (Heterodontiformes).

The most important development in jaw design was the freeing of the upper jaw from the cranium. This made the upper jaw more mobile and enabled the shark to protrude its jaws. The ventral position of the jaws of modern sharks resulted from further shortening of the jaws together with expansion of the snout, which was then able to take on a sensory function. The flattened ventral surface of the head was also able to act as a planing surface, providing additional lift in swimming.

The success of this design is best seen in a requiem shark feeding on prey too large to be eaten in one or two bites. As the shark approaches, it tilts its head back and the lower jaw makes contact first with the prey. The teeth of the lower jaw are often pronglike, so they can gain an initial purchase. The upper jaw then moves forward and down; the upper teeth are sunk into the prey and the head is moved in a sawing motion that scoops a chunk out of the prey. The biting force of a 2- to 3-meter requiem shark has been measured at 3 tonnes per square centimeter. Such a powerful bite imposes considerable forces on the body, and to counteract this, the dorsal and ventral processes have been expanded to protect the spine and to

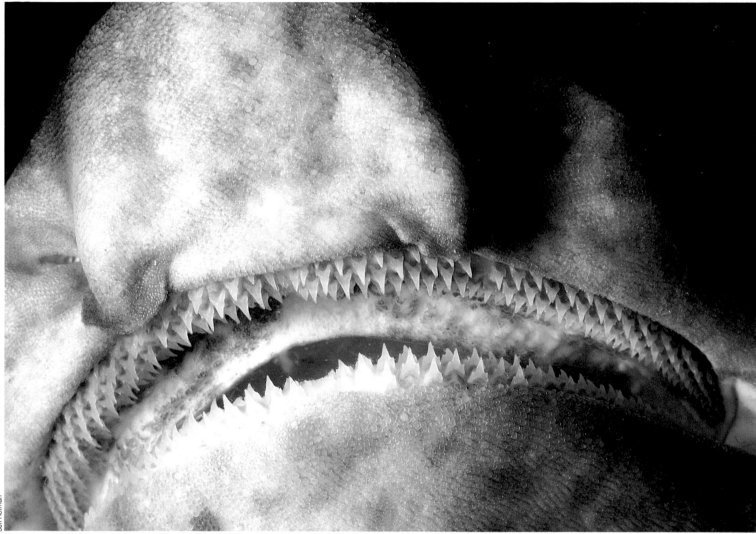

Jeff Rotman

improve its stability. This improved shock-absorber system also makes the body muscles more effective while swimming.

FOOD AND FEEDING

One unusual and highly successful feature of sharks is their teeth, which are continuously replaced through life. The teeth are not attached directly to the jaw cartilage but instead are embedded in a membrane called a tooth bed. Teeth are formed in a groove on the inside of the jaw cartilage and move progressively forward on the tooth bed. Eventually they erupt through the soft tissue overlying the replacement teeth to fold into place in the functional row. Measurement of replacement rates in requiem sharks shows that each tooth is replaced every eight to 15 days during the first year of life. Because the bite is so powerful, teeth become blunt and are often broken. Frequent replacement overcomes this problem and also allows the teeth to grow along with the shark.

The popular belief that sharks are scavengers, eating anything and everything, is far from the truth. Most species are selective about what they eat. Pelagic requiem sharks, for example, feed mainly on small fish and squid. Port Jackson

sharks largely on echinoderms (especially sea urchins) and shellfish, and gummy sharks on crustaceans. The sicklefin weasel shark *Hemigaleus microstoma* is a highly specialized feeder: of stomachs examined from Australian specimens, 99 percent contained cephalopods, mostly octopus.

Not all sharks are so specialized in their diet, and many will take other food if their usual prey is scarce. The diet of some species changes as they grow. Shortfin mako sharks weighing less than around 150 kilograms feed mainly on small fish and cephalopods, for which they are equipped with long, pointed teeth. Larger specimens have broader, more bladelike teeth, which they use for cutting up large prey such as swordfish, marlin, dolphins or porpoises. Small great white sharks have quite pointed teeth like a small mako and feed mainly on fish, while larger individuals have triangular cutting teeth for dealing with their prey—mainly marine mammals such as seals, sea lions and dolphins. The tiger shark *Galeocerdo cuvier* is one of the more omnivorous species, which is partly why it can be dangerous to humans. Juveniles have a liking for seasnakes and adults for seabirds and turtles, which they are able to cut up with their massive jaws and teeth.

ABOVE: The swellshark *Cephaloscyllium ventriosum*—a sluggish, nocturnal bottom dweller—has a huge mouth but relatively small, pointed teeth that help it capture its prey of crustaceans and fish.

Ron & Valerie Taylor

ABOVE: The teeth of the great white shark are triangular and serrated, enabling it to handle relatively tough mammals, such as seals, as well as fish. Its eyes roll back during a feeding lunge to provide extra protection.

RIGHT: The bizarre cookiecutter shark *Isistius brasiliensis* feeds on squid or attaches itself to whale sharks, basking and megamouth sharks, tuna and marlin, or whales and dolphins, using its suction cuplike lips and muscular pharynx for a tight grip.

David Doubilet

From the ancestral feeding mode of seizing and swallowing, modern sharks have developed an enormous range of appropriate feeding mechanisms: the gouging of the requiems and the crushing of the gummy and Port Jackson sharks have already been mentioned. Some of the dogfish sharks such as the piked dogfish have bladelike teeth that overlap to form a continuous cutting edge ideal for slicing fish and squid into pieces that are small enough to swallow.

A small deepwater dogfish, the cookiecutter shark *Isistius brasiliensis*, has one of the most bizarre feeding modes. The cookiecutter uses its sucking lips to attach itself to the bodies of large fish such as marlin, sharks or whales. It then "bores" out a plug of flesh with its teeth. This shark has even optimistically attacked the rubber-coated sonar domes of nuclear submarines. The cookiecutter is luminescent, perhaps to attract smaller prey or would-be predators, which it then attacks. A second species, the largetooth cookiecutter *Isistius plutodus* which grows to around 40 centimeters, has proportionally larger teeth than any other species (around twice the tooth height to body length ratio of the great white shark).

The bottom-living nurse shark employs another feeding strategy. It utilizes suction feeding to extract prey from holes and crevices: its thick lips create a seal and by rapidly expanding its muscular pharyngeal cavity, the shark produces a suction pressure of up to 1 kilogram per square centimeter, equivalent to 1 atmosphere of pressure at sea level.

MUNCHING THEIR WAY THROUGH THE NIGHT

MARTY SNYDERMAN

Market squid *Opalescens loligo* play an important role in many oceanic food chains. These squid are heavily preyed on by pilot whales, sea lions and many other species that live in the open sea. Market squid, sometimes called common squid, are normally found far from shore in the open ocean off the coast of western North America, but when they mate the squid come into shallow water. A favorite mating site is the west end of Catalina Island, about 42 kilometers from the city of Los Angeles. Market squid live only a year or so, and have a strong drive to mate before they perish. During heavy spawning, on moonless winter nights, the squid are literally present by the millions as they seek partners to perpetuate their species.

Because they are so preoccupied, the squid are particularly vulnerable to predation when mating. After the mating ritual has been completed the females lay their eggs on the sandy bottom, and then both the males and females quickly deteriorate and die. In some places the bottom is several meters thick with dead and dying squid. Before long a host of predators and scavengers appear to feed on the live and dead squid and the eggs. Each squid egg-casing contains approximately 200 eggs and it is estimated that on average only one of the potential hatchlings will survive to complete the lifecycle and mate as an adult. Odds are that the remaining 199 will be devoured by a variety of sea creatures.

Blue sharks prey heavily on mating squid, especially at night when the concentrations of squid are at their highest. During those times the blue sharks simply swim, mouths agape,

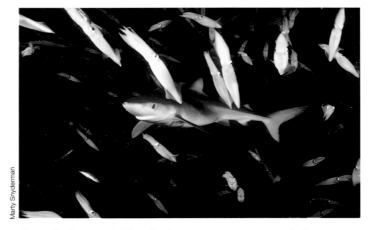

Marty Snyderman

through the squid. The sharks continue to eat until their stomachs are totally distended, they have squid hanging out of their mouths and they simply cannot cram any more into their systems. At that point the sharks begin to vomit and create more room so they can once again begin to feed on the squid.

While this type of behavior might seem obnoxious to you and me, we must remember that in the wilderness meals are never guaranteed. Blue sharks eat only when they can procure a meal and once the chance presents itself, they—like many predators—do all they can to take full advantage of the opportunity. That means the sharks take in as much nutrition as possible. In the final analysis, this voracious consumption plays a vital part in enabling these predators to survive from one meal to the next.

One of the most spectacular specializations is the planktonic filter-feeding of the basking, whale and megamouth sharks. These species have greatly reduced teeth; their gill rakers, situated on the inner sides of the gill arch, are modified into a straining apparatus and the mouth has moved forward to a nearly terminal position. Basking sharks cruise near the surface at around two knots with their mouths open wide; using this feeding method, large individuals filter more than 1,000 tonnes of water an hour. The gill rakers, like the teeth, are shed periodically, which may explain why basking sharks apparently disappear in winter from the temperate waters in which they live. Possibly the rakers are lost during winter when there is not enough plankton in the water to sustain the shark's energy requirements, so during this time they hibernate on the seafloor to conserve energy.

The whale shark supplements its diet of plankton with small fish. It has been seen rising vertically through a school of fish until its head is sufficiently clear of the water to drain its mouth, then sinking back with its mouth agape, allowing water and fish to pour in.

Some sharks use more than their mouths to catch food. Thresher sharks use their enormously elongated tails to stun fish; the vertebrae in the tip of the tail have expanded dorsal and ventral processes that make it an effective club. Sawsharks (Pristiophoridae) apparently use their toothed saw in a slashing action to cut and disable prey.

DIGESTING FOOD

Whatever the feeding method, prey passes to the stomach where it is acted on by the digestive juices. The products of digestion are absorbed in the intestine, which in sharks is called the spiral valve because its internal surface resembles a spiral staircase. This spiral arrangement provides maximum absorptive area in a small space, allowing more room for a large stomach and liver and, in females, for the development of a litter of live young.

Examination of the stomach contents of sharks shows that few have full stomachs. A study of shortfin mako sharks, for example, revealed that their average stomach capacity was 10 percent of the body weight, while the amount of food in their stomachs averaged only 2.6 percent of body weight. A mako weighing 63 kilograms would therefore need to eat 2 kilograms of food a day—11.5 times its body weight a year. Young lemon sharks *Negaprion brevirostris* are reported to have a maintenance requirement—the amount of food needed just to maintain body weight, allowing none for growth—of 20,600 calories or 16.5 grams of food a day. For a 1 kilogram shark, this requirement is equivalent to 1.7 percent of its body weight per day.

Ron & Valerie Taylor

LEFT: Active predators such as the gray reef shark *Carcharhinus amblyrhynchos* use the more pointed teeth in their lower jaws to grab and hold prey. The teeth of the upper jaw, which is tilted back during he first strike at food, then hold the prey and help to draw it into the mouth, while the lower jaw moves forward to gain further purchase.

Herwarth Voigtmann/Seaphot

Sharks in captivity consume between 3 and 14 percent of their body weight a week. They may stop feeding for several months, during which time they presumably live off reserves in the liver. Great white sharks are able to ingest large amounts of food at a time, and it has been calculated from stomachs containing whale blubber that one meal could sustain the shark for up to two months. However, most sharks appear to eat at one or two day intervals, with an average meal weighing 3 to 5 percent of their body weight.

Studies on lemon, sandbar *Carcharhinus plumbeus* and blue sharks have shown that initial digestion of the meals is fairly rapid, taking around 24 hours, but that it takes three to four days for the meal to be completely voided. It may take longer when the water is colder: piked dogfish, for example, take five days to completely digest a meal of herring when the temperature is

ABOVE: In the same way that antelope, for example, ignore lions when they are not hunting, reef fish pay little discernible attention to sharks that are simply patrolling. Many reef sharks will investigate anything novel in their environment and their increased alertness will cause potential prey to move to a safe distance.

RIGHT: The tope shark *Galeorhinus galeus*, one of the most commercially important species of sharks, is widely distributed in cold and temperate waters in both hemispheres. It is ovoviviparous, giving birth to live young that hatch inside the uterus and are nourished from yolk.

10° Celsius. Mackerel sharks, in addition to having elevated muscle temperatures, also have a heat exchange system in the blood vessels supplying the viscera. The warm gut of these active sharks presumably enables them to digest food more rapidly.

GROWING AND AGING

In a unique study of young lemon sharks it was found that new tissue is produced slowly compared with predatory bony fish, and this was reflected in a slow rate of growth.

Lower growth rates in sharks may be a consequence of their slower digestion times and feeding rates. Newborn lemon sharks of 1.2 kilograms weigh 2.6 kilograms after a year; to achieve this weight gain they must eat six times their birth weight during this period. Fish grow fastest during the first few years, then slow as they age. Lemon sharks grow about 15 centimeters a year initially, but do not mature until around 2.4 meters, which means they may

take 15 years to reach maturity. However, lemon sharks kept in captivity and fed to satiation under ideal conditions can grow at 10 times their natural growth rate.

Growth rates show considerable variation between species and sometimes even between different populations of the same species. The majority of sharks seems to have a maximum lifespan of 20 to 30 years: the Atlantic sharpnose shark *Rhizoprionodon terraenovae* and the starspotted smoothhound *Mustelus manazo*, both fairly small sharks that grow to just over a meter, have relatively short lifespans of around 10 to 15 years respectively. The piked dogfish currently holds the longevity record, with a maximum age of at least 70, and possibly closer to 100 for north Pacific specimens. The tope shark *Galeorhinus galeus* is also a longlived species: the recapture of a tagged individual after 40 years indicates that this shark could live to around sixty.

Not surprisingly, the longest-lived species grow the most slowly. The piked dogfish grows at around 4 centimeters a year to sexual maturity which, in females, may not be reached for 20 years. While the Atlantic sharpnose shark and starspotted smoothhound can reach maturity in two or three years, most sharks do not mature until they are six or seven years old. The fastest absolute growth rates are found in some of the large pelagic sharks such as the blue, mako and white, which grow about 30 centimeters a year to maturity.

REPRODUCING THE SPECIES

Most bony fishes produce very large numbers of small eggs, which are spawned into the water where they are fertilized externally by sperm liberated from the males. This tends to be a wasteful process, with high initial mortality among the unprotected eggs and larvae, and widely fluctuating survival rates due to variations in environmental conditions. Sharks have opted

BELOW: Requiem sharks, such as these blacktip reef sharks *Carcharhinus melanopterus*, are viviparous, producing live young nourished in the uterus by a placenta analogous to that of mammals. Most requiem sharks have a long gestation period—up to a year—and produce relatively small numbers of young, from one or two to a dozen.

for an alternative reproductive strategy: the eggs are fertilized internally and more energy is invested in producing fewer, but better protected young, with a consequently higher survival rate. Their reproductive methods range from oviparous forms that lay large, well-protected eggs to viviparous species that give birth to living young nourished via a placenta analogous to our own.

Male sharks have a pair of claspers, cylindrical organs formed from modified pelvic fins. In immature sharks the claspers are short and soft, while in a mature individual they are elongated and rigid from calcification. During copulation, one clasper is inserted into the female genital opening and in some species (such as the sandbar shark) the tip spreads out, anchoring the clasper and holding the oviduct open to facilitate sperm passage. During copulation the sperm flows from the genital pore into a groove that runs along the clasper. Associated with the claspers are two muscular sacs that run forward under the skin of the belly. Before copulation these fill with seawater which, during copulation, is squirted out to flush the sperm from the clasper into the female oviduct. Sperm is produced from paired testes and stored either in the collecting ducts or in accessory sperm sacs. In some species, such as the blue shark, the sperm is enclosed in protective packets called spermatophores.

Mating in smaller, flexible species such as the smallspotted catshark is accomplished by the male coiling around the female's body. In larger stiffer-bodied forms such as the requiem sharks, the male is oriented parallel and head to head with the female. Whatever method is used, the clasper is rotated toward the front before it is inserted.

In a number of species "love bites" or mating scars can be seen on the females—tooth nicks,

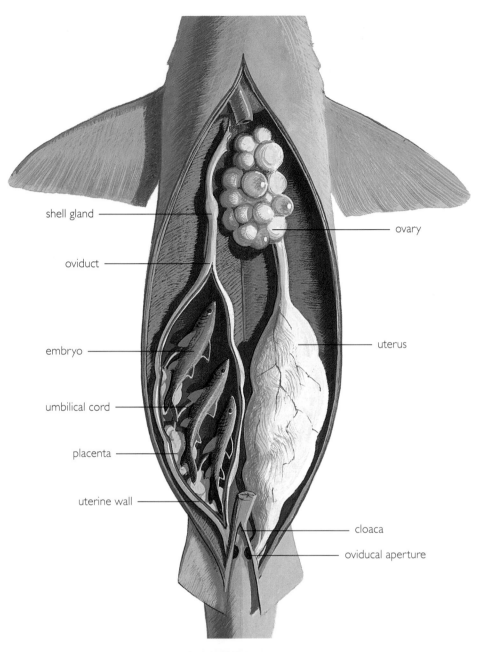

shell gland — ovary
oviduct
embryo — uterus
umbilical cord
placenta
uterine wall
cloaca
oviducal aperture

ABOVE: The reproductive system of a placental shark. Females have paired oviducts which widen posteriorly into the uteri in which the young are nurtured. In most sharks, only the right ovary is developed.

LEFT: Most female sharks display mating scars caused by males grasping a female's back, or her pectoral or dorsal fins, during courtship behavior. Biting is thought to stimulate copulation and many male sharks and rays have longer teeth as an adaptation for courtship; females have evolved thicker, tougher skin to protect them during mating.

RIGHT: The Tasmanian spotted catshark *Parascyllium multimaculatum* is a small shark restricted to waters around Tasmania. Its small, flanged egg case is equipped with prehensile tendrils that wind around seaweed and sea lily "stems" to anchor the egg case.

ABOVE; Bullhead sharks (family Heterodontidae) produce eggs in unique spiral-flanged cases. The Port Jackson shark lays 10 to 16 eggs each year, favoring traditional sites and sometimes actively pushing the leathery egg cases into rock crevices.

BELOW: Four stages in the development of the swellshark *Cephaloscyllium ventriosum*.
1 Eggs are laid in amber cases known as mermaid's purses and take seven to 10 months to hatch.
2 The large yolk sac is gradually reduced as the developing embryo uses its contents.
3 The hatchling has a double row of enlarged denticles on its back that help it force its way out of the egg case.
4 Newly hatched sharks are active, can swim strongly and are ready to search for food.

slashes and semicircular jaw impressions on the flanks, the back, pectoral fins and above the gill area. Biting by the male stimulates the female to copulate and, in species such as the whitetip reef shark *Triaenodon obesus* to hold on to the females pectoral fin during mating. Although the male's biting action is partially inhibited during mating, wounds can be severe, and the female blue shark has developed a thicker skin for protection.

Mating normally precedes ovulation by around a month and sperm are stored for this period in the shell gland of the female: in some species, such as the blue shark, sperm may be stored in a viable condition for a year or more. The female produces eggs either in paired ovaries (for example, the piked dogfish) or in a single functional right ovary (in requiems and hammerheads). The eggs are around 5 millimeters in diameter at the resting stage, but increase to 30 to 40 millimeters at ovulation, when they rupture out of the ovary and are swept down the oviducts to the shell gland, where the sperm are stored and where fertilization takes

place. The shell gland also secretes an egg membrane that is a tough, horny egg case in oviparous forms, but is reduced to a cellophane-like membrane enclosing the embryo in viviparous species.

Until recently, the reproductive method of the whale shark was a mystery: a single egg case had been found but it was so unusually thin that it was not clear whether the whale shark was oviparous or whether this egg was aborted and the species was viviparous. In 1995 an 11-meter female was captured off Taiwain. She contained nearly 300 embryos, each 42–63 centimeters, confirming that reproduction was viviparous.

In oviparous species (mainly the catsharks, carpetsharks and Port Jackson sharks), the eggs are laid on the seafloor where they complete their development nourished by their yolk supply. In some species the egg cases are rectangular with tendrils at each corner to anchor them in weed. In most of the Port Jackson sharks, the egg cases have spiral flanges that wedge them into crevices in rocks. Eggs are usually laid in pairs and in the case of the smallspotted catshark, 20 to 25 are laid each year. Hatching is dependent on water temperature, and is usually over a period of several months.

Viviparous sharks can be divided into those species, such as the piked dogfish, in which the embryos are nourished solely by yolk reserves and those in which additional food reserves are obtained from the mother. In the piked dogfish, several fertilized eggs are jointly enclosed by the egg membrane in the uterus, forming a thin egg case. This ruptures after six months and each embryo develops in the uterus, living off its attached yolk sac, which is completely resorbed just before birth. Ten or so 25-centimeter-long pups are produced after a gestation period of 22 months, which is the longest known pregnancy of any shark.

A form of viviparity in which the embryo receives maternal nutrients, but not through a placenta, is most common in the rays and

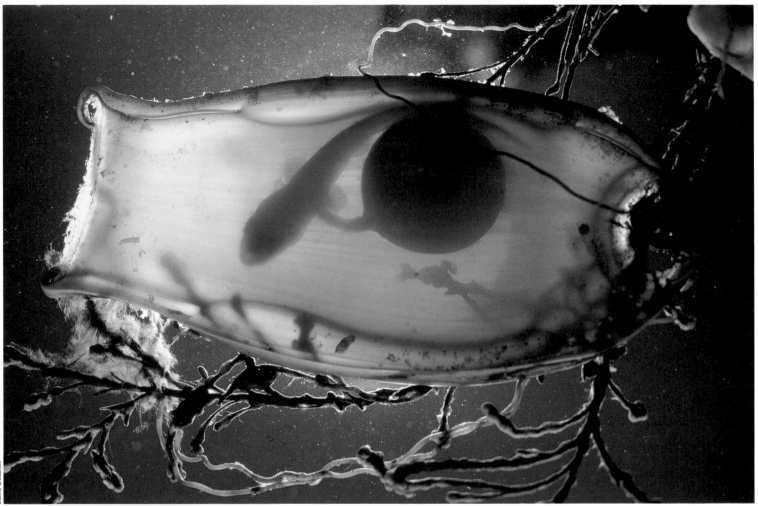

David Doubilet

probably also occurs in the tiger shark. In this group, the eggs are encased in a thin membrane within which the embryos complete their development inside the uterus. Nutrients are apparently secreted by the uterus and absorbed by the embryos to supplement nutrients from the egg yolk itself. Tiger sharks produce between 10 and 80 young, each 60 to 70 centimeters long.

In the requiem and hammerhead sharks, the embryos initially take up oxygen (and possibly additional nutrients) from the yolk sac and also through external gill tufts. During the third or fourth month of pregnancy, the yolk sac is modified into a placenta that becomes attached to the uterus. Nutrients and oxygen are then passed from the mother across the placenta and through the umbilical stalk to the embryo; waste products go in the reverse direction. In viviparous species, the embryos are surrounded by the egg membrane and are contained within separate compartments in the uterus. Litter sizes vary from two in some species to more than a hundred in some blue sharks. Gestation periods are usually nine to 12 months.

ABOVE: The draughtboard swellshark *Cephaloscyllium isabellum* is common on rocky and sandy reefs off New Zealand. Its egg case is attached to underwater forests of kelp and seaweed, providing the newborn sharks with ready access to their prey of crabs, worms, marine invertebrates and slow-moving fish.

A. Kerstitch/Seaphot

A. Kerstitch/Seaphot

Some species (such as the gray nurse, mako, porbeagle, threshers, white and basking sharks) have a bizarre form of viviparity known as oophagy. The ovaries of these sharks resemble those of bony fish, containing many thousands of very small eggs. The embryos feed on a supply of eggs which the female continues to ovulate. During intermediate states of pregnancy, the embryos develop an enormously distended stomach full of yolk from these ingested eggs. Litter sizes are small, mostly between two and 16, although the shortfin mako may have as many as thirty.

Oophagy is taken one step further in the gray nurse, which produces only one large pup per uterus: in this shark, after initially feeding on the supply of eggs, one embryo from the initial batch of hatchlings in each uterus attacks and devours its siblings.

The great white and basking sharks pose an enigma as few pregnant white sharks, and no pregnant basking sharks, have been reliably recorded. This is even more amazing in view of their large size, the curiosity which they arouse and the fact that there have been many commercial fisheries for basking sharks.

Within their variety of reproductive methods sharks exhibit different breeding cycles. Some species reproduce throughout the year, while others have a distinctly seasonal cycle with mating, ovulation and birth occurring in certain months. In some species pregnant females have a batch of ova ripening in the ovary at the same time as embryos are developing. Soon after these "pups" are born the female is ready to ovulate again, so a litter is produced every year. In other sharks only a proportion of the mature females breed every year; the others enter a resting stage for a year or possibly longer. The sicklefin weasel shark is unusual in that mature females produce two litters each year after a gestation period of five to six months.

RIGHT AND BELOW: Active and apparently more highly evolved sharks such as the lemon shark *Negaprion brevirostris* give birth to live young rather than laying eggs. Lemon shark litter sizes vary from four to 17, and newborn sharks remain close to where they were born for some time. In this series of photographs, a female lemon shark was hooked off Bimini, in the Bahamas. The stress of capture may have caused her to give birth prematurely, though the baby sharks were well developed, active and about 60 centimeters long.

David Doubilet

David Doubilet

It appears that ancestral sharks had internal fertilization and were oviparous, and that the trend has been toward the development of viviparity. Viviparity may be favored because it allows production of larger, better-protected young, and because it does not impose habitat restrictions for egg laying. This flexibility is obviously advantageous for wideranging pelagic species.

To protect the young from predation by other sharks of the same species and to avoid competition for food, most sharks show some form of sex and size segregation. Newborn young may be restricted to specific nursing areas separate from the adult population. In certain locations only mature males may be found, while in another area only mature females will occur. Evidence suggests that sharks have a clearly defined and well-executed protocol for protecting their young.

Some sharks undertake extensive migrations associated with their reproductive needs and feeding requirements. Tagging studies have demonstrated that blue sharks utilize currents to travel right around the north Atlantic, and even into the south Atlantic. Sharks tagged off southwest England have been recaptured off South America and New York, while specimens marked in the northeastern United States have been recovered off Europe. At the other extreme, tagging studies on Aldabra Atoll, in the Indian Ocean, have shown that blacktip reef sharks normally live in a restricted area of only a few square kilometers.

The earliest sharks lived some 450 million years ago in the warm, shallow waters that covered most of what is now North America.

Already large—some species were more than 2 meters long—they were streamlined and fast-swimming predators whose success is highlighted by the appearance of modern sharks as much as 170 million years ago. Since then they have evolved to exploit a variety of marine (and even some freshwater) habitats, lifestyles and feeding methods that reflect the efficiency of their hydrodynamic design, reproductive biology and sophisticated sensory systems. They are, indeed, masters of the aquatic environment to which they have become superbly adapted.

ABOVE AND LEFT: As each of the pups was born, assisted from its mother's cloaca by a diver, it would rest briefly on the bottom of the shallow lagoon before swimming away and breaking the umbilical cord. Several small remoras that had accompanied the female shark, even after her capture, moved from their grip on her body and darted forward to consume each placenta as it was delivered.

A DIVERSITY OF FORM AND SIZE

Contrary to their popular image, most sharks are small and harmless to humans. Fifty percent of living species reach a maximum length of between 15 centimeters and 1 meter, and 82 percent do not reach 2 meters. The average maximum length for living sharks is about 1.5 meters. Only about 4 percent of sharks are gigantic—4 to 12 or more meters long. These include the largest living fishes, the whale and basking sharks, which broadly overlap the larger cetaceans in size.

BELOW: Despite their fearsome reputation, some sharks are dwarfs, and mature at lengths of 15 to 20 centimeters.

David Doublet

GREAT WHITE SHARK
This large, active, torpedo-shaped mackerel shark is a powerful and efficient predator.

BONNETHEAD SHARK
This small hammerhead is an active coastal shark. It has a smooth, rounded shovel-shaped head.

TASSELLED WOBBEGONG
This small, patterned, bottom-dwelling carpetshark has fleshy tassels on its chin and jaw.

BIGEYE THRESHER SHARK
This streamlined, spindle-shaped mackerel shark is one of three species of threshers. Like all threshers, it has an elongated caudal fin.

PACIFIC SLEEPER SHARK
This large but slow-moving dogfish has a stout, rounded body and inhabits cold to temperate waters.

SILKY SHARK
This slender, oceanic requiem shark is a fast swimmer, capable of dramatic turns and darting movements.

LONGNOSE CATSHARK
This small, slender groundshark inhabits deep ocean and shelf waters.

WHALE SHARK
This massive, spindle-shaped carpetshark is the largest living fish. Despite its size it is harmless, filter feeding on plankton and small fishes.

SPINED PYGMY SHARK
At 8 centimeters this deepwater dogfish is one of the smallest living sharks.

HABITATS AND DISTRIBUTION

GUIDO DINGERKUS

The distribution of sharks around the world can be largely explained in terms of water temperature, depth and currents. In some cases there is a positive correlation between these factors; in other cases there is not. When classified according to water temperature, sharks can be divided into three groups: tropical, temperate and cold water sharks.

ACTIVE TROPICAL SHARKS

Tropical sharks live in areas where the water is usually warmer than 21°Celsius. Sharks living in these regions include most of the carcharhinids (typical or requiem sharks), the sphyrnids (hammerhead sharks), many of the triakids (smooth houndsharks), the orectolobids (wobbegongs or carpetsharks), the rhincodontids (nurse and whale sharks), the hemiscylliids (banded catsharks), and some of the squatinids (angelsharks). These sharks can further be separated into the active types, which swim almost continuously, and the bottom-dwelling or benthic types, which move relatively little.

In the active group are included the requiem sharks, hammerhead sharks, triakids and the whale shark. Individuals in this group travel considerable distances every day and undertake seasonal migrations, in which they follow changes in water temperatures and currents. In winter active tropical sharks will be closer to the equator, whereas in summer they will be found much further north or south, depending on the hemisphere in which they occur.

Being such active swimmers, and following the seasonable water currents, many of the larger members of these species are found in all the world's tropical waters. Examples are the tiger shark *Galeocerdo cuvier*, bull shark *Carcharhinus leucas*, sandbar shark *C. plumbeus*, dusky shark *C. obscurus*, oceanic whitetip *C. longimanus*, blacktip *C. limbatus*, silky shark *C. falciformis*, scalloped hammerhead *Sphyrna lewini*, great hammerhead *S. mokarran*, smooth hammerhead *S. zygaena* and the whale shark *Rhincodon typus*. Most of these species grow to larger than 3 meters, a factor that helps to explain their common and worldwide distribution in tropical seas.

BELOW: Tropical sharks such as the great hammerhead *Sphyrna mokarran* favor warmer waters and are found in all oceans. A significant factor in the success of active tropical species is their size.

Ron & Valerie Taylor/Australasian Nature Transparencies

DISTRIBUTION OF THE WINGHEAD SHARK, *Eusphyra blochii*

The winghead shark is restricted to the Indo-Pacific region. It typifies the limited range of many smaller active species of sharks.

DISTRIBUTION OF THE BULL SHARK, *Carcharhinus leucas*

The bull shark is widespread along continental coasts and will penetrate deeply and for prolonged periods into fresh water.

One of these species, the bull shark *Carcharhinus leucas*, is also sometimes called the freshwater shark because of its habit of entering freshwater rivers and lakes in most of its range around the world. It has been recorded in such waters as the Amazon River, the Rio San Juan and Lake Nicaragua, the Mississippi River, the Congo River, the Zambezi River, the Bombay River, the Brisbane River, Lake Jamoer and the Panama Canal. In the Amazon River the bull shark has been recorded more than 3,000 kilometers upstream from the ocean.

The bull shark and the much more rare Ganges shark are the only species that invade fresh water to such an extent, and will spend long periods of time in fresh water. However, studies by Dr. Thomas B. Thorson, mainly on the Lake Nicaragua–Rio San Juan area, have shown that the bull shark does not spend its entire life in fresh water, but enters it for periods of up to several weeks. Just why it enters fresh water for these periods is not known, but it has been suggested that it is to exploit food resources there or to breed—perhaps even to rid itself of marine parasites. It should be mentioned here that various fishes sold in pet shops as freshwater "sharks" are not sharks at all; they are species of large minnows or catfishes.

Smaller species of tropical marine sharks (usually less than 3 meters in length) tend to have smaller ranges. Many species are restricted to the Indo-Pacific region. These include the winghead shark *Eusphyra blochii*, whitetip reef shark *Triaenodon obesus*, sharptooth lemon shark *Negaprion acutidens*, blackspot shark *C. sealei*, blacktip reef shark *C. melanopterus*, gray reef shark *C. amblyrhynchos* and snaggletooth shark *Hemipristis elongatus*.

An interesting pattern is found in the western Atlantic and eastern Pacific oceans, where many of these smaller species have populations in the

David Doubilet

tropical coastal waters on either side of Central America. These species include the bonnethead shark *Sphyrna tiburo*, scoophead shark *S. media*, lemon shark *Negaprion brevirostris* and smalltail shark *Carcharhinus porosus*. Such a distribution is probably due to a geological upheaval in Central America that occurred about 3 million years ago. Before then the western Atlantic and eastern Pacific oceans were one uninterrupted body of water and these species formed one continuous population throughout the area. Given enough time, and assuming that the Central American barrier remains, the two populations will probably diverge and become distinct species. These will then become sister species pairs, with one sister species on the Atlantic side and the other on the Pacific side.

LEFT: It has often been said that we know more about outer space than the oceans. The bizarre filter-feeding megamouth shark *Megachasma pelagios*, discovered in 1982, is known from only 10 specimens but may be wideranging, though rare, in the midwater zone of the ocean.

DISTRIBUTION OF THE TIGER SHARK, *Galeocerdo cuvier*

Like many of the larger sharks, the tiger shark is an active swimmer, traveling considerable distances each day and migrating according to seasonal changes.

DISTRIBUTION OF THE WHALE SHARK, *Rhincodon typus*

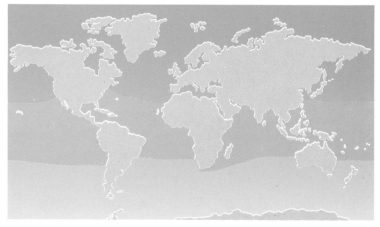

The whale shark—the largest of all—also has one of the widest distributions. It is one of a small group of large sharks that is both continental and oceanic.

Indeed this already seems to have occurred with some species that diverge more rapidly. Examples of already existing sister species pairs on opposite sides of Central America are the mallethead shark *Sphyrna corona* and the smalleye hammerhead *S. tudes*; the Pacific sharpnose shark *Rhizoprionodon longurio* and the Brazilian sharpnose shark *R. lalandei*; the sharpnose smoothhound *Mustelus dorsalis* and the smalleye smoothhound *M. higmani*; and the whitenose shark *Nasolamia velox* and the blacknose shark *Carcharhinus acronotus*. (In each of the above pairs the Pacific species is given first.)

The smallest species of tropical sharks, reaching only about a meter in length, have very small ranges and, hence, limited distributions. These forms occur only around a particular archipelago or in one region of an ocean. Their limited range may be due to their small size and their inability to swim long distances. Examples of such species in the Indo–Pacific region are the spadenose shark *Scoliodon laticaudus*, Australian sharpnose shark *Rhizoprionodon taylori*, gray sharpnose shark *R. oligolinx*, broadfin shark *Lamiopsis temmincki*, speartooth shark *Glyphis glyphis*, Ganges shark *G. gangeticus*, blacktail reef shark *Carcharhinus wheeleri*, Pondicherry shark *C. hemiodon*, creek whaler shark *C. fitzroyensis*, whitecheek shark *C. dussumieri*, nervous shark *C. cautus*, Borneo shark *C. borneensis*, sicklefin weasel shark *Hemigaleus microstoma*, hooktooth shark *H. macrostoma*, banded houndshark *Triakis scyllium*, spotted gully shark *T.megalopterus*, spotted houndshark *T. maculata*, sharpfin houndshark *T. acutipinna*, Arabian smoothhound *Mustelus mosis*, starspotted smoothhound *M. manazo* and the spotless smoothhound *M. griseus*.

In the Atlantic, examples of these species with small range and limited distribution include the Caribbean sharpnose shark *Rhizoprionodon porosus*, daggernose shark *Isogomphodon oxyrhynchus*, Caribbean reef shark *Carcharhinus perezi*, Atlantic weasel shark *Paragaleus pectoralis*, blackspot smoothhound *Mustelus punctulatus*, narrowfin smoothhound *M. norrisi*, starry smoothhound *M. asterias* and barbeled houndshark *Leptocharias smithii*.

BOTTOM-DWELLING TROPICAL SHARKS

The bottom-dwelling tropical sharks have, on the whole, relatively small ranges. They spend most of their time on the ocean floor, moving only to hunt their food. Indeed, many of them do not

BELOW: The nurse shark *Ginglymostoma cirratum* is common off western Africa, the east coast of both North and South America, and from California to Peru in the Pacific. All three populations differ somewhat in body measurements and color, but not enough to consider them different species.

H. G. de Couet/Auscape

actively hunt. They simply sit, camouflaged, on the bottom, waiting for an appropriate meal to come up to them. When the prey comes close enough they dart out, seize it and then settle back to await more prey. As a result, they do not swim great distances. Data suggests that in their lifetime many of these sharks do not travel more than several kilometers from where they were born. Many of them are fairly small, growing to less than 2 meters long. Like the small active swimming sharks discussed above, most of these bottom-dwelling species will be restricted to a particular archipelago or a region of a sea. Examples of tropical bottom-dwellers are the banded catsharks, species of the genera *Hemiscyllium* and *Chiloscyllium*; the carpetsharks or wobbegongs, species of the genera *Orectolobus*, *Sutorectus* and *Eucrossorhinus*; and species of angelsharks, genus *Squatina*.

Three species of fairly large bottom-dwelling sharks—the nurse shark *Ginglymostoma cirratum*, zebra shark *Stegostoma fasciatum* and tawny nurse *Nebrius ferrugineus*—do not fit this pattern. Being much larger sharks, growing on average to between 3 and 4 meters, and good swimmers when they need to be, they appear to travel much more than the smaller bottom-dwelling sharks. The zebra shark and the tawny nurse are both found throughout the Indo-Pacific region. They range from South Africa up to and throughout the Red and Arabian seas, along the coasts of India and China to as far north as the southernmost part of Japan, throughout the Indonesian archipelago to Australia and even as far as Pacific islands such as Fiji. The nurse shark has a very interesting distribution. In the eastern Atlantic Ocean it extends along the west coast of tropical Africa from around Senegal to Angola; in the western Atlantic Ocean it is found in tropical waters from the southern United States to Brazil, including the Caribbean and the Gulf of Mexico; and in the tropical eastern Pacific it is found from California to Peru.

These three populations are somewhat distinct and can be distinguished on the basis of morphometric measurements and differences in coloration. The western Atlantic and eastern Pacific populations are more similar to one another than either is to the eastern Atlantic population. This suggests that, as with some of the active swimming sharks, the western Atlantic and eastern Pacific populations were separated between 1 and 3 million years ago when Central America arose. Since then they have changed, but the differences are not enough to warrant calling them separate species.

ABOVE: One of the most attractive sharks, the 3-meter-long zebra shark *Stegostoma fasciatum* is common in shallow continental and island waters and on coral reefs throughout the eastern Pacific and Indian Ocean, from the Red Sea to Madagascar, southern Japan and Australia. Its diet consists mainly of mollusks, crabs, shrimp and small fish.

The eastern Atlantic population differs quite markedly from both of these and it does not appear that the nurse sharks cross the Atlantic Ocean. Nor have they ever been caught at the Azores islands or Ascension Island. As they are restricted to relatively shallow waters, the best explanation for their distribution may be in terms of continental drift. It is possible that before the Atlantic Ocean spread to its present width, the nurse shark lived in the quite shallow waters between Africa and South America. Then, over centuries, as the continents drifted apart and the Atlantic Ocean attained its great depths, the populations may have been separated. These two populations would, then, have been separated for about 10 million years and in that time the differences between them would have developed. Further studies should show whether this hypothesis is accurate.

TEMPERATE WATER SHARKS

Temperate water sharks live mostly at water temperatures between 10 and 21°Celsius. They include some of the carcharhinids (requiem sharks), heterodontids (hornsharks), triakids (smooth houndsharks), scyliorhinids (catsharks), lamnids (mackerel sharks), alopiids (thresher sharks), odontaspidids (sand tigers), many of the squalids (dogfish sharks), some of the squatinids (angelsharks) and the pristiophorids (sawsharks).

As with the tropical sharks, temperate water sharks can be divided into active swimmers and bottom dwellers. The active swimmers follow water currents or temperature changes. In winter they tend to be closer to the equator, and in summer they will be further away from it; depending on the hemisphere, they will be further north, or further south, than tropical sharks. Reflecting the patterns of tropical sharks, the larger species (more than 3 meters) are found virtually worldwide. However, because of their preference for cooler waters, they have what is

LEFT: The Pacific angelshark *Squatina californica* is one of the most widely distributed members of the family Squatinidae, and is common to abundant from southern Alaska to Chile. Like other angelsharks, it is an ambush predator of the seafloor.

DISTRIBUTION OF ANGELSHARKS, *genus Squatina*

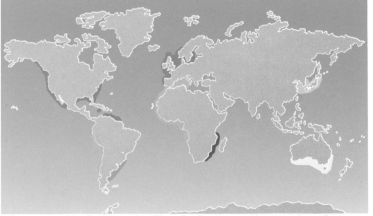

Like most other bottom-dwelling sharks, the various species of angelsharks are limited in their distribution.

called an antitropical distribution. This means that while there are Northern Hemisphere and Southern Hemisphere populations, they are generally absent in tropical or equatorial seas. Species with wide distribution include most of the lamnids: the basking shark *Cetorhinus maximus*, mako *Isurus oxyrinchus*, great white shark *Carcharodon carcharias*, and the blue shark *Prionace glauca* as well as the alopid thresher sharks (species of the genus *Alopias*) and odontaspidid sand tigers (species of the genus *Carcharias* and *Odontaspis*). The blue shark is probably one of the widest traveling species. Individuals tagged off Long Island, New York, have been recaptured off Spain, and individuals tagged off England have been recaptured off Brazil and New York. With individual animals traveling such distances, it is no wonder that the species is found worldwide!

Although these species are most common

LEFT: Although they are often encountered resting on the bottom close to shore, sand tigers *Carcharias taurus* are active predators from the surfline to depths of at least 190 meters. They are found in tropical and temperate waters of the Atlantic, Indian and western Pacific oceans, and many populations appear to be strongly migratory.

north or south of tropical or equatorial regions, they are also sometimes present in the deeper, cooler waters of tropical regions. In some tropical areas where the temperature of the surface water may be 27°Celsius at depths of between 30 and 60 meters, the water temperature may be as low as 15°Celsius. The blue shark, for example, is quite common near the surface in temperate areas and at depths of 60 meters in the tropics.

Other temperate water sharks also venture into tropical water, but to a lesser extent than the blue shark. Two species of lamnids, the porbeagle *Lamna nasus* and the salmon shark *L. ditropis*, are very similar and have exclusive ranges. The salmon shark is found only in the cold and temperate waters of the northern Pacific Ocean. The porbeagle has an amphitemperate distribution in the North and South Atlantic, the Indian Ocean and the southern fringes of the Pacific basin.

ABOVE: *Prionace glauca*, the blue shark, is a wideranging open ocean and coastal species that is found from the surface to depths of 150 meters. Although it is primarily an offshore species, it may venture close to shore at night and in temperate waters has been netted at the edges of littoral kelp forests, where it hunts fish, squid and pelagic crabs.

ABOVE: Collared catsharks are restricted to the island and continental shelves of Australia, the China Sea and Japan, and each species is known from a very small range. The Tasmanian spotted catshark *Parasyllium multimaculatum*, as its name suggests, is restricted to the inshore waters of Tasmania.

As they move very little, their distributions are quite limited. Usually they are only found around one archipelago or in only a restricted portion of one sea. Examples include angelsharks (species of the genus *Squatina*); sawsharks (species of the genera *Pristiophorus* and *Pliotrema*); hornsharks (species of the genus *Heterodontus*); and catsharks (species of the genera *Scyliorhinus*, *Atelomycterus*, *Poroderma*, *Halaelurus* and *Cephaloscyllium*).

ACTIVE COLD WATER SHARKS

Cold water sharks inhabit water colder than 10° Celsius. Many of them live very far north or south, in or close to arctic or antarctic waters. Others live in the deep, cold waters of temperate and even tropical regions. One species, the Taiwan dogfish *Centrophorus niaukang* has been caught at a depth of 2,500 meters. Another species, the Greenland, or sleeper, shark *Somniosus microcephalus* has actually been reported from under polar icefloes. Sharks found in cold water include cowsharks (family Hexanchidae); the frilled shark Chlamydoselachidae; some of the catsharks Scyliohinidae; the false catshark Pseudotriakidae; the goblin shark Mitsukurinidae; and some of the dogfish sharks (families Squalidae and Oxynotidae). These sharks can be divided into active swimmers and bottom dwellers.

Among the active swimming cold water sharks, large forms (more than 2 meters in length) were once thought to be found only very far north or very far south. As more deepwater research is done, we are finding that these species seem to be almost worldwide in distribution. In the far north and far south, they seem to come into shallow water, especially during winter months. However, in other areas they are found at depths of 300 meters and more. Some species also seem to follow seasonal migrations or currents, as they are found in one area at one

Like the smaller tropical species, the smaller active temperate sharks (usually less than 2 meters in length) have more limited ranges than the larger species. However, like the larger forms, they have Northern and Southern Hemisphere populations and are more or less absent in tropical water. If they are occasionally found in tropical areas, it is in deeper cooler waters. Examples of these sharks are the piked dogfish *Squalus acanthias*, Cuban dogfish S. *cubensis*, Japanese spurdog S. *japonicus*, shortspine spurdog S. *mitsukurii* and tope shark *Galeorhinus galeus* as well as houndsharks, genus *Triakis*, and smoothhound sharks, genus *Mustelus*.

Bottom-dwelling sharks in temperate waters are small, growing to less than 2 meters in length.

DISTRIBUTION OF THE GREAT WHITE SHARK, *Carcharodon carcharias*

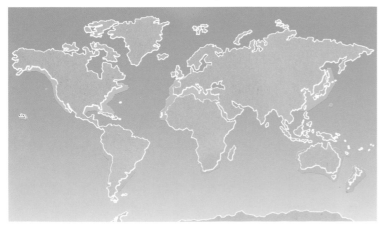

The great white, the killer shark of so many legends, has a relatively wide but distinctly coastal distribution.

DISTRIBUTION OF THE BONNETHEAD SHARK, *Sphyrna tiburo*

A geographical upheaval may account for the appearance of distinct populations of this species on either side of Central America.

Esther Beaton/Auscape

time of the year and another area another time of the year. There are depths at which the water temperature is almost the same as that of arctic or antarctic waters.

Among the larger active cold water sharks are the six- and seven-gilled sharks (species of the genera *Hexanchus* and *Notorynchus*), frilled shark *Chlamydoselachus anguineus*, false catshark *Pseudotriakis microdon*, goblin shark *Mitsukurina owstoni* and the sleeper sharks (species of the genus *Somniosus*). Although tagging or tracking studies of these species have not yet been done, it is possible that when they are, we will find that individuals travel great distances, because food is relatively scarce in such cold waters.

The smaller species of active cold water sharks (less than 1 meter in length) all live in depths of 300 meters or more. Even in the far north and south they are not known to come close to the surface. Originally they were thought to be rather rare and to have only limited distributions. However, recent research at greater depths has shown them to be more common and to be much more widely distributed than was once thought. In fact, most recent studies suggest that most of these species have global distributions in the deep seas. Further studies may show that, like the larger species, these smaller cold water sharks travel extensively in order to find enough prey to sustain themselves. All the smaller cold water

ABOVE: Hornsharks (family Heterodontidae) are necessarily restricted in their ranges, since their diet of mollusks, sea urchins and crustaceans can only be found relatively close to shore in temperate and tropical waters. The Port Jackson shark *Heterodontus portusjacksoni* is strongly migratory and returns each year to favored breeding sites.

DISTRIBUTION OF THE SPOTTED GULLY SHARK *Triakis megalopterus*, ●
AND SPOTTED HOUNDSHARK, *Triakis maculata* ●

The very limited distribution of these sharks is typical of many active temperate and tropical sharks.

DISTRIBUTION OF THE COOKIECUTTER SHARK, genus *Isistius*

The cookiecutters exemplify "spotty" distribution. Although widespread, their distribution appears to be limited to specific depths.

David Doublet

ABOVE: One of the many reasons for sharks' evolutionary success stems from the fact that unrelated species occupy similar niches in different environments. Thus, the blue shark *Prionace glauca* occupies the same freeranging, predatory niche in temperate seas as the oceanic whitetip *Carcharhinus longimanus* does in tropical waters.

worldwide in distribution, but there are at least 31 species (according to some estimates there might be twice that number) and each seems to have its own small "pocket" on the ocean floor. The only other group of bottom-dwelling cold water sharks, the roughsharks (species of the genus *Oxynotus*, family Oxynotidae), has only five species which, however, have somewhat larger distributions. The one exception is the false catshark *Pseudotriakis microdon* which grows to a fairly large size, 2 to 3 meters, and seems to be fairly widely spread, but rare.

Because in certain areas sharks live at different depths, according to the water temperature, a stratification often occurs. It occurs most frequently in tropical areas where variations in water temperature are most marked with depth. In the same general area tropical, temperate and cold water shark species will be found at different depths. Some species, however, live only in areas where particular temperatures and depths coincide. For these species, both the temperature and the water depth must be right. For example, most requiem sharks (family Carcharhinidae) and hammerheads (family Sphyrnidae) prefer tropical shallow waters. In the middle of a tropical ocean—say the Pacific—where the water depth is 1,500 meters, one will not find hammerheads or most species of requiem sharks, even near the surface. On the other hand, the oceanic whitetip *Carcharhinus longimanus*, a pelagic species of requiem shark, prefers tropical waters that are, on average, at least 60 meters deep. This species does not come close into shore in shallow tropical water, but remains in the upper, tropical layers in the middle of all oceans where the depth is 1,500 meters.

In temperate water, the oceanic whitetip is replaced by the blue shark, a temperate pelagic species. Most species of temperate and tropical sharks are shallower water species that inhabit

sharks are dogfish, species of the genera *Squalus*, *Isistius*, *Etmopterus*, *Deania*, *Dalatias*, *Centroscymnus* and *Centrophorus*.

BOTTOM-DWELLING COLD WATER SHARKS

The bottom-dwelling cold water sharks, too, are found only in deep cold waters and never come close to the surface, even in the far north or south. Most are less than 1 meter in length but unlike the active swimming species, have small distributions. They seem to be sedentary and to move only short distances during their entire lives. Indeed, many species seem to have ranges that cover only a few thousand square kilometers. The deepwater catsharks, genus *Apristurus*, are

DISTRIBUTION OF THE OCEANIC WHITETIP, *Carcharhinus longimanus*

The oceanic whitetip has a very wide distribution that is typical of many of the larger species of sharks.

DISTRIBUTION OF THE BASKING SHARK, *Cetorhinus maximus*

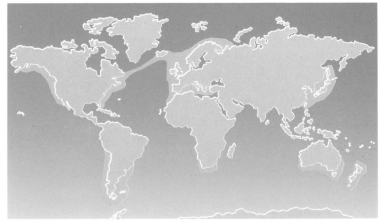

The basking shark has an antitropical distribution. It is typical of a number of species that are more common away from tropical and equatorial seas.

Ken Lucas/Seaphot

water less than 30 meters deep. Pelagic sharks form only a small group: as well as the blue shark and oceanic whitetip, pelagic species include the whale shark *Rhincodon typus*, mako *Isurus oxyrinchus*, basking shark *Cetorhinus maximus*, porbeagle *Lamna nasus* and salmon shark *L. ditropis*. As well, all species of the family Lamnidae, including the great white shark *Carcharodon carcharias* and all the species of thresher shark *Alopias* are pelagic.

When active swimming species from temperate and cold waters move into deeper waters, they stratify themselves in the water layers. When in this stratified condition they are

called midwater sharks, as they are at neither the water's surface nor near the bottom. The active swimming species of cold water sharks, except for the few species that come into cold shallow water in the far north or south, always behave as midwater species, finding the depth where the water temperature suits them.

A survey of the distribution patterns that have been outlined in this chapter will show that sharks are found in all of the world's marine waters—from the deepest parts of the oceans to the shallowest tropical waters, from the coldest arctic and antarctic waters to temperate and tropical rivers and lakes.

ABOVE: Wideranging in temperate and cold waters, the broadnose sevengill shark *Notorhynchus cepedianus* is a powerful and indiscriminate predator whose diet of other sharks, bony fishes, stingrays and carrion has enabled it to thrive in a range of habitats from the surface to at least 46 meters deep.

DISTRIBUTION OF THE SALMON SHARK, *Lamna ditropis*

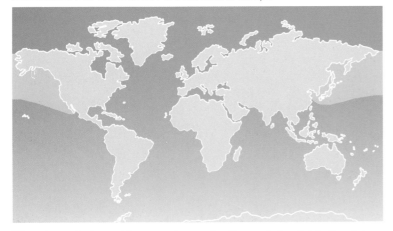

The salmon shark provides a good example of an exclusive distribution. It is found only in the northern Pacific Ocean.

DISTRIBUTION OF THE GREENLAND SHARK, *Somniosus microcephalus*

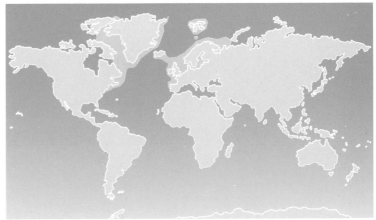

This cold water shark has been recorded underneath polar icefloes. Although it may reach 7 meters, it is sluggish when captured.

ABOVE: Despite common belief, remoras are active and strong-swimming fish that do not rely on sharks to provide them with food; indeed, they seem to "hitch a ride" only when it suits them and are often found attached to turtles, which are vegetarians and do not provide food for their companions.

FRIENDS AND ENEMIES

CARSON CREAGH

Sharks do not exist in an ecological vacuum: as predators, they play a vital part in the complex web of interactions that make up the oceanic food chain and, like all organisms, associate with other species in symbiotic relationships.

Symbiosis is popularly defined as mutual dependence, but in its widest sense can be regarded simply as "living together." Where one organism benefits from the relationship and the other is not affected, the relationship is called commensalism; where both parties benefit it is called mutualism; and if one organism benefits at the expense of the other, the relationship is called parasitism.

The relationship between sharks and pilotfish is a classic case of commensalism. It was once believed that pilotfish guided—literally piloted—their shortsighted and dimwitted "masters" to food, and in return were protected from other predators and spared by their grateful companions.

Unfortunately, pilotfish neither direct sharks to food, nor are their lives spared if they are slow, ill or weak. The fish themselves certainly benefit from the relationship by stealing scraps of food, and it has recently been suggested that they derive other advantages from the relationship. Smaller pilotfish gain some hydrodynamic benefits, riding the shark's "bow wave" in much the same way as dolphins will with a ship. More intriguing is the idea that pilotfish, being schooling fishes, are attracted to moving objects that offer contrasts in brightness—a diver, a school of other pilotfish, a manta ray … or a shark. They are more robots than guides, attracted to sharks merely through instinctive schooling responses rather than any knowledge of feeding advantages.

Diskfish, commonly known as remoras or suckerfish (family Echeneidae) were once thought to "take advantage" of sharks in the same way as their relatives the pilotfish—simply attaching themselves by their louvered suction cups (actually highly modified dorsal fins) and "hitching a ride" in order to steal food scraps.

The truth is more complex, and demonstrates some of the adaptations bony fishes made to take advantage of their supposedly more primitive relatives. The eight species of diskfish have evolved to live with more or less specific hosts: the remora *Remora remora*, sharksucker *Echeneis naucrates* and white suckerfish *Remorina*

ABOVE: The remora or suckerfish grows to 60 centimeters in length and smaller specimens are sometimes found living inside the gill cavities of sharks, manta rays or marlin without causing any harm to their hosts.

albescens are usually found with sharks or rays, and the whalesucker *Remorina australis* with baleen whales and larger toothed whales. The sharksucker does not spend most of its time attached to a shark. Instead, like the pilotfish, it rides the shark's bow wave, only using its suction disk to attach itself when its host changes direction or slows down.

However, the stomach contents of both sharksuckers and remoras reveal that their relationship with sharks must be regarded as mutualism. Almost all of their food consists of parasitic copepods, and the remora and white suckerfish have adapted so well to their role as cleaners that they have short, stumpy bodies and reduced fins, and are most often found inside the mouths or gill chambers of sharks and rays.

Other organisms also provide a service to sharks, apparently ridding them of external parasites, or ectoparasites, that are too small for diskfish to remove. Most tropical reefs have a resident population of cleaner fishes (usually wrasses or blennies) and shrimps that earn a living by removing parasites from a range of elasmobranchs and bony fishes. These animals move purposefully over the shark's skin, picking off copepods and often entering the mouths or gill chambers of their "clients." Both lemon sharks and nurse sharks will rest on the bottom to be cleaned and nurse sharks have been observed to halt the movements of their gills for up to two minutes while they are served by cleaners. This is a remarkable example of mutualism.

Just as "big fleas have little fleas," so sharks, like all other organisms, have parasites that survive at the expense of their unwilling host. As well as flatworms and roundworms, there are specialized marine leeches that live only around the cloaca and claspers of sharks. But the most common ectoparasites are undoubtedly the copepods, highly evolved crustaceans that range

from less than a millimeter to around 30 millimeters in length. Copepods usually feed on the skin tissues of their hosts, especially on the trailing surfaces of fins, but one species, *Ommatokoita elongata*, attaches itself to the cornea of Greenland shark eyes. Even more strangely, this minuscule species of parasite is bioluminescent and may therefore act as a lure to attract prey to these lethargic bottom-dwelling sharks.

The trend in shark evolution toward urea retention as a means of establishing a chemical balance between the interior of the body and the surrounding seawater has made life difficult for most parasites, but tapeworms appear to have rallied to the challenge and comprise the most abundant—more than 400 species—internal parasites, or endoparasites, of elasmobranchs. Although few grow to more than 20 centimeters long, thousands of smaller tapeworms have been recovered from the intestine of a single shark. They are indeed successful parasites!

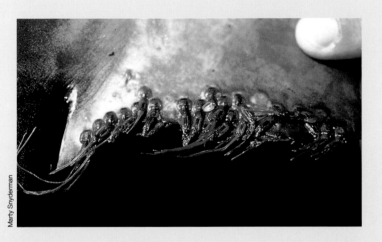

Marty Snyderman

ABOVE: Among the most common body and skin parasites of sharks are copepods, crustaceans often referred to as sea lice. Most of the 4,500 species of copepods are free-living, but 1,000 or so are parasites ranging in size from less than one millimeter to 30 millimeters long. These are usually found attached to the fins or gills of their hosts.

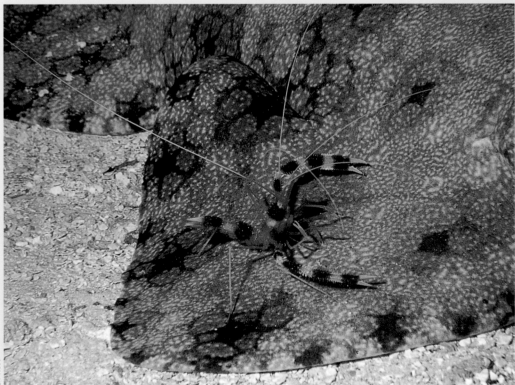

Bill Wood

LEFT: A banded coral shrimp *Stenopus hispidus* removes tiny parasites from the skin of a wobbegong as it rests on the seafloor. These shrimps set up "cleaning stations" near coral outcrops and clean parasites from the skin and mouths of fish and sharks, which will even cease breathing to allow the shrimps to rid their gills of parasites.

Sensory Systems

Edward S. Hodgson

Fascination and fear usually dominate human reactions to the behavior of sharks. Both these reactions lead to questions about the senses of sharks. What "triggers" a shark to feed or attack? How does a shark detect a triggering stimulus? Can we, through understanding the sense organs involved, interfere with their functions and block shark behavior that is hazardous to humans?

Early attempts to answer such questions concentrated upon the shark's sense of smell (olfaction). Nineteenth-century biologists plugged the nasal openings in the snouts of sharks and observed that the animals then failed to detect food. If only one nasal opening was blocked, the shark typically veered toward the normal unblocked side, swimming in circles. Dr. George Parker of Harvard University, who did many of these experiments on "circus movements," concluded that sharks tried to balance the amounts of chemical stimulation they detected on the two sides of the snout—a behavior that would normally enable the swimming shark to home in on a source of odors, such as a bleeding fish. Sharks were viewed as "swimming noses," with the other senses being of minor importance. More recent studies show that feeding and attack behaviors depend upon several important senses, including at least one that is absent or poorly understood in most other animals.

BELOW: Sharks were once thought to have poor eyesight, but research has demonstrated that many species can hunt by sight and, in fact, have excellent vision. In bottom-dwelling species, however, such as this Port Jackson shark, the eye is relatively small and vision is not as important as smell or electroreception for feeding or social behavior.

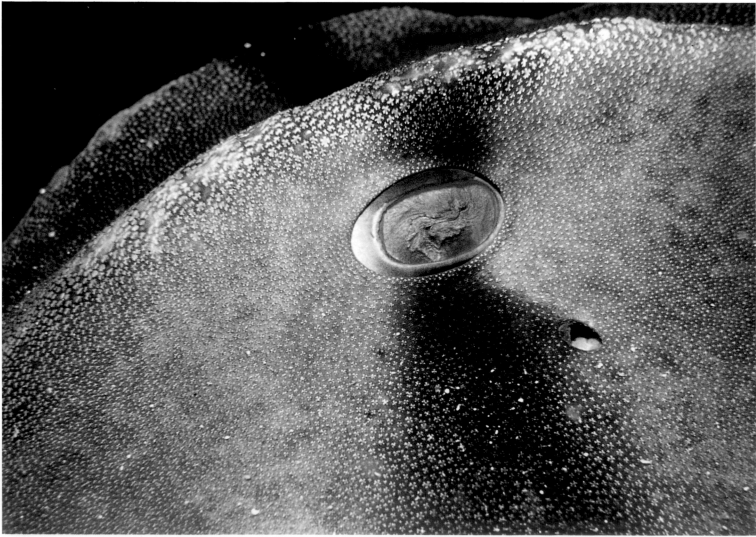

MECHANICAL AND ACOUSTIC SENSES

The senses of touch and hearing in sharks involve stimulation of specialized hairlike cells located in, or very near, the body surface. Most hair cells of sharks occur in pits, grooves or canals which make up the lateral line, extending along the shark's side and branching throughout the head. Mechanical strain on the largest hairlike projection from one of these sensory cells produces an electrical change within the cell. That electrical change stimulates an attached nerve fiber, which passes the "information" to the shark's central nervous system.

Since the information carried along nerves is in the form of brief electrical impulses, it has been possible to record that information by connecting amplifiers and oscilloscopes to the nerves. Such recordings made from lateral line nerves have shown that the hair cells detect the direction as well as the amount of movement in their fine projections (cilia). If the smaller cilia are bent toward the largest one, the hair cell is highly stimulated and many nerve impulses are sent to the brain. If the smaller cilia are bent away from the largest one, fewer nerve impulses go to the brain. It appears that the shark uses this characteristic of its hair cells to detect water currents, monitor its swimming direction or localize vibrations in the water.

The importance of the lateral line sensory system is indicated by the large number of nerve fibers running between it and the brain. Dr. Barry Roberts, of Amsterdam University, The Netherlands, counted about 6,000 sensory nerve fibers from the lateral line that fed into the brain of a dogfish shark *Scyliorhinus*.

Curiously, sharks also have nerves that carry impulses in the opposite direction toward the hair cell sense organs. Impulses in these outgoing nerves inhibit the lateral line sense cells whenever the shark makes violent movements, as in escape or attack behavior. Dr. Roberts and his co-workers believe that this is a safety mechanism to prevent overloading and fatigue in the hair cell receptors. In effect, the mechanical senses are kept in fully rested and responsive condition, ready to resume their usual jobs the instant that violent behavior stops.

The ear of the shark is closely related to the lateral line system. Patches of hair cells lie within the inner ear, and are stimulated by vibrations having frequencies below a thousand cycles per second (1,000 Hz). Field studies confirm that some sharks are attracted to sounds in the frequency range of 25 to 100 Hz, especially if the sounds are pulsed, like the low-frequency sounds made by struggling fish.

Traditional folk wisdom of Pacific Islanders recognizes and exploits the shark's sensitivity to sound. Fishermen in the Society, Fiji, Tonga and Caroline islands, among others, commonly shake coconut shell rattles underwater to produce intermittent bursts of low-frequency sound that attract sharks. There are also reports of Pacific Islanders repelling sharks with underwater sounds, but scientists have not yet been able to use sound to accomplish this consistently.

CHEMICAL SENSES (SMELL AND TASTE)

The sensitivity of sharks to chemicals is attested by many examples: the spearfisherman's loss of a freshly punctured catch to an attracted shark; the injured survivors of boating mishaps being circled or attacked by sharks; or the use of chum by fishermen and photographers to lure sharks within range of their hooks or lenses. Early

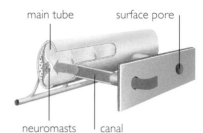

ABOVE: The shark's lateral line. This line, which extends along the shark's side and branches throughout the head, marks the position of most of the specialized hair cell receptors that are central to the shark's sensory system.

ABOVE: The diagram shows how vibrations enter through the skin pores and stimulate the sensory hair cells, or neuromasts, which are connected to the nervous system.

BELOW: Sharks' hearing is particularly sensitive to low-frequency vibrations, a fact exploited by local fishermen in New Ireland (left) and the Solomons (below), where coconut shell rattles are used to attract sharks.

RIGHT; Sharks can detect incredibly low concentrations of chemicals through the nasal sacs inside the nostrils. The sacs are lined with folded sensory tissues arranged in rows. A fleshy flap across the center of each nasal sac channels water flow over the receptor-bearing olfactory tissue. In this photograph the flap has been surgically removed to expose the underlying folded sensory tissue.

Edward S. Hodgson

BELOW: Bottom-dwelling species such as the Port Jackson shark hunt in darkness and often feed on animals that try to escape detection by burying themselves in sand. The small eyes of these sharks are of limited use and their nostrils have evolved into elaborately folded structures that expose the maximum surface area to water to detect faint odors.

experiments, mentioned above, ruled out visual cues to the sharks in many of these cases. The olfactory sacs on the shark's snout are the location of greatest chemical sensitivity (smell), while taste receptors occur in the mouth and pharynx, enabling the shark to make a final discrimination of food before it is swallowed. Modern investigations of the chemical senses of sharks generally use pure chemical stimuli, tested in precisely determined amounts under carefully controlled conditions. Since these test requirements are not easily achieved under field conditions, such work must be done in

laboratories. Electrical changes in olfactory organs, or in the brain, are recorded to detect responses of the shark's nervous system while chemicals are applied to the sense organs.

As a follow-up, behavior of unrestrained sharks may be studied in natural field conditions, using the same chemicals that were tested in the laboratory. Comparisons between observations in the laboratory and in the field have been particularly revealing. They show what kinds of chemicals have the most powerful effects upon sense organs and upon behavior, and how attractants and repellents differ in their effects upon the shark's sense organs.

The most extensive recent experiments of this kind were conducted at the Lerner Marine Laboratory in the Bahamas, as part of the US Navy's research program on sharks. Wires were connected to smell organs or brains of lemon sharks *Negaprion brevirostris* and nurse sharks *Ginglymostoma cirratum* at various positions. While patterns of electrical activities at these sites were being monitored, chemicals mixed in seawater were allowed to flow through the olfactory sac. Chemicals that attract sharks produce characteristic changes in the olfactory organs and the front part of the shark's brain.

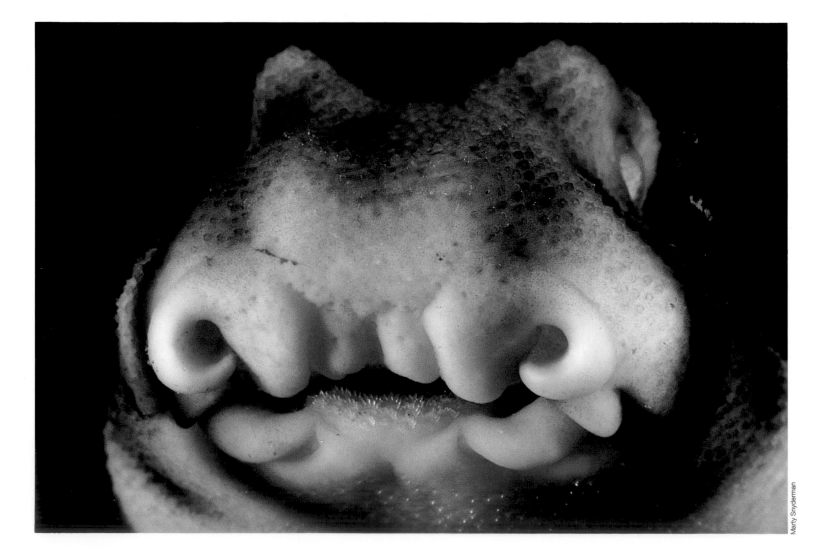

Marty Snyderman

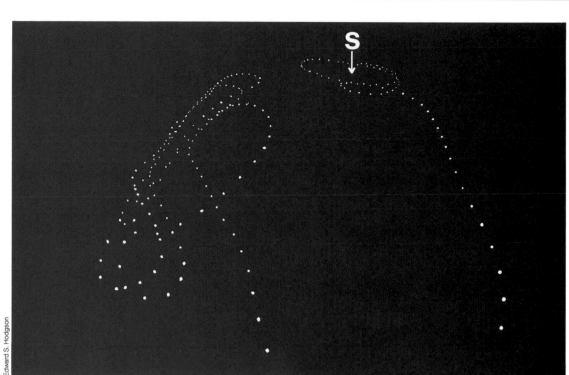

Edward S. Hodgson

Several components of meat (amino acids) and chemicals found in the skin or excretions of fish (betaine, trimethylamine) and components of blood (hemoglobin and serum albumen) produced changes in nerve activity, as well as eliciting approach and feeding reactions in free-swimming sharks.

Unexpectedly, it was found that a more posterior part of the brain (medulla) also showed changes in nerve activity during stimulation; this proved to be a change in the nerve centers that control the contraction of gill muscles. When the shark first senses an attractive chemical stimulus, the gills give an extra "beat," pumping extra water through the gill openings. Then, for several seconds while the shark lunges ahead, the gills are closed down against the body, apparently an advantage in providing maximum streamlining during the first few seconds of pursuit or attack.

Behavior of free-swimming sharks was studied at Bimini by photographing the trails of blinker lights attached to sharks, or by using underwater television to monitor shark activities in the open ocean. Fortunately, there was good correlation between the types of chemicals (amino acids and amines) that produced the greatest changes in a shark's brain activity in the laboratory and those chemicals that triggered orientation and approach behavior in the sea. The actual orientation mechanisms used by sharks to approach chemical stimuli, however, were found to differ. Nurse sharks *Ginglymostoma* home in on the stimulus by swimming criss-cross through the olfactory corridor toward the greatest concentration of chemical. Lemon sharks *Negaprion*, and closely related species, react to chemical stimuli by swimming into the strongest water current and using that current as their main

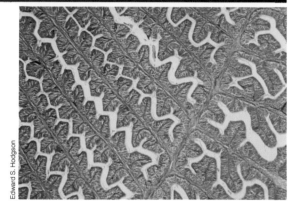

Edward S. Hodgson

"guide" until they are near the chemical source. Under normal circumstances, either method works to bring the shark near its prey.

Some of the most stimulating chemical attractants, components of meat or blood, may affect a shark's brain activity and behavior at concentrations as low as one-millionth part of a molar solution in seawater. To explain how such low thresholds could possibly stimulate olfactory receptors, some biologists have suggested that chemicals might become bound to the nasal sac lining and thereby reach higher accumulated amounts. However, when radioactive chemical stimuli were injected into the shark's nasal sac, and the densely packed receptor cells were examined for radioactive accumulation, nothing of the sort was found. Evidently the stimuli flow freely through the smell organs, exciting the smell receptors in no more than a few thousandths of a second, and then pass out of the nasal sac.

When stronger concentrations of effective chemical stimuli are encountered, sharks generally attempt to bite anything visible in their immediate area. Such a case is shown in the

Edward S. Hodgson

ABOVE: Scientists at the Lerner Marine Laboratory anesthetize a dusky shark *Carcharhinus obscurus* by pumping a diluted solution of anesthetic into the mouth so that it will flow into the gills and inhibit the shark's respiration.

BELOW: A group of lemon sharks engages in social circling in the shark testing pool at the Lerner Marine Laboratory.

photograph opposite, where a large lemon shark, after stimulation with an invisible amine and amino acid mixture, is making a frenzied attack upon air bubbles at the ocean surface. Plastic bottles containing mixtures of amino acids and amines that are allowed to diffuse slowly in the water may be attacked by sharks passing nearby on coral reefs. This is another confirmation of the relevance of laboratory findings to the understanding of shark behavior in natural surroundings.

Attempts to find an "ultimate" chemical repellent have now largely been abandoned. Instead attention has shifted to naturally occurring repellents. These are found in various animals that appear to have no defense against predators, but which are not attacked by other fish or sharks.

One of the earliest recognized natural repellents is holothurian, found in sea cucumbers *Actinopyga agassizi*, relatives of the beche-de-mer used in some Asian soups. When a shark attempts to grasp a living sea cucumber—an event that happens rarely—the cucumber is quickly ejected from the mouth and is not disturbed again. Both the shark's smell and taste receptors are affected by the sea cucumber's protective secretion. In the

laboratory, nerve recordings show that holothurian disrupts, and later blocks chemoreceptor responses. A dilution of one part in 600,000 of holothurian can kill a 20-kilogram shark in a tank, but in the open ocean any shark is likely to swim away before receiving such a toxic dose of the repellent.

A similar case involves the relatively immobile fish *Pardachirus marmoratus*, the Moses sole from the Red Sea. A milky secretion, which is retained in the mucous covering of the fish's skin, deters sharks from biting the sole. The repellent is an acidic protein that reduces water surface tension and upsets the crucial stability of receptor cell membranes.

Still more effective natural repellents may be found in the large numbers of relatively slow-moving invertebrate animals in many marine environments such as coral reefs. Naturally occurring repellents, evolved specifically for their effects upon the chemical senses and behaviors of predatory sharks and fish, may be safer to use and more effective than many chemicals tested in the past. Nevertheless, remembering the lessons learned from excessive claims for previous products, scientists have become more cautious in evaluating potential shark repellents.

Edward S. Hodgson

EYES AND VISION

The eyes of sharks are basically similar to those found in many backboned animals, with a rigid eyeball enclosing a light-sensitive receptor area (retina). Shark retinas are populated largely by rod cells (functioning in dim light) but they also include cone cells (functioning in bright light). Dr. Samuel Gruber of the University of Miami, who devised a behavioral test for color vision in sharks, reported that at least one species appears to be capable of responding to color cues. Many shark species have been shown to be capable of distinguishing between different

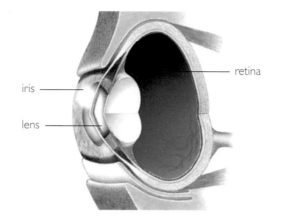

LEFT: A cross-section of a shark's eye. Eye size and position vary widely.

iris

lens

retina

LEFT: Unlike lemon sharks, nurse sharks *Ginglymostoma cirratum* track down chemical stimuli by criss-crossing through the "olfactory corridor" toward the source. A high concentration may even stimulate this normally placid species into a feeding frenzy.

BELOW: An invisible but, to the shark, potent mixture of amino acids and amines—components, respectively, of meat and fish skin or excretions—has stimulated this lemon shark into a frenzied attack on air bubbles at the ocean surface, confirming in field conditions results obtained in laboratory experiments.

intensities of light and between different shapes of test patterns.

Although there have been few surprises from studies on the eyes of sharks, an interesting assortment of anatomical variations, related to the particular habitats or behavior of various species, has been revealed. Eye size and position, for example, vary over a wide range. Relatively inactive sharks inhabiting shallow waters—such as hornsharks and carpetsharks—have eyes that usually measure less than 1 percent of their body length, suggesting that they rely far less upon vision than other senses.

More active, midwater predatory species have larger eyes. Extreme eye enlargement is found in the big-eyed thresher sharks that inhabit deep water. They have upwardly directed eyes that may be as large as one-fifth the size of the head. Extremely large eye size is typical of deep-dwelling fishes, and the upward aim of the thresher shark's eyes may provide it with a better view of prey that it is attacking with the elongated upper lobe of its tail.

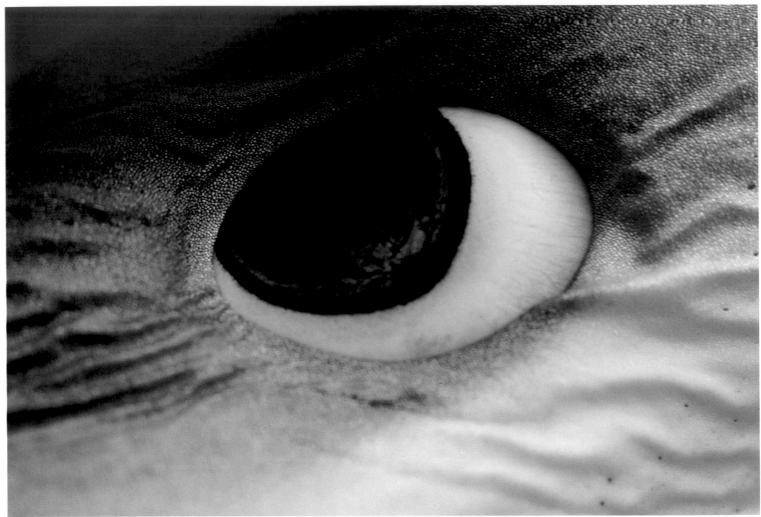

Ron & Valerie Taylor

ABOVE: Active, fast-moving sharks that live in the open ocean make use of sight for hunting and have much larger eyes than bottom-dwelling species. Many, such as this pelagic blue shark *Prionace glauca*, have eyes equipped with a tapetum—a layer of mirrorlike cells on the retina that reflect light back to receptor cells.

The eyes of most sharks are rimmed with immovable eyelids. However, some (particularly the carcharhinid sharks) have the lower lid folded into a nictitating membrane. This tough, movable membrane closes over the eye during feeding and protects it from damage. There is no need for eyelids to close and lubricate the eye or to reduce the amount of light that enters. Opening and contracting the pupil of the shark's eye regulate the light that is admitted.

Perhaps the most remarkable feature of the shark's eye is a series of reflecting plates (tapetum) just behind the retina. The tapetal plates function like mirrors, reflecting up to 90 percent of certain colors of light back into the light receptor cells of the eye. This increases the sensitivity of the eye and produces "eyeshine" similar to that seen in cats. Sharks that live in brightly lit shallow waters can darken the tapetum with movable pigments, much as a curtain might be pulled across a mirror. All these eye specializations clearly refute the old assumption that vision plays only a minor part in the shark's sensitivity to its environment.

ELECTRICAL AND MAGNETIC SENSES

The most unusual senses used by sharks allow them to detect weak electrical voltages. Such electrical cues may emanate from prey animals or be produced by currents flowing through the earth's magnetic field. Sharks may employ their "electrical sense" in ordinary daily orientation during long-distance migration and in locating nearby prey. Experiments that reveal these abilities and analyze the operation of the sense organs that make them possible are among the most exciting in the modern study of sensory systems.

Since the 1930s, there have been reports that dogfish sharks *Scyliorhinus*, as well as skates and other relatives of sharks, are sensitive to metallic objects in the water. Drs. Dijkgraaf and Kalmijn, working in the Netherlands, found that skates could detect voltage gradients as low as 0.01 microvolt per centimeter, the greatest electrical sensitivity known in the whole animal kingdom! They showed that the sense organs detecting these weak electric fields are the so-called ampullae of Lorenzini—delicate jelly-filled canals connected to pores in the skin of the shark's or skate's snout.

In an ingenious extension of laboratory tests to events in the open sea, Kalmijn recently tested the responses of the dogfish shark *Mustelus canis* to underwater electrical stimuli off the coast of Massachusetts, USA. Two electrodes were fastened to an underwater cable and energized from an electrical simulator in a rubber raft that floated above the test area. A fish extract was allowed to flow out of a chumming tube, also fastened to the underwater cable. When the fish odor attracted sharks into the area, Kalmijn observed their behavior through a glass-bottomed viewing box next to the raft.

He describes typical dogfish behavior as follows: "After entering the test area, the dogfish began randomly searching the sand, evidently trying to locate the odor source … when nearing the underwater setup, the animals did not bite at the opening of the chumming tube, but turned sharply toward the current electrodes from distances up to 25 centimeters, viciously attacking the electrically stimulated prey." On the basis of several hundred observations of shark attacks on the source of electric current, Kalmijn concluded that odor stimuli attracted the sharks from a distance but at close range the electrical fields were much more compelling to the animals.

An intriguing possibility is that sharks may have an inbuilt electromagnetic compass sense that they can use for orientation. When swimming through the earth's magnetic field, a shark induces electric fields that depend upon the direction of the shark's movement. Experiments on the leopard shark *Triakis semifasciata* and also on stingrays, related to sharks, show that these animals change their swimming directions when the earth's normal magnetic field in their area is changed by energizing a nearby induction coil.

In fact, when the earth's magnetic field was approximately neutralized, the animals appeared to lose their sense of position and moved randomly. These observations open up questions of enormous importance for understanding shark behavior. They also suggest that we have a long way to go in research before claiming even an approximate understanding of the shark's total sensory world.

THE SENSES AND BEHAVIOR

Human imagination is inevitably strained when attempting to comprehend the total sensory input that influences a shark's behavior at any given moment. It is most unlikely that a shark ever relies upon one type of sense organ alone; the animal's brain presumably integrates the nerve impulses from thousands of receptor cells which, more or less simultaneously, signal detection of mechanical, chemical, visual and electric stimuli. Different sensory systems may temporarily dominate during the various stages of behavioral patterns, such as the feeding or attack patterns.

As a final illustration, consider a shark that orients toward a potential food source and eventually eats it. Underwater sounds (the struggles of an injured fish, or some similar low-frequency vibrations) can attract the shark from a

great distance. Approaching the sound source, the shark may cross an odor corridor emanating from a wound or excretion. The smell may trigger a more precise orientation that will depend upon the shark species—some will home in by criss-crossing the odor trail; others will simply swim upstream against the odor-carrying current.

Once close to the potential food, electrical potentials from the prey's heartbeat or muscle contractions may provide cues for a more precise aim. The shark may obtain further information visually, while circling the prey, or get tactile information by bumping the prey with the snout. The actual attack will be a superbly integrated affair with nictitating membranes closed over the eyes and gill movements giving an extra charge of oxygen and then maximum streamlining even as the jaw begins to open and close.

No one pattern will fit all sharks, for the sense organs and sensory worlds of each species are somewhat different. In every case, however, we can be sure that both sense organs and the behavior they influence are superbly adapted to the habitat and needs of the species—one of the chief reasons sharks have been successful for some 450 million years.

ABOVE: The shark's sensitive electroreceptor system is based on delicate jelly-filled canals called the ampullae of Lorenzini, connected to pores on the surface of the skin.

BELOW: The shark's brain. Hundreds of thousands of specialized cells—called neurons—receive impulses from the sensory systems. The information is processed in different parts of the brain. Mechanical, chemical, visual and electric stimuli are integrated to determine the shark's behavior.

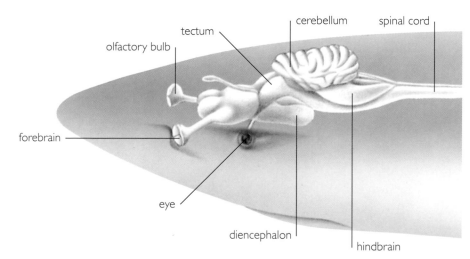

olfactory bulb

tectum

cerebellum

spinal cord

forebrain

eye

diencephalon

hindbrain

SHARK BEHAVIOR

Ron & Valerie Taylor

ABOVE: When a number of sharks (especially highly social gray reef sharks) feed together, the sheer volume of sensory input—from smell to sight, vibration and electrosense—builds to a crescendo that sometimes overwhelms normal inhibitions. The result—a feeding frenzy that is the equivalent of violent mob behavior in humans.

Arthur A. Myrberg Jr.

Sharks' behavior is inextricably linked to their remarkable sensory systems that influence every aspect of their lives and may be responsible for what often seems to be erratic or dangerous behavior. The longstanding myth that sharks are mindless, destructive automatons has been destroyed by studies that show them to be sophisticated and remarkably intelligent animals, capable of learning and possessing subtle social systems.

CHANGING PERSPECTIVES

Sharks have been raised to mythic status whenever they have directly influenced human endeavor. Pacific Islanders, for example, have long been acquainted with the habits and movements of sharks and can predict when and where they can be found. Interest in sharks was minimal, however, in the great population centers of the world through much of the twentieth century. Human–shark interactions were not only rarely reported, but relatively little public news media existed to disseminate information rapidly to outlying regions. Science also had little interest in the ways of sharks.

Nevertheless, coastal fishermen were often highly interested in sharks, since they were familiar with not only reduced catches due to shark predation but also the reasonable prices paid for sharks in certain regions. That interest, in turn, generated sporadic investigations by fishery scientists from several countries between the early 1920s and mid-1960s, particularly the United States, England and Australia.

Progress in understanding shark behavior accelerated following the establishment of the Shark Research Panel by the American Institute of Biological Sciences in 1958. The panel, supported in large measure by the US Navy's Office of Naval Research, was concerned with all aspects of the biology of elasmobranch fishes but emphasis was directed at the shark hazard problem. Although that problem had long been recognized in certain regions of the world before World War II, little concern existed elsewhere until the war brought about global use of the oceans. The shark hazard problem continued after the end to hostilities because of the increasing importance of the oceans for recreational purposes.

STUDYING SHARKS

Sharks are inherently difficult to study: they are wideranging and inhabit a concealing medium; they are relatively swift swimmers and often move alone or in small groups. Many species can be found only in remote locations. Members of most species are fragile, requiring careful capture

and transport, large holding facilities, high water quality and an appropriate diet. The number of scientists working on the behavior of sharks remains small. And, finally, many of the most interesting species, from the standpoint of humans, are formidable and potentially dangerous creatures.

These considerations suggest that behavioral and ecological studies must be long-term, with information accumulating slowly. One important advance has been the use of ultrasonic underwater telemetry. Other tools include small one- or two-man submersibles, underwater television, stereophotography, data loggers, various types of internal and external tags, specially designed boats and even tethered balloons. Much of our knowledge about the behavior of sharks is based on observations of precious few species. Yet that knowledge is vastly greater than what was available 10 years ago. Facts have replaced the speculations and myths that were so intimately associated with these animals for so many years.

A 1997 report prepared by Alan Henningsen of the National Aquarium, Baltimore, Maryland, noted that, with 98 institutions from 13 countries reporting, 60 species of sharks were presently being held in captivity with the number of individuals at 2,682. This compares with a 1983 review, listing more than 50 species in captivity at that time. Hardy benthic species usually survive under such conditions for up to one year or more: bullhead sharks *Heterodontus* spp., leopard sharks *Triakis* spp., catsharks *Scyliorhinus* spp., the sand tiger *Carcharias taurus*, and the nurse shark *Ginglymostoma cirratum*. Despite these successes, many species are not only difficult to collect and transport but, once in captivity, individuals often refuse to feed. Severe hematological changes can occur during and after capture, and important research findings may actually have been based on unhealthy animals.

Increasing knowledge about the maintenance of good health in captive sharks has now resulted in many species—even the larger and more pelagic species of the genera *Carcharhinus* and *Sphyrna*—being kept in large public aquaria for more than a year. Proven techniques for transporting sharks to distant locations are now available, as are the means for maintaining high water quality during captivity. Sufficient space for unimpeded movement, prophylaxis and the use of supplements to correct dietary deficiencies are just a few of the practises now used to keep sharks at a level of health comparable to that found under natural conditions.

A REMARKABLE SENSORY WORLD

Sharks presumably use smell and taste to aid them in conducting many of their activities. For example, two common species found along the coast of the southeastern United States, the lemon shark *Negaprion brevirostris* and the nurse shark *Ginglymostoma cirratum*, can distinguish waters of differing salinity. This ability could assist them in locating different water masses during daily seasonal movements, in maintaining the segregation of the sexes shown by various species and in locating appropriate pupping areas.

Another remarkable ability, chemically based recognition of the members of one's own species, has been shown by the catshark *Scyliorhinus stellaris*. Males of the gray reef shark *Carcharhinus amblyrhynchos* have also been observed moving along apparent odor trails produced by females.

The visual systems of many sharks are highly developed. The abundance of low light photoreceptors (rods) in the eyes of all species points to the importance of night time and twilight for these animals but the presence of high light photoreceptors (cones) suggests that many species are also active during the daylight hours. Brightly colored objects seem to be especially attractive; survival gear, painted yellow, is known to attract freeranging sharks, while the same gear, painted black, is ignored.

Sharks are also well endowed for sensing mechanical disturbances. Not only do they have specialized receptors in the deep layers of their skin and muscle, they also have well-developed inner ears (similar to those found in other vertebrates) as well as thousands of hair cells, called neuromasts, in specialized pits along the sides, on the head and in canals—the so-called lateral lines. Neuromasts are sensitive to underwater vibrations and probably play an important role in sensing water movements close to the body. The inner ears are sensitive to underwater sounds that originate from sources many meters away.

Studies have shown that although hearing abilities vary among species, some sharks can hear sounds as low as 10 Hz (cycles per second) and as high as 800 Hz, in other words, from about 1.5 octaves below the frequency of the lowest key on a piano to just below high C on the piano. Since adult human hearing extends from about 25 Hz to around 16,000 Hz, humans hear many

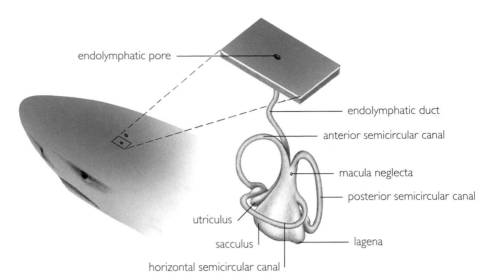

sounds that sharks cannot. On the other hand, sharks can detect low-frequency sounds unheard by humans.

Many species move rapidly to specific sound sources, which explains why nearby sharks often appear shortly after a speared or hooked fish begins struggling, thereby transmitting low-frequency sounds. Similar irregularly pulsed, low-frequency vibrations are also produced by the strumming of cables and set lines—and by humans when struggling in the water.

Some freeranging Carcharhinid sharks have been observed suddenly withdrawing from the near vicinity of a sound source when audible sounds of high intensity and sudden onset are transmitted. This response is not unique to sharks. Many other animals respond in the same way when confronted by a similar stimulus.

Still another function of hearing has also been recently suggested in the case of nurse sharks. Splashing sounds produced by pairs during sexual encounters in shallow water appear to attract nearby adult males to the locations of such encounters.

Electroreception is a profoundly important dimension of the sensory world of sharks, but one that we cannot easily identify with, since humans possess no comparable system. The significance of the electrical sensitivity became evident when sharks were observed to "home in" on bioelectrical fields measured at 0.005 microvolts per centimeter—the highest known electrical sensitivity in the animal kingdom! All sharks and other elasmobranchs possess ampullae of Lorenzini, small saclike structures beneath the skin of the head that house the electrical receptors. Field experiments on the dusky smoothound *Mustelus canis*, the blue shark *Prionace glauca* and the swellshark *Cephaloscyllium ventriosum* have clearly demonstrated that these predators detect the tiny bioelectric fields generated by the bodies of their prey, and are thereby able to capture them. Fortunately, the strength of a bioelectrical field falls off very

ABOVE: Although sharks lack external evidence of well-developed ears, their hearing is acute. The inner ear, shown diagramatically above, provides both balance and hearing.

Arthur A. Myrberg, Jr

ABOVE: Silky sharks *Carcharhinus falciformis* approach a hydrophone broadcasting low-frequency sounds at a depth of 20 meters. This species is a fast and relatively aggressive open-ocean feeder whose superb hearing enables it to detect prey—primarily schools of mackerel, ocean mullet, tuna and squid—at great distances.

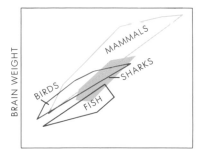

ABOVE: Brain weight compared with body weight in four major groups of vertebrates. Sharks' brains, represented by the shaded area, are surprisingly large in relation to their body weight out of water and demonstrate the fallacy of the traditional view of sharks as killers incapable of learning.

steeply over distance and even in the case of a human body, the field is undetectable by a shark beyond a distance of 1 or 2 meters.

Other tiny electrical fields, well within the dynamic range of sharks, include not only those generated by ocean currents as they flow through the earth's magnetic field, but also those created by a shark's own body as it swims through that same electrical field. As the shark moves, it induces a tiny electrical field whose strength depends on the direction in which it is heading. Laboratory experiments have shown that the round stingray *Urolophus halleri* is capable of such geomagnetic orientation. Based on our knowledge about long-distance movements by sharks, it is reasonable to speculate that such travels are the result not of lost and aimlessly wandering animals, but of well-oriented individuals moving purposefully to distant regions by attending to their "built-in" compass.

Experiments seeking to establish just how sensitive members of a species are to a particular visual object, sound or electrical field have almost invariably required subjects to learn a specific task to demonstrate their sensitivity. Such studies have shown that sharks can indeed learn through experience—a capability that may explain behavioral differences between juvenile and adult sharks. Juveniles generally appear clearly more inquisitive than adults. Their activity levels are often higher and their actions are often more erratic and unpredictable than those of conspecific adults. Such youthful high spirits— clearly ill-suited for a long life in many of the world's habitats—change as individuals grow to maturity through learning experiences, not unlike those of many other young animals.

Since we are now aware that sharks and their relatives possess many of the attributes ascribed to the so-called higher vertebrates, it is only fitting that another myth be thrown out. Sharks were long considered insatiable feeding machines, driven only by primitive instincts. It was, therefore, not unreasonable to assume that they must have only pea-sized brains. We now know, however, that many sharks and rays have brains comparable in size with those of many birds and mammals.

FEEDING BEHAVIOR

The natural feeding behavior of sharks has rarely been observed during the day. This strongly suggests that twilight and darkness are the most important times for feeding in the majority of these predators. Such cycles of activity come as no surprise, since sharks are certainly no exception to the universality of rhythms of activities in biological systems. The few experiments that have been conducted demonstrate clear rhythms within a 24-hour period (even in total darkness).

Evidence has accumulated that white sharks *Carcharodon carcharias* off the west coast of California, particularly those greater than 4 meters in length, often feed on pinnipeds and move to specific areas where such prey haul out both inshore and offshore north of Point Conception, California. A swimmer at the surface, wearing a dark wetsuit and holding onto a short surfboard, appears, from the shark's perspective, to mimic such prey items and is thus vulnerable to attack based on mistaken identity.

Most of the early literature about shark attack maintained the view that shark attack is

RIGHT: Because of its inoffensive nature and ready adaptation to captivity, the sand tiger *Carcharias taurus* has provided scientists with an ideal subject for observation and experiment. Experience with such hardy species has contributed a great deal to our understanding of shark biology, behavior and maintenance in captivity.

Ben Cropp

motivated by hunger. That view was initially challenged in 1969 when American researchers Baldridge and Williams noted consistent peculiarities in cases listed in the International Shark Attack File. These cases often involved severe wounding but little or no loss of flesh. The wounds appeared to have been caused solely by the teeth of the upper jaw during an apparent bite-and-run or slashing attack: wounds that were inconsistent with the idea that hunger was the underlying motivation for the attack. As Baldridge and Williams pointed out in analyzing their research: "If hunger motivated [such] attacks, then the shark or sharks involved were certainly inefficient feeders."

Yet, such slashing attacks may indeed be a strategy used by some sharks when confronting powerful prey. Such behavior apparently occurs when white sharks attack pinnipeds. The predator is less likely to be injured if it first slashes its prey and then waits nearby until the prey dies of blood loss.

DISPLAY PATTERNS

The gray reef shark *Carcharhinus amblyrhynchos* is unique in its highly stereotyped behavior pattern, termed the exaggerated swimming display. The display varies in intensity; its peak occurs when a shark is approached closely, especially if it is cornered and without an escape route. The display, though not seen during feeding, resembles the actions of the body and the head during an exaggerated bite and is apparently derived from the feeding act itself. Although only the gray reef shark performs the full display, components of the display are shown by Galapagos sharks *Carcharhinus galapagensis*, silky sharks *Carcharhinus falciformis*, blacknose sharks *Carcharhinus acronotus* and bonnethead sharks *Sphyrna tiburo*.

Since these displays are neither dependent on location nor related to feeding, their significance remains unclear. That gray reef sharks are so aggressive despite their relatively small size (usually 1 to 1.5 meters long) stands in contrast to the behavior of other sharks. Overt aggression, attacks, chasing or apparent threat are rarely observed. Even during active feeding, including the infamous "feeding frenzies," sharks seem interested only in getting the food (sometimes biting one another apparently by mistake).

Aggressive behavior could be expected if sharks defended exclusive areas, but there is no evidence to suggest that they are territorial. Such behavior may be the result of individuals attempting to maintain a position of relative dominance in specific areas. Observations suggest that female gray reef sharks show elevated aggression and exaggerated swimming displays in pupping areas. Perhaps they are simply defending themselves from possible predation.

Ron & Valerie Taylor

ABOVE: Increasing knowledge of the dietary, spatial and social needs of sharks means that even such delicate pelagic species as the oceanic blue shark may soon be captured, transported and kept in good health for research.

front view

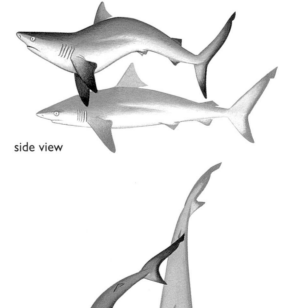

side view

top view

LEFT: When persistently startled by unusual sounds or rapid movements, or when approached, gray reef sharks perform a threat display that consists of an exaggerated swimming pattern in which the shark wags its head and tail in broad sweeps, arches its back, lifts its head, depresses its pectoral fins and sometimes swims in a horizontal spiral or a series of figure-eight loops that bring it closer to the source of its anxiety. These illustrations compare display behavior (top) with the shark's normal non-threatening behavior (bottom).

Ron & Valerie Taylor

LEFT AND BELOW: Stimulated by blood and bait in the water, more than a dozen gray reef sharks gather and their behavior becomes increasingly aggressive until they are involved in a feeding frenzy. In a bizarre and savage climax, one shark that had been bitten accidentally during the frenzy is followed, attacked and killed by a larger comrade.

SHARKS IN GROUPS

The classical view of the shark is that of a solitary hunter, ranging the oceans in search of food. Although this is probable for large species such as the great white shark, the tiger shark *Galeocerdo cuvier* and megamouth *Megachasma pelagios*, many other species move in groups, at least during part of their lives. One of the most spectacular instances of such behavior is that of the scalloped hammerhead *Sphyrna lewini*. Daytime schools of more than 100 individuals gather near islands and over seamounts in the the Sea of Cortez, between Baja California and the western coast of Mexico. Such refuging behavior may well reflect a common strategy to minimize activity when not foraging by remaining at a single location in their home range. A remarkable aspect of such behavior is the consistent return to the same location—a seamount, for example—each day after nocturnal movements take individuals many kilometers from the refuging site.

Dominant–subordinate associations (social hierarchies) have been reported between different species. Oceanic whitetip sharks *Carcharhinus longimanus* dominate silky sharks of comparable size when both species are feeding. Silvertip sharks *Carcharhinus albimarginatus* dominate Galapagos sharks, while both dominate blacktip sharks *Carcharhinus limbatus*. Such interactions, however, may actually reflect antipredatory behavior by the subordinate species.

Social hierarchies among members of the same species have also been reported and in bonnethead sharks, females tend to shy away from males, regardless of size. The reason for such shyness is unclear, but the harassment and bites that males of many species inflict on conspecific

Ron & Valerie Taylor

females during mating may explain why females give them such a wide berth.

It should be mentioned, however, that such biting is not the sole domain of males: females of the scalloped hammerhead inflict such bites on other females during non-feeding periods and even males of that species occasionally show similar wounds. The social hierarchies noted among members of a given species—be they dogfish, bonnetheads, silvertips or great white sharks—are clearly size-dependent; smaller individuals move away from larger individuals.

One might question why adult sharks would move about in packs or schools at any time. It is easy to understand why small sharks might do so, since a tight aggregation would reduce the chance of any given individual becoming a prey item. This argument wanes in importance,

FACING PAGE: The popular image of the shark as a lone hunter is shaken by the spectacular and mystifying congregations of scalloped hammerheads *Sphyrna lewini* that occur near seamounts in the Sea of Cortez, off western Mexico. The function of these gatherings—often of hundreds of individuals—is unknown, but may be related to mating.

Marty Snyderman

however, as individuals become large enough that the risk of predation is severely reduced. Perhaps the answer rests with the fact that food often occurs in widely separated patches and individuals may be able to take advantage of the extended sensory capabilities of the group. That advantage disappears if there isn't enough food to support the group. So, apart from the mating season (when aggregations form for purposes of reproduction), the size of a shark pack may indicate the abundance of prey.

The ultimate social activity in sexually reproducing animals is mating. The scarcity of observations of mating in sharks suggests that it either occurs rarely or that it occurs primarily at night. Except for the nurse shark, where numerous matings have been witnessed during the day, the relatively few cases observed during daylight show that mating pairs of unrelated species demonstrate strong similarities in position and activities.

Mating behavior has been observed in catsharks *Scyliorhinus canicula* and *S. torazame*, the hornshark *Heterodontus francisci*, the blackfin reef shark *Carcharhinus melanopterus*, the whitetip reef shark *Triaenodon obesus*, the nurse shark and the lemon shark. All occurred on the ocean floor, except for one report of lemon sharks

RIGHT AND BELOW: Although copulation has rarely been observed in the wild, most sharks engage in elaborate courtship behavior that commonly involves the male biting the female on the dorsal or pectoral fins before inserting a single clasper into the cloaca. Copulation may last from 10 seconds to two hours, depending on the species.

copulating at the surface. In most instances, the male maintains a bite-hold on one of the pectoral fins of the female during copulation, no doubt to assist the placement of the clasper in the female's genital opening. Copulation may last from 10 seconds to two hours, depending on the species.

The importance of an undisturbed area for mating and nursery purposes was recently recognized by the US National Park Service. A small (0.8 hectare) region within the Dry Tortugas National Park, approximately 75 nautical miles west of Key West, Florida, was closed to public access during the breeding season of the nurse shark. This may serve as a model for other shark species when important breeding and nursery areas are identified.

THE PUZZLE OF THE WHITETIP

We are well aware that sharks can intercept a variety of sensory signs from their prey and use them for their own benefit. However, we are almost totally ignorant about the ways sharks use signals to communicate with each other. Is it possible that certain sharks might even attempt to communicate with their prey, using deceptive signals? Body markings, for example, are used throughout the animal kingdom for communication. Markings such as those possessed by the angelsharks are clearly used as camouflage. However, many sharks show specific regions of pigmentation—such as along the edges and the tips of fins—that do not suggest functional camouflage. Might such markings have a communication function?

As I dived among oceanic whitetip sharks *Carcharhinus longimanus*, I was intrigued by what possible function could be served by their large, white-tipped fins. Although my answer to the riddle is based on communication, I believe the markings are not related to providing information among members of that particular species; instead they facilitate another type of communication—providing deceptive information to prey so as to benefit the predator itself.

While conducting acoustical experiments on epipelagic sharks over the deep waters of the Bahamas during the mid 1970s, we often encountered oceanic whitetips. These sharks moved slowly, almost lethargically; their movements appeared uncommonly effortless compared with other sharks we had observed over the years. But the slow movements were deceptive. Oceanic whitetips can move with astounding speed over distances of more than 30 meters. Attaining such high speeds can explain, at least in part, something long known about these sharks—their prey includes some of the fastest moving oceanic fishes: tuna, mackerel, dolphinfish and even white marlin.

It is highly unlikely that this shark could overtake such fast-moving prey from behind, nor

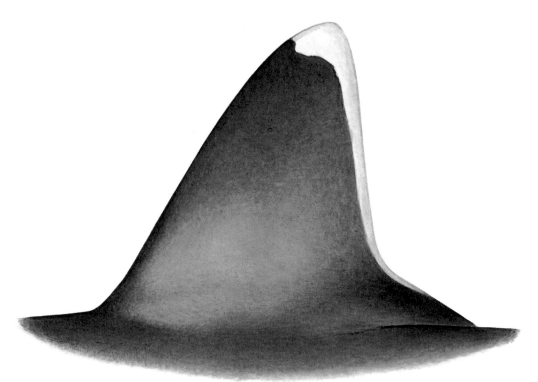

is it likely that it could sneak up on them in clear, open water. One suggestion has been advanced to answer this intriguing problem: oceanic whitetips move into surface schools of small fishes when these schools are being preyed on by tuna, mackerel or marlin. As the predators leap about feeding on their prey, they literally jump into the open mouths of the sharks. I can't help but wonder, however, what the chances are that a shark could position itself precisely at the end of the trajectory of a speeding, leaping fish.

My theory is based on a visual effect I often experienced while observing oceanic whitetips; other divers have confirmed the same effect. As long as whitetips remained close by, their body shape was unmistakable. As they moved to the limit of visibility, however, one's eyes were constantly drawn to their white-tipped fins, with the result that the sharks' grayish, countershaded bodies became indistinct. Indeed, the shark seemed to disappear unless one concentrated on it. And when the form became indistinct, attention was forced to focus on the three to five white fin spots, moving in close formation. Occasionally, when two whitetips moved closely together at such distances, a "school" of white spots could be seen moving through the clear water and near the surface, where the species is often found. The effect of this optical illusion was particularly striking during periods of moderate or low light, since under these conditions the spots stood out in far greater contrast to the background light.

Now comes the speculation. If the eyes of a human and those of the fishes mentioned are not too dissimilar in terms of their general levels of sensitivity, the perceptual change that occurs—

ABOVE: Coloration and body markings seem to play a part in enabling members of the same species to recognize each other. Silvertips are so named because of the distinctive white tips and margins on all their fins.

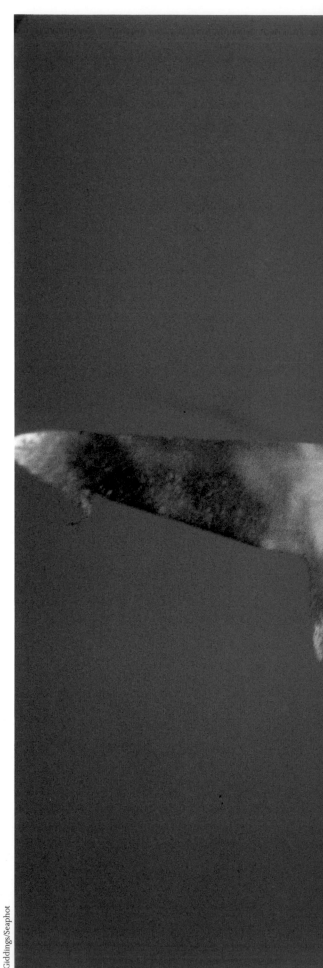

Al Giddings/Seaphot

RIGHT: An intriguing explanation for the white-spotted dorsal and pectoral fins of the oceanic whitetip *Carcharhinus longimanus* involves an optical effect whereby the neutral gray of the shark's body can barely be seen in low light. The white spots may appear to predators (themselves prey for this species) like a school of small, edible fishes.

that is, the white-tipped fins of a shark becoming a "school" of white spots—holds the explanation for how such rapidly moving fishes are caught by oceanic whitetip sharks. If the white spots are considered, at a distance, to be a small school of appropriately sized prey, rapidly moving, predatory fishes might well move toward such "prey" and, if they were to reach a point where the sudden acceleration by the oceanic whitetip could overcome their attempts to escape, they could become the unexpected prey of the "spots." The white spots of the oceanic whitetip shark might well be species-recognition marks. However, they appear to have another function as well—they are lures for attracting fast-moving fishes that hunt by sight.

This may also explain why the first dorsal and the pectoral fins of this shark are so conspicuously large. One way to improve the effectiveness of such a lure is to increase its size so that it can be seen over a larger area, increasing the probability of prey noting the lure. The large pectoral fins play an important role in the effortless gliding movements of such sharks and the large median dorsal fin adds stabilization to sudden, rapid forward movement. Nevertheless, whatever forces initiated the increase in fin size, the spots seem to have benefited since their increasing size could lure prey from ever greater distances.

BELOW: The distinctive markings of an oceanic whitetip. Are they an ingenious way to confuse and lure prey?

Marty Snyderman

DO SEA LIONS EAT SHARKS?

MARTY SNYDERMAN

Our boat, the *Sand Dollar*, was drifting well out of sight of land about 30 kilometers off the coast of San Diego, California, over a bottom that is several hundred meters deep. As I looked over the side I could see at least a dozen blue sharks and four mako sharks cruising in and out of the chum line created by our bait.

Most blue sharks—the most commonly encountered open-ocean sharks off the coast of southern California—are sleek, graceful animals, while makos look like torpedoes whose teeth do not fit into their mouths. Blue sharks can generally be baited in at any time throughout the year, but makos are much more common in summer and fall.

At the time I was working on a documentary film about sharks with Stan Waterman and Howard Hall. Howard and I had worked with blue sharks and mako sharks for several years, and we considered ourselves to be rather well versed in their behavior. Stan is acknowledged as a superb underwater cinematographer. Several accredited scientists were also aboard as part of the film crew.

Most of the sharks had been on the scene for several hours and all were obviously interested in the chunks of fish we were throwing in the water. To that point our day had been routine. We began baiting early in the morning and the sharks had begun to gather around the boat as soon as the wind had picked up and spread the chum line. The mixture of blues and makos was typical for summer and conditions were near perfect for a good day of film work.

We were refilling our tanks between dives when a medium-sized California sea lion suddenly appeared at the bait basket. For a moment we stared in utter amazement as the sea lion swam among the sharks. Then our professional training overtook us and we hurriedly suited up so that we could get into the water and film a sea lion being attacked by sharks, an event we thought was certain to occur. This type of animal behavior is precisely what documentary filmmakers pray for.

Cameras running, we jumped into the water; but we were not prepared for the sequence of events that took place before our eyes. The sea lion constantly stole our bait from the sharks. Whenever a shark moved closer to the mammal than it cared for, the sea lion would maneuver to a position behind and above the shark, and then swoop down and bite it on the top of its body just in front of the tail. Try as they might, none of the sharks could turn the game on the sea lion.

As the scene unfolded, the sea lion simply outmaneuvered each and every shark every time we placed a bait in the water. Several of the blue sharks and all the makos became so annoyed at being bitten by the sea lion that they departed. The sea lion remained behind and feasted on our bait, making it impossible to film any "marauding" sharks.

Needless to say, all of us—filmmakers and scientists alike—were completely surprised that the expected pattern of events had been reversed. Since that dive I have witnessed many similar situations and every time the results have been the same: the sea lions were able to outmaneuver the sharks and compete successfully with them for the bait.

Do sea lions eat sharks? Obviously not. But certainly all sharks, even large ones, don't have an easy time preying upon sea lions. While many species of seals are known to have been taken by sharks, very few examples have been reported of sharks successfully preying on sea lions.

Three cases of sea lions being taken by great white sharks have been documented. Great whites are known to prey heavily on a variety of seals but sea lions, being better swimmers are, therefore, much more demanding prey.

SHARK ECOLOGY

TIMOTHY C. TRICAS

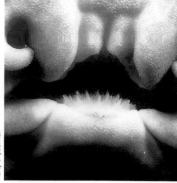

ABOVE: Although modern sharks share many characteristics with their ancestors, variations in the style of predation have seen extensive changes in anatomy. The Port Jackson shark, for example, has teeth modified for crushing hard-shelled prey such as oysters, sea urchins and crustaceans.

BELOW: The great white shark's teeth are flat, triangular, minutely serrated and fearsomely sharp—the classic tooth shape of a powerful predator. Younger great whites, however, have narrower, doglike teeth designed to grasp smaller prey that can be swallowed whole.

*S*harks are prominent members of nearly all marine ecosystems. They occur in shallow bays and estuaries, cold waters of rocky coastlines, tropical coral reefs, in the center of oceans and abyssal plains of the deep. Each shark species is well adapted to the physical conditions and assemblage of biological organisms that share its environment.

Sharks are the top predators in marine communities and are the equivalent of large carnivores in terrestrial ecosystems. Studies in shark ecology encompass many aspects of the relationships between sharks and their environment. These include factors that influence the numbers and distribution of sharks, links between different species of sharks, their predators and prey, and ways in which they compete with other species for food and space. Because they range over large areas and live in an environment that limits prolonged observation and experimental study, sharks present marine ecologists with unique challenges. Our understanding of their roles in marine ecosystems is still surprisingly limited and much research remains to be done.

The most obvious differences between shark species are seen in the shape of the head and tail, the articulation of the jaw and head, and the shape of the teeth. Scientists believe these variations can be explained as adaptations to the differing environments in which species must feed, avoid predators and reproduce. An ecological approach to the study of sharks helps us better to understand the dynamics of marine communities and the environmental factors that shape patterns of shark evolution.

This chapter is divided into two main sections. The first deals with the feeding habits and the environmental adaptations that allow sharks to feed efficiently on their prey. The second looks at the structure of the shark community on a typical Pacific coral reef and provides insights into how sharks of different species may coexist within the same ecosystem.

FEEDING ECOLOGY

One of the most remarkable features of living sharks is the large number of characteristics that they share with their ancestors, which inhabited the oceans more than 450 million years ago. Most notable is the striking similarity of body form found in species of vastly different sizes and lifestyles. For example, the whale shark *Rhincodon typus* reaches lengths of more than 14 meters and feeds in tropical seas by straining plankton and small fishes through its gill rakers. This large species has a body plan very similar to that of the cookiecutter shark *Isistius brasiliensis*, which reaches a maximum length of less than half a meter and is a parasite that feeds by biting small pieces of flesh from tuna, marlin, porpoises and whales. The retention of this similar body form in sharks with very different lifestyles suggests that they developed these characteristics early in their evolutionary history.

On closer examination of individual species, distinct morphological (physical and anatomic) differences that relate to their feeding become

goblin shark

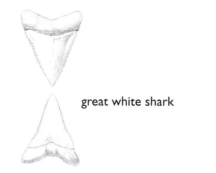

great white shark

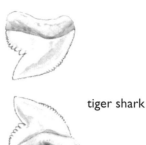

tiger shark

apparent. Perhaps the most marked differences are in tooth shapes, which in most species seem well adapted to take prey in their environment. Some bottom-dwelling species, such as the horn sharks *Heterodontus* spp. and smooth dogfishes *Mustelus* spp., have teeth modified for crushing hard-shelled invertebrate prey such as crustaceans (crabs and lobsters) and mollusks (clams). Other species have flat, triangular teeth with sharp serrated edges for cutting prey. This latter tooth structure is found in many species, including the requiem (family Carcharhinidae), great white

(family Lamnidae) and hammerhead (family Sphyrnidae) sharks. These species feed heavily on fishes and cephalopods.

A third general tooth class is long and narrow in profile, double-edged and usually without serrations. This form is best suited for grasping fish prey, which is usually swallowed whole. Narrow teeth are found in the bottom-dwelling sand tiger (family Odontaspididae) and the oceanic porbeagle and mako (family Lamnidae) sharks. Many additional tooth forms exist, some of which are unique to particular species. For example, the tiger shark *Galeocerdo cuvier* has a flat, highly serrated, triangular tooth with a large primary notch on the outer margin. This configuration functions well to cut through the hard shell of turtles and to take bites out of very large prey items such as tropical marine mammals and other sharks.

The importance of tooth shape to feeding habits is illustrated by the dynamic changes in dietary patterns that occur during the lifetime of

a shark. For example, great white sharks *Carcharodon carcharias* less than about 3 meters long feed on small fish, which they usually swallow whole. Larger great whites feed primarily on large marine mammals, which they consume in pieces. Small white sharks have very narrow teeth that are very similar to those of adult makos and are best suited to grasping small fish—captured young white sharks are often mistaken for makos because of the tooth shape! In contrast, when white sharks grow longer than 3 meters, they develop triangular serrated teeth best suited to gouging and cutting pieces from their prey that are too large to swallow whole. Thus, the feeding habits and predatory success of the great white are intimately related to its tooth structure. Changing tooth morphologies in association with shark growth have also been reported for requiem and hammerhead sharks, but their feeding function remains to be demonstrated.

Similarities and contrasts in ecological adaptations are found among species that frequent the same habitats. The blue shark *Prionace glauca* is common in the surface waters of the northeast Pacific and north Atlantic oceans.

It planes gracefully through the water on broad pectoral fins by slow, sinuous undulations of its long body and tail. It feeds primarily upon small fishes such as anchovies and sardines, and small squid that migrate from deep water to the surface at night. Blue sharks have small mouths and small serrated triangular teeth for feeding on small prey. A summer visitor to the same waters is the shortfin mako *Isurus oxyrinchus*. This species has short, stout pectoral fins, a fusiform body, and a tail with upper and lower lobes of almost equal

ABOVE: A selection of shark teeth. Their shapes reflect the feeding ecologies of the various species. The teeth of the goblin shark are long and needlelike, ideal for grasping small fish. The great white has powerful, almost triangular teeth with serrated edges, while the teeth of the tiger shark are shaped somewhat like a coxcomb.

LEFT: Bottom-dwelling and relatively sluggish sand tigers have teeth similar in shape to those of fast-moving oceanic predators such as makos and porbeagles. In both cases, this tooth shape is superbly evolved to hold fish (and in the case of makos, pelagic squid) that do not have to be bitten into smaller pieces.

LEFT: Requiem sharks are opportunistic feeders that will take advantage of almost any food resource, from fish and crustaceans to seabirds, turtles and carrion. Their teeth are designed to cope with a variety of textures and are replaced constantly through the shark's life as they wear or are broken.

ABOVE: Tropical reefs support a range of shark species, some of which are active in daylight hours. Others, which rest in crevices and coral caves during the day, hunt at night. The remora accompanying this small requiem shark *Carcharhinus* sp. cleans parasites from the skin and gill chambers of its host.

length. In contrast to the blue shark, it is adapted to swim extremely fast and feeds on schools of mackerel and other fishes. It has long needlelike teeth for grasping its prey. Despite their morphological differences, these two sharks are remarkably similar in color. Both have dark blue backs that are countershaded by a white undersurface. This color pattern serves to make both species blend into their open-water environment, and to render them virtually invisible to their prey (and predators) at a distance. Thus, while species may exhibit different specializations, they may also share adaptations that maximize their success.

SHARK COMMUNITIES ON PACIFIC REEFS

Most islands and coral atolls in the central Pacific have a similar submarine reef profile. There is usually a shallow reef flat that separates the seaward reef from shallow backwaters or a large lagoon. The reef flat is often exposed at low tide, and is frequented by large fish only when flooded. The backreef and lagoon areas are usually scattered with patch reefs of living coral across a sandy bottom. On the seaward side of the reef crest is the forereef area, which rapidly falls off into deeper waters. The seaward and back regions of the reef are usually connected by a series of deep channels that cut through the reef flat.

The species composition and distribution of sharks on different tropical reefs in the Pacific are remarkably similar. The most common visitor to the reef flat during flood tide is the blacktip reef shark *Carcharhinus melanopterus*. Juvenile and adult sharks of this species often frequent waters so shallow that their dorsal fins are completely exposed above the surface. This relatively small shark grows to an average length of around 1.5 meters and feeds upon a broad range of small fishes, crustaceans and cephalopods that inhabit the reef flat and adjacent shallow waters. It is an active species, capable of quick and rapid turns, and often moves about the reef flat in large aggregations.

These schools often exhibit high levels of excitement when feeding. Its relatively small size permits this species to forage efficiently for prey over shallow areas that are less accessible to larger sharks. Although the blacktip is the most common visitor to the shallow reef flat, it is also found in shallow waters—usually less than 15 meters deep—on both sides of the reef flat. Telemetry and conventional tagging studies indicate that blackfin reef sharks have a limited home range, frequent the same areas of the reef, and forage for food mainly at night.

Another shark common to most Pacific reefs is the whitetip reef shark *Triaenodon obesus*. This species is slightly larger than the blacktip reef shark and reaches a maximum length of around 2 meters. It has a slender, flexible body and swims close to the bottom where it moves among reef crevices and caves in search of food. Whitetip sharks are usually most abundant between depths of 5 and 40 meters but appear to prefer habitats

with high vertical relief and abundant reef interstices. Only rarely are they observed on the reef flat or very shallow waters. Their diet includes a wide variety of reef fishes, octopuses and crustaceans. During the day, they often rest (sometimes in groups) in caves or on the open reef with mouths open and oriented upstream, taking advantage of water currents to ventilate their gills.

Various telemetry and tagging studies show that individual whitetip sharks are strongly attached to specific geographical areas of the reef, and individuals can be observed in the same area over periods of many years. Although daytime feeding by this species is reported, activity increases during the night and indicates hunting may be more intense then. It is well known that olfaction is used by whitetip reef sharks during hunting, and their ability to detect the electric fields of prey by use of electroreceptor organs on the snout (the ampullae of Lorenzini) may be especially important for this species while hunting in caves and crevices

The shark most familiar to divers in deep waters of central Pacific reefs is the gray reef

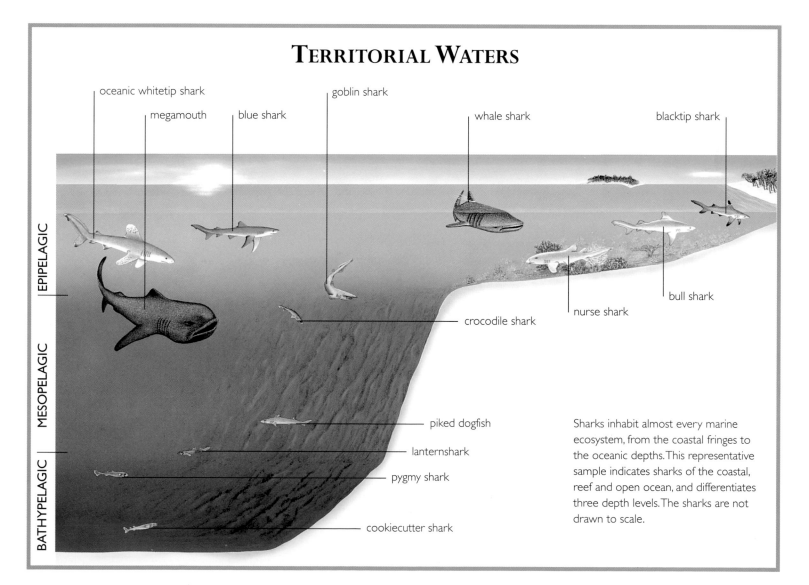

TERRITORIAL WATERS

oceanic whitetip shark

megamouth   blue shark

goblin shark

whale shark

blacktip shark

EPIPELAGIC

MESOPELAGIC

BATHYPELAGIC

crocodile shark

nurse shark

bull shark

piked dogfish

lanternshark

pygmy shark

cookiecutter shark

Sharks inhabit almost every marine ecosystem, from the coastal fringes to the oceanic depths. This representative sample indicates sharks of the coastal, reef and open ocean, and differentiates three depth levels. The sharks are not drawn to scale.

ABOVE: Tagging studies of the whitetip reef shark *Triaenodon obesus* indicate that this species is most active at night and at slack tides. Whitetips spend most of the day resting in caves; individuals favor particular caves and have narrow home ranges.

shark *Carcharhinus amblyrhynchos*. It is slightly larger then the whitetip, reaching lengths of more than 2 meters. Its distribution overlaps considerably with that of the whitetip reef shark, but it is more abundant in deep areas on the seaward side of the reef flat and also in deep areas of the backreef or lagoon. Particularly large aggregations of gray reef sharks are reported in deep passes and channels that transect fringing reefs. Their diet consists primarily of reef fishes and cephalopods. At Enewetak Atoll, gray reef sharks will strike rubber squid lures during the daytime, a good indication that they feed naturally at that time. Apparently this species (like most other reef sharks) does not feed every day, since most stomachs of live sharks examined by the author were empty.

The behavior of the gray reef shark is well studied. It is best known for its threat display,

which is characterized by an exaggerated swimming motion with back arched, pectoral fins depressed and snout lifted. This behavior can be elicited if gray reef sharks are cornered on the reef by divers and often precedes an attack. Sometimes, however, these sharks are extremely aggressive to divers without apparent provocation. This unique behavior may function in more natural situations as a means of defending a territory or personal space against other sharks, or perhaps as a defense against large predators such as tiger sharks. Its importance in spacing individuals of the same or different species, however, remains to be scientifically investigated and recorded.

A large shark commonly encountered on the seaward reef is the silvertip *Carcharhinus albimarginatus*. This species is larger than the gray reef shark, and adults typically inhabit waters below 25 meters. It feeds largely on small fishes, squid and octopuses associated with the reef.

Other sharks found on the outer reef, but less well studied, are the blacktip shark *Carcharhinus limbatus*, bull shark *C. leucas* and hammerheads *Sphyrna* spp. Unfortunately, relatively little is known about the ecology of these species on Pacific reefs and the factors that influence their distributions and abundance.

The largest shark on most Pacific reefs is the tiger shark *Galeocerdo cuvier*, which can grow to more than 5 meters. It has a blunt snout, very large mouth, and the flat, triangular, serrated teeth described earlier. Tiger sharks feed on a wide variety of prey items from many habitats and have perhaps the most diverse diet of all sharks. They usually occur in deep water on the seaward side of the reef flats, but also frequent deep channels and passes. Individuals will enter shallow waters adjacent to the reef flat to feed on seabirds at rest on the water surface. Smaller prey such as bottom-dwelling crustaceans, cephalopods and small fishes are also commonly taken, probably in deeper waters near the reef.

This species is also a voracious predator on large stingrays and other sharks. Because of its large size and wideranging habits, little is known about its movement patterns. A 4-meter female tracked with ultrasonic telemetry by the author and associates for two days on a reef in Hawaii moved a distance of around 80 kilometers per day and covered an area of around 100 square kilometers. This particular shark was also observed making deep excursions during the night along the steep reef slope, where it presumably fed on fishes or invertebrate prey.

The distribution and abundance of sharks in marine communities is strongly influenced by the morphological and behavioral adaptations of each species to its physical environment and to its prey. In this chapter we have looked at one particular environment, but similar adaptations determine the feeding ecologies and predatory success of shark species in other habitats. A great deal of work remains to be done to extend our knowledge and appreciation of the role of sharks as predators in marine ecosystems throughout the world.

BELOW: The gray reef shark *Carcharhinus amblyrhynchos* shares reef habitats with the smaller blacktip reef shark *C. melanopterus* but prefers deeper waters on the seaward side of the reef. The blacktip is usually found on shallow sand flats inside lagoons.

Ron & Valerie Taylor

WHEN SHARKS AND DOLPHINS CROSS PATHS

MARTY SNYDERMAN

Many of us know of instances where sharks have been killed by dolphins when the animals were together in captivity. Those who have witnessed such events report that the dolphins kill the sharks by repeatedly ramming the sharks' soft underbellies with their snouts.

But what happens when sharks and dolphins encounter one another in the wild? Do fierce fights occur? Do the animals simply swim their separate ways? I am not sure that anyone can claim to be an expert in this matter, but I will never forget one night when I watched dolphins and sharks swimming side-by-side as they fed on flying fish.

I was aboard the *Ambar II* at Socorro Island, just over 300 kilometers south of Land's End at the southern tip of Mexico's Baja Peninsula. Our diving day had ended, and we were sitting on deck an hour or so after sunset watching the squid that were attracted by the light of our boat. Several flying fish had landed on deck, and the water around the boat was rapidly becoming populated with them. We were shooting a film about sharks for the television series "Wild Kingdom." We had seen plenty of sharks during our dives—hammerheads, duskies, blacktips and silvertips—so it was no surprise when several duskies showed up that evening to feed on the squid and flying fish.

In order to catch a flying fish, a dusky would single one out and then swim at it from behind until the flying fish was only 30 centimeters or so directly in front of the shark's snout. As the shark closed in, the flying fish would move off to its side. Then the dusky would "thrust" its head to the side and snare the flying fish. I watched the sharks repeatedly pursue the flying fish in this manner, and to my utter amazement the duskies never missed their prey.

After I had been watching the sharks for about 45 minutes, a dozen bottlenose dolphins appeared in the lights under the boat. They, too, were interested in feeding on the flying fish, though they were not nearly as successful as the dusky sharks. It seemed as if the flying fish were able to detect the dolphins' sonar and were often able to avoid the dolphins because of this early warning.

The dolphins and sharks swam in close proximity to one another throughout the night without a single incident of aggression. Both groups fed on the flying fish, but competition was not evident even when sharks and dolphins were within a few meters of one another. In short, it was a case of "You go your way and I'll go my mine." In captivity, where close quarters might lead to conflict, the situation might have been different, but in the open sea on the night in question, the dolphins and sharks simply left each other alone.

Marty Snyderman

Ron & Valerie Tay

ABOVE: Protected by a unique suit of
stainless "chain mail," Valerie Taylor
provokes an attack by a blue shark.

ENCOUNTERS WITH SHARKS

RELATIVE WORLDWIDE DISTRIBUTION OF SHARK ATTACKS

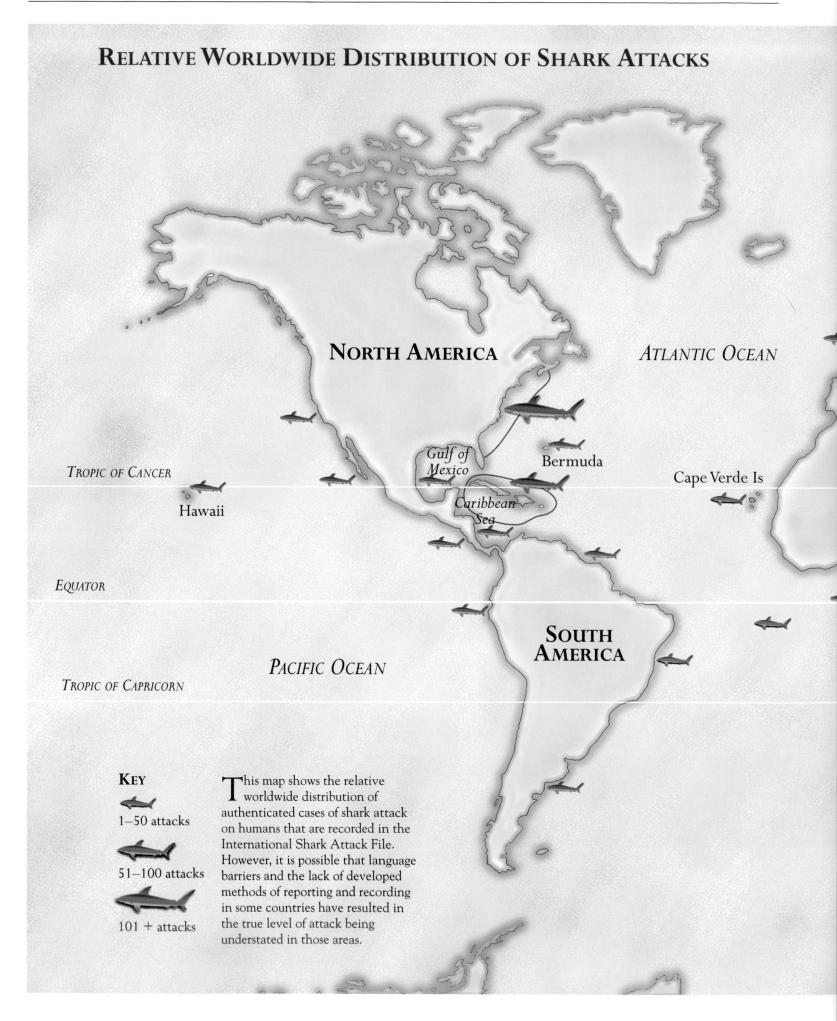

NORTH AMERICA

ATLANTIC OCEAN

Gulf of
Mexico

Bermuda

TROPIC OF CANCER

Cape Verde Is

Hawaii

Caribbean
Sea

EQUATOR

PACIFIC OCEAN

SOUTH
AMERICA

TROPIC OF CAPRICORN

KEY

1–50 attacks

51–100 attacks

101 + attacks

This map shows the relative worldwide distribution of authenticated cases of shark attack on humans that are recorded in the International Shark Attack File. However, it is possible that language barriers and the lack of developed methods of reporting and recording in some countries have resulted in the true level of attack being understated in those areas.

EUROPE

ASIA

Mediterranean
Sea

Persian
Gulf

Red Sea

India

Japan

AFRICA

Philippines

INDIAN OCEAN

Papua New
Guinea

Pacific
Islands

AUSTRALIA

kwaZulu-
Natal

New Zealand

SOUTHERN OCEAN

ENCOUNTERS WITH SHARKS IN NORTH AND CENTRAL AMERICA

GEORGE H. BURGESS AND
CHADWICK S. MACFIE

Until recently, the traditional view of the shark held by most North Americans was that of a relentless killing machine that should always be feared. Fueled by extensive media hype portraying sharks in this distorted fashion following the spectacular success of the provocative novel and movie Jaws *(and cinematic sequels), a marked upswing in recreational fishing for sharks occurred in the Atlantic waters of the United States in the mid-1970s and 1980s. Governmental promotion of sharks as an underutilized resource, which coincided with a sharp decline in regional swordfish stocks and the emergence of a strong east Asian market for shark fins, resulted in the development of a large commercial fishery in the 1980s and 1990s. Concurrently, commercial and artisanal shark fisheries developed or expanded rapidly along the US Pacific coast, in Mexico, and in numerous Central American and Caribbean countries. The result of the combined commercial and recreational fishing has been a drastic decline in shark populations from this region.*

While shark stocks were declining, the region's human population continued its upward spiral with synchronous increases in marine recreational activities. Such aquatic sports as surfing, boogieboarding, sailboarding, kayaking, and skin and scuba diving became increasingly popular with residents of and visitors to the region. The consequent increases in time spent in the sea have resulted in increased opportunities for shark–human interactions.

ABOVE: A shark swimming in shallow water inspires fear but represents far less danger than being struck by lightning. Nevertheless, almost 90 percent of attacks in American waters occur either at the surface or at depths of less than 1.5 meters.

SOURCES OF INFORMATION ABOUT SHARKS

In this chapter we will discuss the volatile relationship between human and shark in North and Central America. Shark attack data has been obtained from the International Shark Attack File (ISAF) and information about the conservation of sharks has been derived from the International Union for the Conservation of Nature's (IUCN) Shark Specialist Group.

The International Shark Attack File is a compilation of all known shark attacks that is administered by the American Elasmobranch Society and the Florida Museum of Natural History. More than 3,000 individual investigations are currently housed in the ISAF, covering the period from mid-1500s to present. Many of the data in the ISAF originate from the voluntary submissions of numerous cooperating scientists who serve worldwide as regional observers. Regional observers forward investigations of attacks in their areas for integration into the ISAF. Data submitted to the ISAF is screened, coded and entered into an electronic database. Hard copy documentation, including original notes, press clippings, photographs, audio/video tapes and medical/autopsy reports, is permanently archived. The ISAF is utilized by biological researchers and research physicians and access to the data is granted only after careful screening on a case-by-case basis. Direct access by the press and general public is forbidden since much information is sensitive in nature and considered privileged.

The International Union for Conservation of Nature and Natural Resources is an umbrella

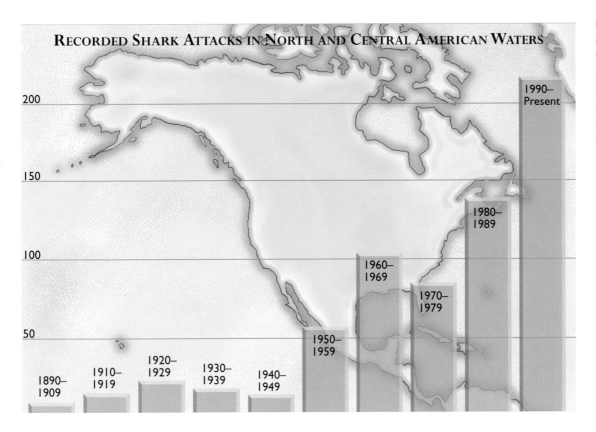

RECORDED SHARK ATTACKS IN NORTH AND CENTRAL AMERICAN WATERS

LEFT: The graph shows the number of unprovoked attacks in North and Central American waters in 10-year spans from 1890 to the present. The higher number of recent attacks reflects the greater number of people using the oceans for recreation.

organization of the world's conservation agencies and institutions. It includes both governmental and non-governmental members. The IUCN actively supports the conservation of biological diversity, the preservation of life-support systems, and the sustainable use of living resources. The IUCN has six Commissions, including the Species Survival Commission (SSC), the largest and most active unit. Within the SSC are a series of specialist groups, composed of conservation experts, which promote action to arrest the loss of the world's biological diversity and to restore threatened species to safe and productive population levels.

The Shark Specialist Group (SSG) has a regional network composed of elasmobranch specialists willing to donate their time to identify the problems associated with the maintenance of elasmobranch stocks in their regions. One of the SSG's goals upon formation was to consolidate regional status reports into a global Action Plan for the conservation of sharks. The Action Plan will highlight global and regional problem areas and is anticipated to be a useful tool in developing funding to support needed elasmobranch research programs.

THREE KINDS OF ATTACKS

The ISAF classifies its investigations of shark attack incidents as either "provoked" or "unprovoked" and additionally segregates attacks on boats from those directly involving humans. Provoked attacks typically involve bites presumably incited by contact—either intentional or unintentional—between divers,

waders, swimmers or fishers and free-swimming or captured sharks. Throughout this chapter we will address only unprovoked attacks on humans—those cases where an attack occurs in the shark's natural habitat without human provocation. Attacks related to spearfishing and ecotourism shark feeding dives currently are placed in the unprovoked category, but compelling arguments may be made to consider them as provoked and they may be reallocated as such in the future.

Three types of unprovoked attacks are encountered in the region. The most common is what we have coined a "hit-and-run" attack, which usually transpires in the surf or wash zone in water depths of 2 meters or less. The victim, most often a surfer, swimmer or wader, is grabbed and quickly released by a shark. Injuries typically occur on extremities of the body, usually the lower leg, and the shark does not return to make a repeat attack. Our observations of the shape and size of bite patterns and the testimony of victims confirm that small sharks measuring 1 to 2 meters in length are the primary attackers. Sharks feeding in this habitat are faced with low water visibility and challenging physical conditions—breaking waves and strong currents—necessitating swift predatory strikes.

We believe that hit-and-run attacks are largely cases of mistaken identity when sharks interpret provocative human actions (such as splashing of hands and feet at water surface) as schooling bait fishes breaking the water's surface. Hit-and-run attacks are most common along the US Atlantic coast. Trauma from this type of attack generally is not too severe, usually

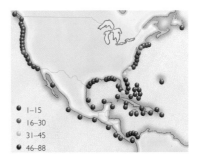

●	1–15
●	16–30
●	31–45
●	46–88

Unprovoked shark attacks

Attacks by bull sharks
Carcharhinus leucas

Attacks by blacktip sharks
Carcharhinus limbatus

constituting lacerations and not accompanied with tissue loss. Occasionally tendon or nerve damage occurs on hands or feet.

More severe injuries and occasional deaths are recorded from "sneak" and "bump-and-bite" attacks. Sharks are larger in size in these types of attacks, which generally occur in deeper water, typically involve swimmers and divers, and frequently include repetitive bites. In a sneak attack the shark is not observed prior to the violent and unexpected first bite. In a bump-and-bite attack, the shark circles and often bumps the victim before biting. We believe these types of shark attacks intentionally target humans and represent feeding or aggressive behaviors. It seems unlikely that sharks seek out rarely appearing humans as prey items. It is more likely that humans simply approximate, in size and shape, normal food items, or, alternatively, that sharks may be attracted to novel biotic elements in their environment. All regional deaths recorded to date have been the result of bump-and-bite and sneak attacks.

Historically, there have been 87 deaths in the region attributable to unprovoked shark attack (12 percent of 703 attacks). The highest mortality rate has occurred in Mexico and Central American countries, where emergency medical care lags behind that available in other areas of the region. By contrast, fatalities are much less common on the Atlantic and Pacific coasts of the United States where lifeguards are common, emergency medical services and immediate care facilities abound, and physicians are well trained in dealing with trauma. In parts of the region fatality rates have declined dramatically over the years with improvements

in medical treatment techniques and facilities. As evidence of this, the pre-1950 fatality rate of 44 percent for attacks in the insular Atlantic and US East Coast has been reduced to 2 percent since 1950.

WHERE AND WHEN SHARKS ATTACK

Shark attacks have been reported from all North and Central American countries except Belize, Guatemala, Honduras and Nicaragua. It is likely that attacks have occurred in these countries but incidents have not been reported to the ISAF or have not been authenticated; there are, for example, unverified Lake Nicaragua attack cases in the ISAF. As might be expected, attacks are more common in the warmer water sections of the region where sharks and aquatically active humans are more abundant.

The sole Canadian Atlantic coast attack was reported from Newfoundland. Twelve attacks have occurred in the northeastern United States from Massachusetts to New York and 26 have taken place in the Middle Atlantic Bight from New Jersey to Virginia. There have been 49 attacks in the South Atlantic Bight from North Carolina to Georgia. Of those, 32 occurred in South Carolina, more than any state other than Florida and California. The high number is probably a result of its long coastline and the traditionally high recreational usage of its beaches. All but one US East Coast attack occurring north of Florida has happened during the warm water months of May to October. The northwestern Gulf of Mexico, bordered by Texas, Louisiana, Mississippi and Alabama, has had 23 attacks, most occurring in the months from June to October.

RIGHT: A tiger shark *Galeocerdo cuvier* tears at a chunk of meat, proffered by a dive operator. The frequency and location of attacks by sharks on humans are linked with aquatic human activity.

Ron & Valerie Taylor

Florida annually leads the region in shark attacks and has averaged 17 attacks per year since 1990. Florida's total of 341 attacks joins Australia, South Africa and California as world leaders in historic attacks. The high number of attacks in Florida is attributable in part to its very long coastline and inshore waters that are high in biological productivity and habitat diversity.

The shark fauna is rich and populations, until recently, have been robust. The state has a large, rapidly growing resident human population augmented by ever-increasing year-round influxes of tourists drawn to the area's subtropical and tropical waters, attractive beaches and accessible coral reefs. Two-thirds of Florida's attacks have occurred in the last two decades, mirroring the trends in population and tourism growth. Most attacks occur along Florida's Atlantic coast and the southerly Florida Keys. Far fewer incidents take place along its Gulf of Mexico shoreline. This dichotomy is reflective of the easterly location of the state's most popular beaches, such as Daytona Beach and Palm Beach, and many of its major population centers. Perhaps more importantly, virtually all surfing occurs in this area since surf conditions are poor in the Gulf of

Mexico, and surfers are the recreational user group most often attacked in Florida. Attacks occur year round, but are most frequent from May to October when maximum human recreational utilization takes place in Florida's waters. This summer incidence is typical of shark attack patterns in other parts of the world.

The remaining countries in the southeastern portion of the region have had 95 attacks with the Bahamas (33) and Mexico (19) recording the most activity. More than 80 percent of Bahamian attacks have occurred in the 1980s and 1990s, chiefly associated with increased spearfishing and ecotourism shark feeding dives. Most Mexican attacks have taken place in the state of Veracruz. Attacks are most common regionally in the warmer months from May to August.

Shark attacks are rare in the cold waters of the Pacific Northwest with just 20 attacks reported from Canada to Oregon. California leads all eastern Pacific areas with 100 total attacks, averaging three attacks per year since 1990. California's cool waters attract few large inshore shark species and most historic attacks are credited to the great white shark *Carcharodon carcharias*. Attacks occur year round, but most

ABOVE: Hammerhead sharks *Sphyrna* spp. have been implicated in unprovoked attacks on humans. They are probably over-represented in attack statistics because of their easily recognizable shape.

Attacks by hammerhead sharks *Sphyrna* spp.

have been recorded from the July to October period, coinciding with observed times of peak white shark and human abundance. There have been only 31 attacks in the eastern Pacific between Mexico and Panama.

About 90 percent of attacks in the region occur at the water's surface or in depths of 1.5 meters or less. This indicates that either humans tend to stay near the surface while in the sea or that sharks preferentially attack near the surface. Both probably are true. The normal feeding pattern of great white sharks involves attacking prey near the surface, and many other species do the same. However, the depth of attack varies greatly within the region based on human utilization patterns. In the insular Atlantic and throughout the Pacific part of the region most attacks occur in waters greater than 3 meters, reflecting a greater emphasis on surfing and diving than swimming. By contrast, in the continental Atlantic, where swimming is more popular, most attacks occur in depths of less than 1.5 meters.

Attacks are known from a wide variety of habitats, but they occur most frequently off beaches, from just beyond the surfline to the wash zone. This area, of course, is highly utilized by swimmers, waders and surfers. Attacks that occur on reefs and in the open ocean are primarily on divers and are fewer in number. Since humans most commonly enter the water during daylight hours, it comes as no surprise that virtually all attacks occur during this period. Nearly half of the attacks occur during the afternoon, from 2.00 to 6.00 pm. Lest anyone think that this reflects shark feeding patterns, we find that there is a noticeable drop-off in shark attacks in the 12.00 to 2.00 pm time period, coinciding with a well-known land-based human feeding event!

ATTACKING SPECIES

Correct identification of many species of sharks is difficult even for trained scientists carefully examining a specimen, so it is challenging to identify the attacking species of shark from the often sketchy description given by a victim more intent on survival than taxonomic features. Nevertheless, based on more than 200 positive identifications, a large suite of species has been implicated in attacks in the region.

In Atlantic waters the most frequently identified attackers, in descending order of frequency, are blacktip *Carcharhinus limbatus*, hammerhead *Sphyrna* spp., bull *Carcharhinus leucas* and spinner *Carcharhinus brevipinna* sharks. Somewhat less frequently cited are sandbar *Carcharhinus plumbeus*, sand tiger *Carcharias taurus*, Caribbean reef *Carcharhinus perezi*, great white, lemon *Negaprion brevirostris* and tiger *Galeocerdo cuvier* sharks. This listing probably

LEFT AND ABOVE: Blue sharks *Prionace glauca* are a pelagic species with a widespread distribution. Although they are not usually aggressive they are not particularly timid and divers should treat them with caution.

Attacks by Caribbean reef sharks
Carcharhinus perezi

Attacks by tiger sharks
Galeocerdo cuvier

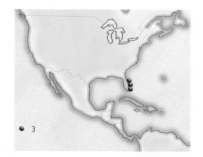

Attacks by spinner sharks
Carcharhinus brevipinna

Al Giddings/Ocean Images

ABOVE: Tiger sharks have been identified in unprovoked attacks in American waters.

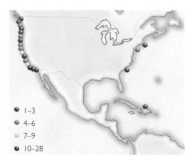

● 1–3
● 4–6
● 7–9
● 10–28

Attacks by great white sharks *Carcharodon carcharias*

FACING PAGE: Although the attack rate in United States waters (primarily northern central California) by great white sharks remains steady, the number of divers meeting great whites underwater is increasing.

accurately reflects the relative frequency of major attacking species, with the exception of the hammerhead sharks. The importance of these species is almost surely overstated because their odd head shape makes them, as a group, the easiest sharks to recognize. By contrast, requiem sharks of the family Carcharhinidae often lack patently obvious distinguishing features and cannot be specifically identified by most attack victims.

There are some regional patterns involving attacking species, with blacktip shark attacks most commonly occurring in northern continental waters and Caribbean reef shark attacks most likely in southern insular areas. More than 90 percent of attacks from the continental northeastern Pacific having positive identification of the attacking shark are attributable to great white sharks. Attacks by blue sharks *Prionace glauca* occasionally occur, usually involving baited sharks.

THE HUMAN FACTOR

When the region is looked at as a whole, attack victims are engaged about equally in three recreational activities: surfing (including rafting and kayaking), swimming (including floating and wading) and diving (scuba and snorkeling).

However, there are marked differences in activity emphasis within the region. For example, in the insular Atlantic almost 60 percent of attacks are on divers, but a similar percentage of Mexican and Central American attacks occurring on both coasts involve swimmers. Divers are three times more likely to be attacked on the US Pacific coast than on the US Atlantic coast. Conversely, swimmers are twice as vulnerable on the US Atlantic coast than those on the US Pacific coast. However, when viewed on a statistical basis, one's chances of encountering a shark, much less being killed, are astronomically small, regardless of activity.

Frequently we are asked if one's sex or race plays a role in whether a shark attacks. ISAF data indicate that sharks are indiscriminate in their choices, attacking people in the proportion they appear in the water. Aquatic recreation, especially surfing and diving, has historically been dominated by males and Caucasians. Regionally, 90 percent of the attacks have been on males and 99 percent on Caucasians. Caucasian females, who have become more active aquatically in the last two decades, have been involved in 11 percent of attacks. Women were involved in 20 percent of attacks in the 1990s compared to only 4 percent in the 1960s.

ENVIRONMENTAL FACTORS

Water temperature is an important factor in shark attacks, with 84 percent of attacks from the US Pacific coast reported from temperatures at or below 16°Celsius. This correlates with the water temperature preferences of both the species of attacking sharks and of the human victims. Water temperatures along the US Pacific coast are cold and great white sharks, largely cool-water inhabitants, are responsible for attacks on humans that adapt to these conditions by wearing wetsuits while diving or surfing. Conversely, farther to the south in the Pacific and throughout the Atlantic portion of the region, attacking shark species generally are warm-water denizens that attack humans entering the sea only during warm-water seasons in northern climes and year-round in warmer southern waters.

Water clarity also plays a role in shark attacks. In about two-thirds of the regional attacks the water is described as murky or muddy. This is especially the case along the US Atlantic coast where about three-quarters of attacks occur under murky water conditions, apparently contributing to mistaken identity. By contrast, insular Atlantic and US Pacific coast attacks largely take place in clear waters.

FISHING AND CONSERVATION

As noted earlier, shark populations have declined precipitously in some parts of the region primarily as a result of overfishing. Regional catches are made in directed longline fisheries; bycatches of inshore gillnet, trawl and hook-and-line fisheries; and recreational fisheries. Management regulations for the Atlantic waters of US and Canada have apparently minimized overfishing of large coastal sharks, but reductions of catches of piked dogfishes *Squalus acanthias*, small coastal sharks and pelagic sharks are still necessary. The unregulated Mexican Atlantic shark fishery is of particular concern since it catches many of the same stocks being addressed by US fishery management. In certain other areas of the western North Atlantic and northeastern Pacific, shark populations are probably fully fished or have become overfished, but little scientific data is available and no sustainable management policies are in place.

Most shark landings in Atlantic Canada are the result of bycatches in traditional fisheries, but during the last decade an inshore directed fishery for piked dogfish and an offshore fishery for pelagic sharks have developed, with shortfin mako *Isurus oxyrinchus*, porbeagle *Lamna nasus*, and blue sharks the targeted species in the latter. A management plan addressing these species was enacted in 1994 which included the prohibition of "finning," the wasteful and inhumane practice of removing only the fins for market and returning the carcase to the sea.

In the US Atlantic, the pattern of shark fisheries changed in 1986 when the commercial longline fishery began to develop. Up until this date the recreational catch, which had experienced noticeable declines as early as 1980, greatly exceeded the commercial catch. The addition of a large commercial fishery has resulted in serious declines in shark abundance and reductions in the average size of landed sharks over the last decade.

Management of US Atlantic shark populations is a biologically complex and politically sensitive task. Unlike many managed US fisheries which address a single species, more than 30 species of sharks are involved in the harvest. Although it is scientifically obvious that different management strategies are needed for individual species because of differing life history characteristics, the group is being managed as a whole, partly because biological and population information is lacking for many species.

A US National Marine Fisheries Service management plan aimed at reducing catches, both sport and commercial, was implemented in 1992 to address this pressing problem. Although the initial recovery plan was imperfect in design and grossly over-optimistic in expectation, it has been periodically adjusted as new biological and fishery data became available.

The management plan defined three management groups of sharks and set annual poundage quotas (called TACs) for two of these groups, the large coastal sharks and pelagic sharks. No restrictions were placed on the third group, the small coastal sharks. Recreational anglers were restricted in their daily catches, and sale of recreationally caught sharks was prohibited. The cruel and wasteful practice of "finning" sharks was prohibited for both commercial and sport fishermen.

The large coastal shark assemblage is the group hardest hit by commercial and recreational fishing interests. According to scientific calculations, this group was overfished in four of six years from 1986 to 1991. Some species have undergone marked reductions in abundance. The dusky shark, once a common species, is now uncommon in catches. Other large coastal sharks showing declines are the sandbar, sand tiger and tiger sharks. Currently the sandbar and blacktip sharks constitute the bulk of the commercial catch, with tiger sharks the third most common species caught. Tiger, nurse and sand tiger sharks are usually released. The US Atlantic fishery for piked dogfish has greatly increased in recent years as bony fish stocks became overfished. Piked dogfish are now targeted and marketed primarily in Europe. This species is now fully exploited and stocks are declining; sustainable coordinated management is needed immediately.

FACING PAGE: The nurse shark *Ginglymostoma cirratum*, like the sand tiger, spends a great deal of time resting on the seafloor. Generally regarded as an unaggressive species, it may retaliate if provoked.

- 1
- 2–3
- 4–5
- 6–7

Fatal unprovoked shark attacks

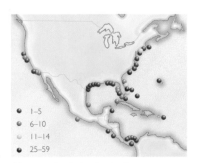

- 1–5
- 6–10
- 11–14
- 25–59

Unprovoked shark attacks on swimmers

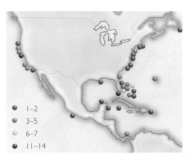

Unprovoked attacks on divers

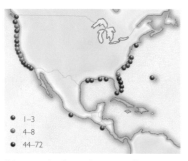

Unprovoked attacks on surfers

RIGHT: Found in tropical and warm temperate seas, the whale shark *Rhincodon typus* is, at nearly 14 meters, the world's largest living fish. As attitudes toward sharks change, humans increasingly understand and appreciate the power and beauty of these sharks.

Artisanal shark fisheries have been present in Mexican waters of the Gulf of Mexico and the Caribbean Sea since pre-Columbian times. Fishing occurs in all Mexican states, but Veracruz and Campeche have the largest catches. Sharks are captured in directed longline and gillnet fisheries and as bycatch in other fisheries. Catches were small until the mid-1970s but grew rapidly in the early 1980s. The extensive capture of juveniles of many species in both the directed and bycatch fisheries is a major threat to the fishery stocks. Changing this practice will be difficult because of the artisinal nature of most of the fisheries and the high esteem in which small sharks are held as a food resource.

WHAT THE FUTURE HOLDS

Attitudes toward sharks in North and Central America may be viewed as a microcosm of how sharks are viewed throughout the world. Through active public education efforts of biologists and conservationists, the perception of sharks by Americans and Canadians has changed markedly over the last decade. Instrumental in this effort has been a gradual change in media depiction of sharks based, at least partially, upon the pragmatic realization that "man bites shark" sells as well as "shark bites man." While shark attacks on humans are still headline material, the relatively low risk of attack and plight of declining shark populations are now more often accurately portrayed by the media. Partly as a result of this reworked public image, growing pro-shark public sentiment has put pressure upon governmental agencies to properly regulate shark fisheries, and while unfortunately late in coming, that management promises to stem the downward slide of shark populations and begin rebuilding of stocks.

To the south, as in much of the Third World, perception of sharks tends to remain on a rather even keel, since the overwhelming influence of the media on popular opinion is reduced in this portion of the region. The large-scale *Jaws* hype of the late 1970s largely failed to make it to much of the populace and the recent upswing in more balanced presentation is also slow to arrive. As a result, residents embrace a more traditional view of sharks as a harvestable resource, balanced with an appropriate appreciation of the risk of attack, gained by years of practical experience passed on from generation to generation.

While enlightened relative to its view of attack, this perception fails to acknowledge the biological vulnerability of sharks to overfishing. The overwhelmingly enticing economic opportunity offered by exportation of shark fins to Asia and the need to provide protein to an often depauperate resident population makes the future of Central American shark conservation quite bleak.

Neville Coleman

ABOVE: A white shark lunges for food hanging from the side of a boat. The great white's ability to rear its head out of the water is one of its most fearsome characteristics.

BELOW: The great white has been implicated in more attacks in Australian waters than any other species. Most attacks have occurred in the summer months, when Australian beaches attract large numbers of swimmers and surfers.

Encounters with Sharks in Australia

Roland Hughes
Revised by John West

For many, the mere mention of the word "shark" is enough to conjure images of a maneater on a horrific killing spree. Whether on the busy streets of New York or London, or on a beach in Australia, the reaction is often the same. But to give Australians credit, their love of the surf and sand, and their abiding interest in the continent's vast marine playground have led, if ever so slowly, to a sophisticated respect for the shark.

It is an undisputed fact that before the introduction of meshing on the eastern seaboard of the continent, Australian waters had the unenviable reputation of being the worst in the world for shark attacks. Recently, a number of fatal attacks off Australia's coast have refueled the popular belief that sharks are savage killers. The facts, however, suggest otherwise. Since records began in 1791, the Australian Shark Attack File has recorded 542 shark attacks on humans in Australian waters, of which 181 were fatalities (an average of one fatality per year). This average is being maintained: in the past 30 years, 31 recorded fatalities have occurred due to shark attack in Australia.

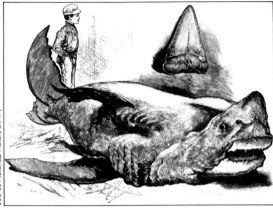

EARLY SHARK ATTACKS

Rock carvings and paintings indicate that the Aborigines were familiar with several kinds of sharks and rays. We will, of course, never know how many Aboriginal people were attacked by sharks while swimming or fishing. Early European navigators, too, quickly became familiar with the sharks of Australian waters. In 1923, the Dutch sailor Jan Carstensz noted the presence of "sharks, sword-fishes and the like unnatural monsters" in the ocean near Cape York, Queensland. Shark Bay in Western Australia was named by the English explorer William Dampier in 1699, reportedly because his men had killed and eaten a shark there.

One of the earliest Australian shark tragedies was recorded by François Peron, a naturalist with Louis Baudin's exploratory expedition to Western Australia. In March 1803 Peron noted:
The eastern side of Faure Island is infested with sharks remarkable for their size and voracity. One of these monsters almost devoured Lefevre, who had saved my life at the Josephine Islands. He was already knocked over: the terrible shark was about to swallow him when three other sailors, running up at his shouts, managed to rescue him. Furious at thus being deprived of its prey, the shark hurled itself several times at the sailor, succeeding in tearing off parts of his clothing.

Although swimming was not popular among the early European convicts and settlers in eastern Australia, a fear of sharks was apparent in the colony from its earliest days. Prisoners were isolated on Pinchgut Island in Sydney Harbor and at Port Arthur in Tasmania because their fear of sharks was a strong deterrent to escape. The *Sydney Gazette* of February 26, 1804, mentions a shark attacking a boat in Port Jackson and two years later the newspaper issued "A Caution to Parents" to keep children away from the hospital wharf where a large shark had been sighted.

The first recorded fatal attack occurred in eastern Australia on January 17, 1837, when Alfred Australia Howe, age 12, was taken in the Macleay River in northern New South Wales. Ironically, the boy had been rescued eight years earlier from Sydney Harbor.

VICTOR COPPLESON'S RESEARCH

It is surprising that, given the significant tally of shark attacks already registered in Australian waters, no local full-time research is being undertaken on what actually provokes sharks to attack humans. However, a comprehensive study of shark attack in Australia was completed in 1958 by Dr. Victor Coppleson.

Although they were made more than 40 years ago, most of Coppleson's findings still apply, even if the interpretations he put on those findings are sometimes now disputed. One of his major discoveries was that most attacks occurred between two and six o'clock in the afternoon and that weather, tides and water clarity were not

ABOVE: While there has been an incredible increase in the number of people using the ocean for sailing, swimming and diving, there is no evidence to suggest a comparable increase in the number of shark attacks. Human attitudes, it seems, have changed more than the behavior of sharks; in the nineteenth century, when these illustrations were published, sharks were recognized as dangerous and predatory animals but were regarded more as curiosities than monstrous killing machines.

Port Lincoln, a seaside town in fear

By TONY HORWITZ

The setting is a small and scenic seaside town. A young woman is attacked in shallow water by a great white shark of mythic proportions. Only limbs — or, in this case, flippers — escape the shark.

And now, sadly, to complete the *Jaws* analogy, the bereaved town takes to the seas to hunt the killer.

"The shark has to be captured and killed," says Mr Brian Wood, treasurer of the Port Lincoln Game Fishing Club, which is co-ordinating the shark hunt.

"It's had a taste of human flesh and it may come back again for more easy prey."

Police are combing the beaches for remains of the body. Offshore, fishing boats ply the waters with nets and bait, hoping to lure the shark back to the scene of Sunday's crime.

The 14 volunteers on board are armed with hooks, oil drums to weigh down and tire a hooked shark, and high-powered rifles to finish off the six-metre monster if its blunt nose appears above water.

An old friend of the victim's

THE VICTIM: Mrs Shirley Durdin, 33.

THE HUNTER: Graham Bauer with the bullet he intends to use on the shark.

THE TOWN: Port Lincoln, where a shark threatens tourism.

LEFT: Today's media coverage only encourages a hysterical response to shark attack. Gun-toting vigilantes were bent on avenging the death of Shirley Anne Durdin in 1985. "It's had a taste of human flesh and it may come back again for more," said one of the hunters.

ABOVE: Wiseman's Beach, Port Lincoln.

A REVIEW OF SHARK ATTACK IN AUSTRALIAN WATERS

The statistics below have been drawn from 542 cases of shark attack recorded in the Australian Shark Attack File between 1791 and 1998. Of these, 181 were fatal. The records include both provoked and unprovoked attacks.

TIME OF ATTACK (131 cases)

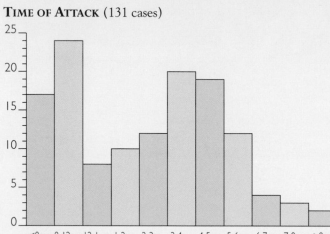

LENGTH OF SHARKS INVOLVED IN ATTACKS

< 1 meter **2%**

1–2 meters **23%**

2–3 meters **30%**

3–4 meters **24%**

4–5 meters **15%**

> 5 meters **6%**

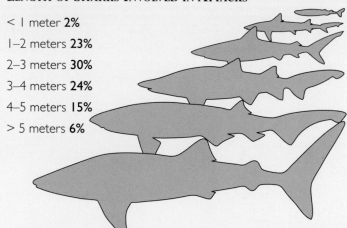

AGE OF VICTIM (217 cases)

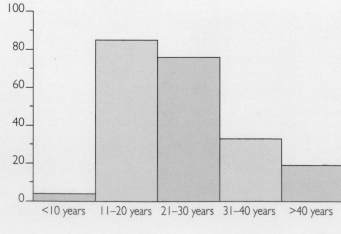

MONTH OF ATTACK (527 cases)

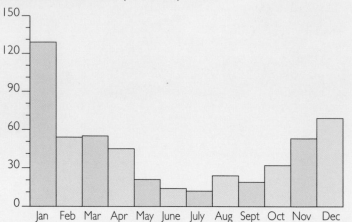

ACTIVITY AT TIME OF ATTACK (259 cases)

Activity	Number of attacks	Number of fatal attacks
Swimming	83	45
Surfboard riding	40	4
Scuba diving	25	7
Hooka	1	1
Spearfishing	36	3
Snorkeling	15	3
Diving into water	1	1
Boat sinking	7	6
In shallow water	11	0
Fishing	13	0
Surf ski/sailboard & blow-up mattress	11	1
Feeding in captivity	6	0
Rescue of others	1	0
Waterskiing	1	1

MOST COMMON SHARK SPECIES IN ATTACKS (168 cases)

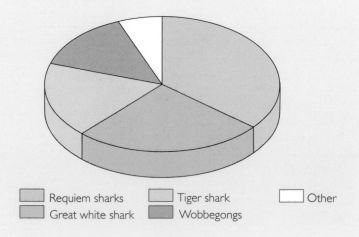

Requiem sharks | Tiger shark | Other
Great white shark | Wobbegongs

Rich Mula/Ocean Images

LEFT: Surfboard riders have sometimes attracted the attention of sharks, perhaps because of their resemblance to seals or fish. The owner of this surfboard was lucky that only his board (which might have looked to a hungry shark like a large and attractive tuna) was damaged in a lightning attack by a great white shark.

factors that influenced the attacks. Coppleson's investigations also confirmed that the majority of Australian attacks were made by lone sharks and that only in a few instances were shark packs involved. He found in many cases the shark would strike the same victim a couple of times while completely ignoring other swimmers nearby. This was the case with a shark attack that occurred off Wiseman's Beach near Port Lincoln in South Australia on March 3, 1985.

Shirley Anne Durdin and her husband Barry were snorkeling for scallops in 2 meters of water, 50 meters from the shore. Nearby, a fisherman trailed a line from the side of a small dinghy and two men and a woman were frolicking in the water with three children and a dog. At 1.30 pm, Shirley Durdin was struck below the waist by a 6-meter white shark. Eyewitnesses said there was a big spray of red froth and bubbles and that one man started yelling, "Help, help, help, she's gone, she's gone." When one of the larger boats in the vicinity rushed over to the scene of the attack to help, the shark resurfaced and made off with the remains of Mrs. Durdin's body.

Local fishermen reported that a "monster" white shark had been feeding in the area for four weeks and blamed rotten bait and burley that had been thrown in the bay for a local fishing competition for attracting it to the scene.

THE ROGUE SHARK THEORY

Coppleson was a strong advocate of the "rogue" shark theory. He found that places that had been free of attack for years would suddenly, within a short period and for no apparent reason, become the scene of two, three or even more attacks. Then, just as suddenly as they began, the attacks would stop and the area would enjoy a long period of freedom from shark attack. This pattern, according to Coppleson's theory, recurred far too often to be a matter of simple coincidence. He blamed individual sharks, which he called "rogues," for the occurrence. One of Australia's most horrific series of shark attacks is attributed to a 5-meter "rogue" tiger shark.

On July 26, 1983, Ray Boundy told how over the preceding 35 hours, after his 14-meter trawler capsized and sank 100 kilometers northeast of Townsville in northern Queensland, he had watched helplessly as a large shark first took a young crewman then came back for the female cook. After managing to escape from the sinking boat, Boundy and the crew, 24-year-old Dennis Murphy and 21-year-old Linda Horton, took a surfboard, lifering and piece of foam from the wreckage and decided to paddle toward Lodestone Reef where they knew help could be found. They set off at 1 pm on July 25 and it was not until after dark that evening that the shark first appeared. On spotting the swimmers, the shark began to follow their progress, surfacing occasionally and pushing at the pieces of foam, lifering and surfboard to which they were clinging. By this time the three crew were only 8 kilometers from Lodestone Reef and tried to ignore the harassing shark in the hope it would eventually leave them alone.

Their wish was not fulfilled. On one of its many passes the shark suddenly turned, lunged at Ray Boundy and grabbed his leg. In a split-second

Ben Cropp

reaction, Ray drove the shark off with an almighty kick. "He got such a fright we thought he had gone," he said later. Ten minutes after the first attack, the shark reappeared and seized Dennis Murphy's leg, pulling him under several times. When the shark let go, Dennis told the others he had lost his leg and that he had no hope. He persuaded them that with the shark's attention on him their opportunity had come to escape. Acting under Murphy's advice, Ray Boundy and Linda Horton paddled off, leaving Dennis Murphy to deal with the shark. "We heard a lot of screaming and kicking and punching, then saw the shark lift his body upsidedown out of the water and eat it," Boundy said after the event.

Two hours later, while Linda Horton was sitting in the sling of the lifering with her feet up on the foam and with Ray beside her, the shark struck again. Grabbing Linda around the arms and chest, the shark shook her three or four times

then disappeared under the water with her body. Terrified, Ray immediately grabbed two remaining pieces of foam for support and paddled as fast as he could for the reef. It was not until after daylight that the shark returned and began circling Ray Boundy. By this time the outer reef, offering safety, was in sight and Ray made a last-ditch effort to reach the reef in one piece. His desperate progress was watched by the shark as it zigzagged behind him. Once Ray had made it to the reef edge, the shark turned and disappeared. Not long afterwards Ray was spotted and rescued by a surveillance helicopter.

Although Ray Boundy did not recognize the species of shark responsible, evidence suggests that it was almost certainly a tiger shark. Following the multiple attack, local fishermen landed a number of large tiger sharks in the area but as the culprit was never proved caught, it was not properly identified. This is a very common problem with shark attacks as positive identification of maneaters can only be made if tooth fragments are found in the victim. More important, while some people have speculated that the "rogue" shark had particularly set its sights on the three crew, no one knows just what triggered the attack. Clearly much more scientific research needs to be undertaken if marine biologists are to understand the reasons for shark attacks.

ATTACKS IN AUSTRALIA

At July 1, 1998, the Australian Shark Attack File had recorded 542 shark attacks in Australian waters (including Torres Strait Islands, Cocos Island and within the 200 nautical mile

Ben Cropp

Ben Cropp

THE SHARK ARM MURDER CASE

Record books around the world abound with bizarre cases and fascinating tales of shark attacks, but none has managed to top what is known internationally as the "Shark Arm Murder" case. On April 18, 1935, Albert Hobson set off in his boat to a point off Coogee Beach in Sydney where he had left a line bait. Pulling up the line, Albert was amazed to find he had hooked not only a small half-eaten shark but also a 4.5-meter tiger shark, entangled in the line and still very much alive. Albert secured the giant shark and towed it to the beach. Once there he decided to turn the prize shark over to the Coogee Aquarium for exhibition. Albert's find soon had Sydneysiders flocking to the aquarium to see the "monster."

For several day the tiger shark slowly cruised around its new home, happily eating all the fish thrown to it. Then on April 25, having not taken food during the morning and early afternoon, the shark, according to observers, went "crazy" and began bumping into the aquarium walls and turning in circles. After 20 minutes of this behavior the shark suddenly startled onlookers by regurgitating a human arm. The shocked aquarium owners immediately called the police, and Dr. Victor Coppleson was asked to examine the arm in the Sydney morgue. According to police, the arm was that of a muscular man. On the forearm was a slightly faded tattoo of two boxers shaping up to each other.

Coppleson reported that in his opinion the arm had not been bitten from the body by a shark because it was so cleanly separated at the shoulder joint. He also stressed that a surgeon had not performed the task because the usual skin flaps a doctor would leave were not present. On learning this, the police decided to publicize the incident in the hope of solving the mystery. They issued a photograph and description of the tattoo. Soon after, a man came forward to identify the arm as that of his brother, 45-year-old James Smith.

Within a short time police had arrested Patrick Brady for murder and questioned another man, Reginald Holmes. Several days after being questioned Holmes was found dead in his car near the Sydney Harbor Bridge. He had a bullet in his head. Smith had last been seen alive on April 8 at 6 pm in a hotel in Cronulla, a Sydney suburb, and police decided that James Smith, Patrick Brady and Reginald Holmes had been involved in standover tactics, murder threats, forgery and conspiracy to defraud an insurance company. A series of murder trials followed, with the Crown alleging that Brady and Holmes had murdered Smith on the night he had been last seen alive. They believed that Smith's body had been cut up, stuffed into a tin trunk and dumped in the ocean. As the arm could not be forced into the trunk, the men decided to tie it to a rope attached to a heavy weight and sink it to the sea bottom beside the trunk. The police conjectured that the shark must have seized the arm sometime between the night of April 8 and April 17, when it was caught off Coogee. Surprisingly, the arm remained intact for another eight days in the shark's stomach until it was dramatically disgorged on April 25.

Three sensational trials later, Patrick Brady was acquitted through lack of evidence; he lived a free man until his death in 1965. As for the tiger shark, it became very sick a couple of days after disgorging the arm and the aquarium owners had to kill it. When police performed an autopsy, they found that the tiger shark's stomach contained a portion of the other shark and some fish bones but no further human remains.

international fishing zone), of which 181 have been fatal. The total number of recorded attacks include provoked and unprovoked encounters, bites while removing sharks from nets, bites on kayaks and small canoes, and bites from sharks kept in captivity.

The activities of victims at the time of the attack were recorded in 259 cases. Swimming was by far the most dangerous activity, with 83 attacks, of which 45 were fatal. The second most dangerous activity was surfboard riding, which resulted in 40 attacks but only four fatalities. Spearfishing, scuba diving and snorkeling figured prominently on the list of activities, provoking a total of 76 attacks, 13 of which were fatal. Six people were attacked while feeding sharks in captivity, and one while trying to rescue others.

The age of the victims was recorded in 217 cases, and ranged from 7 to 70 years old. Four

victims were under 10 years old, 85 between 11 and 20, 76 between 21 and 30, 33 between 31 and 40, and the remaining 19 were over 40 years old. Most of the attacks occurred on males: 486 cases were recorded, compared with only 41 for females. This is a sex ratio of approximately 12:1. The majority of shark attacks occurred in the summer months: November (53), December (69), January (129), February (54) and March (55).

Pearl divers along the Great Barrier Reef figured significantly in an earlier list compiled by Gilbert Whitley in 1963, particularly native "swim divers" who worked without specialized diving equipment or helmets. Iona Asai was one such diver who had a remarkable encounter with a shark. A Torres Strait Islander, Asai was diving from a lugger into just 4 meters of water when he was attacked by a tiger shark. His verbatim account follows.

ABOVE: Meshing is regarded as the most effective method of protecting large numbers of swimmers, but it is so expensive that only restricted areas may be netted. In places, such as Botany Bay in Sydney, authorities can do no more than warn swimmers of potential danger.

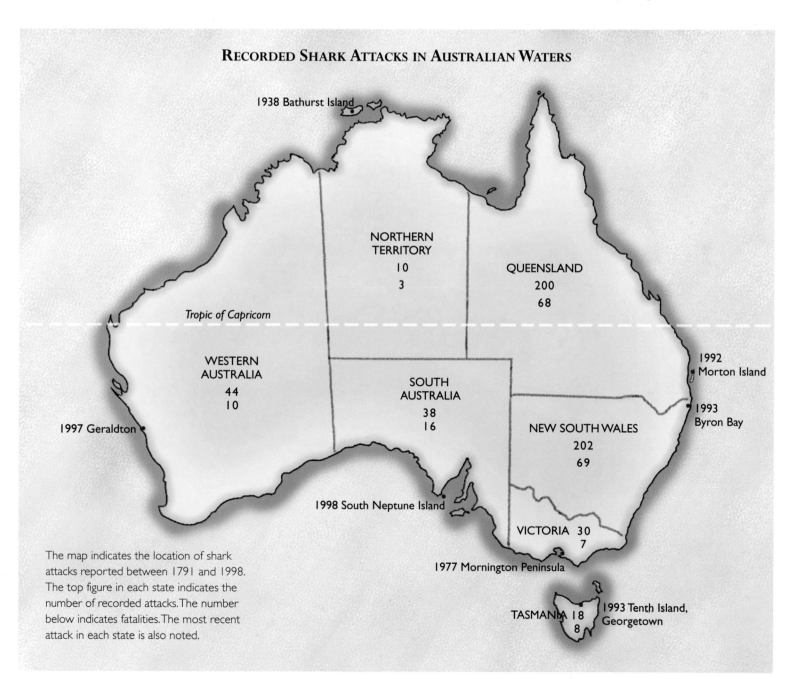

RECORDED SHARK ATTACKS IN AUSTRALIAN WATERS

1938 Bathurst Island

NORTHERN TERRITORY
10
3

QUEENSLAND
200
68

Tropic of Capricorn

WESTERN AUSTRALIA
44
10

SOUTH AUSTRALIA
38
16

NEW SOUTH WALES
202
69

1992 Morton Island

1993 Byron Bay

1997 Geraldton

1998 South Neptune Island

VICTORIA 30
7

1977 Mornington Peninsula

TASMANIA 18
8

1993 Tenth Island, Georgetown

The map indicates the location of shark attacks reported between 1791 and 1998. The top figure in each state indicates the number of recorded attacks. The number below indicates fatalities. The most recent attack in each state is also noted.

POTENTIALLY DANGEROUS SHARKS OF AUSTRALIAN WATERS

GREAT WHITE SHARK
Carcharodon carcharias
Primarily a coastal and offshore species of continental and insular shelves, the great white grows to about 6 meters and is regarded as second only to the orca, or killer whale, as a marine predator. Great whites have accounted for 44 of the 168 cases in which the kind of shark involved in an attack in Australian waters was identified. Despite its reputation, many cases have been reported of great whites inspecting divers without attacking.

TIGER SHARK
Galeocerdo cuvier
Regarded as the most dangerous shark in tropical waters, the tiger shares with the great white and bull sharks membership of the "unholy trinity" of proven maneaters. It grows to about 6 meters and has been responsible for 30 known attacks in Australian waters. The tiger shark is one of the few species that actually consumes human prey—though it also has a reputation as a "garbage can with fins" and will eat bony fishes, other sharks (including tiger sharks), rays, turtles, seabirds, sea snakes, carrion and garbage from ships.

SEVENGILL SHARKS
Family Hexanchidae
One Australian attack has been attributed to a sevengill shark. These sharks are indiscriminate feeders of carrion and prey, but the recorded "attack" may have resulted from careless handling rather than a deliberate assault.

WOBBEGONGS
Family Orectolobidae
The seemingly inoffensive wobbegong has been identified as the culprit in 23 attacks, most of which were probably the accidental results of careless encounters with fishermen and divers. Wobbegongs, of which there are six species, are common on rocky and coral reefs around the Australian coast. Their cryptic coloration provides perfect camouflage on the seabed, thus strengthening the likelihood of accidental encounters.

BLUE SHARK
Prionace glauca

The blue shark has been identified in only one attack in Australian waters. It is found around the world in temperate and tropical waters and grows to around 4 meters. The blue shark is a fast and aggressive predator of the open oceans and has attacked people and boats. Victims of plane crashes and ship sinkings are especially in danger of attack from blue sharks, if only from injury caused by "test-feeding."

SAND TIGER
Carcharias taurus

The sand tiger, known in Australia as the gray nurse, has been identified in only four of the recorded attacks in Australian waters. It is a large shark, with a heavy body typical of the mackerel sharks. Generally sluggish, the sand tiger is drawn to action by disturbance to its habitat, and attacks may have resulted from harassment by divers.

SHORTFIN MAKO
Isurus oxyrinchus

A common, active offshore and pelagic species of temperate and tropical waters around the world, the shortfin mako is famed as the game fish that can leap several meters in a single bound above the water and is capable of high-speed dashes when hooked or in pursuit of prey. The shortfin mako grows to around 4 meters in length and has been identified in one attack in Australia. Its power, aggressiveness and sharp teeth, in combination with speed so great that defensive weapons may be ineffective, make it a real danger to divers.

HAMMERHEAD SHARKS
Sphyrna species

The unique lateral wings that give these warm temperate and tropical sharks their name may provide increased maneuverability and sensory capacities. Of the nine species of hammerheads, only the great hammerhead *S. mokarran* is regarded as dangerous to humans, mainly due to its size—6.1 meters. However, most attacks have been attributed only to "hammerheads" and none of these species is aggressive. Hammerheads have been implicated in only three recorded attacks in Australian waters.

Ron & Valerie Taylor

RIGHT: Despite appearances, the sand tiger is not an aggressive shark and will not attack humans unless provoked.

On the year 1937, day Friday just about 11 o'clock in the morning, the third time I dive and walked in the bottom. I went behind a little high place. The shark was on the other side. I never saw him and he never saw me. I saw a stone like a pearl shell on the north side and when I turned I saw the shark six feet away from me. He opened his mouth. Already I had no chance of escape from him. Then he came and bite me on the head. He felt it was too strong so he swallow my head and put his teeth round my neck. Then he bite me. When I felt his teeth go into my flesh I put my hands round his head and squeeze his eyes until he let go me and I make for the boat. The captain pulled me into the boat and I fainted. They got some medicines from Jervis Island school teacher.

WATER TEMPERATURE AND SHARK ATTACK

One popular misconception is that shark attacks are directly linked to water temperature. Because most Australian attacks have been recorded in summer when the sea is at its warmest, some researchers claim that shark aggression toward humans runs on a set timetable: north of the Tropic of Capricorn, all the months of the year are deemed dangerous; in southern Queensland the risky months are noted as November to May; for Newcastle, Sydney and Perth the danger period is from December to April; for Adelaide it is from December to March; Melbourne is most dangerous between January and March; for Bass Strait and Tasmania January is the problem

the many shark teeth still embedded in the woodwork. As the use of wetsuits increases, divers spend more time in colder water. With more than 300,000 Australians already qualified as scuba divers, and many thousands more snorkeling all year round, the number of shark attacks is likely to increase.

FEEDING AND THREAT BEHAVIOR

According to the Australian Shark Attack File records and other shark research, one of the most common misconceptions about sharks is that they attack people in order to eat them. Analysis of

Ron & Valerie Taylor

ABOVE: The blue shark, an efficient open-ocean predator, has been implicated in only one attack in Australian waters.

1,000 recent shark attacks throughout the world shows that well over 50 percent of these attacks had no direct relationship with feeding. More than 75 percent of victims were struck only once or twice and less than 30 percent of attacks were fatal. A study of wounds made on shark attack survivors supports biologists' claims that these sharks were not trying to remove large portions of flesh from their victims. The sharks were not attacking for food because, despite large amounts of blood and tissue in the water, they rarely pressed home their attack after the initial strike.

Another behavior pattern that is often highly sensationalized is the frenzy some sharks display when, in the presence of food, they appear to lose all control and attack anything in their path. But while this behavior is known to occur, especially among reef sharks, statistics show that it is not relevant to the majority of attacks that take place around Australia.

Attacks by great whites may be more directly related to feeding than attacks by most other species. This is because these sharks habitually prey on marine mammals. The behavior of white sharks is different from that of every other species. Many fishermen report this shark's spine-chilling habit of quietly raising its head out of the water to investigate anything unusual. Marine

month. Of course, as the summer months are obviously the time when most people are in the water and therefore have more chance of being attacked by sharks, one wonders how reliable this timetable is.

Even more serious doubts are raised by the fact that white sharks have often defied this attack pattern theory. On October 15, 1984, for example, a Tasmanian abalone diver reported that he was pinned to the ocean floor for more than an hour as a 6-meter white shark tried to prise him out of a crevice. Two months earlier, on August 13, two Perth fishermen reported an attack on their fishing boat by a "monster" white shark. Their evidence was the smashed boat and

Ben Cropp

Carcharhinus amblyrhynchos, compete with each other as well as with other sharks for food and have developed a ritualized threat display. Marine biologists have found that many of the attacks made on divers by this particular species came about because the shark was cornered and had no means of escape. In every case of shark attack investigated, the shark performed its ritual threat display before it came in for the attack.

The reef shark's threat display consists of an S-shaped swimming pattern followed by a figure of eight as it moves closer to the "threatening" skindiver. As the shark swims, it twists and turns in an exaggerated fashion with its pectoral fins depressed, snout raised, jaws slightly open and back arched. On its direct approach it appears rigid. It frequently breaks off the attack within a meter of contact and repeats the procedure until the offending diver leaves the water. Marine biologists believe this ritualized behavior may be connected with either courtship displays or territorial defense.

biologists believe that this most unsharklike action results from the white shark's search for seals basking on the rocks along the shore. South Australian and Victorian fishermen operating around Phillip and Kangaroo islands claim to have seen white sharks lift their bodies clear of the water to seize a sleeping seal from the rocks.

Extensive work by American researchers on the reactions of reef sharks to divers has added considerably to our knowledge of shark attack. Reef sharks, notably the gray reef shark

Wideranging migratory sharks may have threat responses that are very different from those of the reef sharks. These sharks may be stimulated to attack after swimmers or divers make what the sharks consider to be aggressive incursions into their "living space" as opposed to their geographical territory. While much more work

THE TRAGEDY OF MARCIA HATHAWAY

John Fairfax & Sons

John Fairfax & Sons

One of the most tragic shark attacks to occur in Sydney waters occurred on the Australia Day holiday in January, 1963. It was a humid, overcast day and ironically a headline in that morning's *Sydney Morning Herald* read "Australia Day Surfers Warned of Sharks." Marcia Hathaway, a well-known

32-year-old actress, her fiancé Frederick Knight, and four friends came by boat to Sugarloaf Bay, a stretch of water just north of Balmoral Beach in Sydney Harbor, for a day of swimming and picnicking. Two of the party went off for oysters while Marcia and Frederick cooled themselves and swam in a mere 75 centimeters of water.

The water was lapping at Marcia's hips when suddenly she screamed out, "I've been bitten by an octopus!" Knight was only a couple of arm-lengths away when the shark seized her right leg below the calf. In a second lunge, the shark's teeth were fixed in Marcia's thigh. Another member of the party rushed to assist Frederick and together they managed to release the girl's torn and bloody leg from the shark's jaws.

The beach was inaccessible by road. Marcia was taken back by cruiser to the nearest boatshed while Frederick dived into the water and swam to the nearest house for help. An ambulance was waiting when Marcia's boat drew up. As it started the slippery climb from the water's edge, the tires skidded and the clutch burnt out. Volunteers strained as they tried to push the ambulance up the hill.

A second ambulance was called but Marcia Hathaway had suffered enormous blood loss and was dead on arrival at hospital, less than half an hour after the attack.

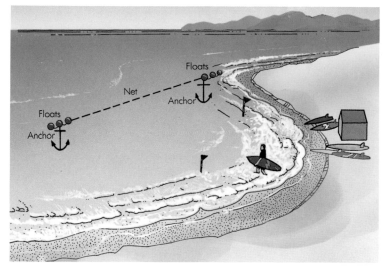

ABOVE: Positioning shark nets to protect a New South Wales surfing beach. In recent years up to 350 sharks have been caught per annum, the most common of which are hammerheads. A shark netting program also operates in Queensland. (After Coppleson 1976)

ABOVE: A shark net in place. Each end of the 150-meter shark net is secured by a 14-kilogram anchor and its position marked by floats, which also help to hold the net upright. The loosely hanging nets, about 6 meters deep, are set by trawler in the late afternoon and usually hauled in the next morning. The frequency of meshing for each beach is determined by a quota system and therefore not all beaches in the program are protected at any one time. (After Coppleson 1976)

Ben Cropp

ABOVE: Meshing of Sydney beaches began in 1936 and 1,500 sharks were caught in the period from October 1937 to February 1939. Since then the number has continued to decline, which probably reflects a relatively steady decrease in the population of potentially dangerous sharks.

needs to be carried out on this aspect of sharks' behavior, the evidence suggests most shark attacks are aggressive threat reactions to the presence of people in the water. The fact that the types of wounds found on victims are often similar to those sharks inflict on each other when they fight supports this explanation.

COPING WITH SHARKS

Mesh netting of beaches is by far the most effective method of reducing shark attack on swimmers. Shark experts advise bathers that if they see a shark while they are in the water they should assume it to be dangerous and head straight for the beach or boat as quickly and quietly as possible.

Kicking wildly and thrashing with the arms in a panic to escape is the worst thing a person can do. It serves only to send vibrations to the shark that suggest the person is a fish in trouble, and therefore easy prey. Probably the best method of stopping a shark once it has decided to attack is to put on a show of aggression and kick or pummel it when it rushes in. Divers separated from their boats should retreat to the sea bottom and wait patiently for the shark to move on.

Any injury from a shark should be considered a medical problem. Such injuries range from slight abrasions to deep punctures, tissue damage and severe bleeding. In coastal areas influenced by human activity, puncture or abrasions of the skin can result in severe infection.

ENCOUNTERS WITH SHARKS IN SOUTH AFRICA

LEONARD J.V. COMPAGNO

T he South African coastline, from the mouth of the Orange River in the eastern South
Atlantic to the Mozambique border in the southwestern Indian Ocean, stretches for only
2,954 kilometers, yet includes in or adjacent to its boundaries (including Namibia and
Mozambique) approximately 111 species of sharks. All eight of the major orders of sharks occur
here, and almost all of the families. There is every likelihood that additional species will continue
to be added, especially from northern incursions of tropical species and discoveries of deepwater
and oceanic species. South African sharks are diverse, and include oceanic, continental shelf and
continental slope species, wideranging circumtropical and circumtemperate sharks, local endemic
species, cold temperate sharks, warm temperate sharks, and tropical-subtropical sharks.

The interaction of two great current systems on the landmass of South Africa constrains and
strongly influences many of these sharks and makes for a great variety of habitats compressed into
a coastline which, when compared with that of Australia or the United States, is relatively short.
The cold Benguela current sweeps the west coast of South Africa and supports cold-water sharks
and bony fishes roughly similar to those of northern California. The warm Agulhas current flows
along the east coast, warming the beaches of kwaZulu-Natal, Transkei and the eastern Cape and
bringing with it many tropical Indo-west Pacific sharks and other fishes. These species extend their
range for varying distances south, depending on their temperature tolerances and the fluctuations
in warm-water masses. One warm-water species, the bull shark Carcharhinus leucas, *readily*
penetrates into fresh water and highly saline bays in the area.

BELOW: South Africa's many
swimming and surfing beaches
present an idyllic scene but, like
Australia, South Africa has an
unenviable record for shark
encounters, though vigorous anti-
shark measures have greatly reduced
the risks to swimmers.

Al Giddings/Ocean Images

POTENTIALLY DANGEROUS SPECIES

Slightly less than a quarter of the shark species in South African waters are large and powerful enough to be capable of seriously injuring people in the water. These are listed in the table on the following page. They include sharks that occur in waters readily accessible to people, but not the large deepwater sharks of the continental slopes that live beyond the range of normal human activities. Omitted also are the giant filter feeders, the whale shark *Rhincodon typus* and basking shark *Cetorhinus maximus*, and the three species of thresher sharks *Alopias* spp., which normally are innocuous unless captured or harassed.

As with shark encounters (usually given the emotionally loaded term "attacks") worldwide, very few of the known shark injuries on people in South African waters can be attributed to particular species. This is because of the difficulty of identifying the species of shark involved, and

from the formerly confused state of classification of the requiem shark family (Carcharhinidae), which contains most of the species identified in shark–people encounters.

Of the species listed, five or so have actually been identified in encounters that resulted in minor to serious injury or death: sand tiger, great white shark, bull shark, oceanic whitetip shark and tiger shark. Of these, the sand tiger is a fairly sluggish fish-eating species that is usually quite docile when approached by divers and is popular for ecotourist shark viewing. It inflicts little injury when biting people and such encounters are most likely the result of aggression, accidental provocation or related to spearfishing. They are emphatically not an attempt to feed on people.

The bull and great white sharks are the species most frequently recorded as having caused injuries or mortalities to South African swimmers and divers. The oceanic whitetip shark does not visit

ABOVE: Despite their size and undoubted capacity to take prey with ease, great white sharks tend to attack in an inhibited fashion. It may be that they are merely "taste-testing" swimmers, wetsuited divers or surfboard riders who look from below like seals—animals high on the list of the great white's most-favored prey.

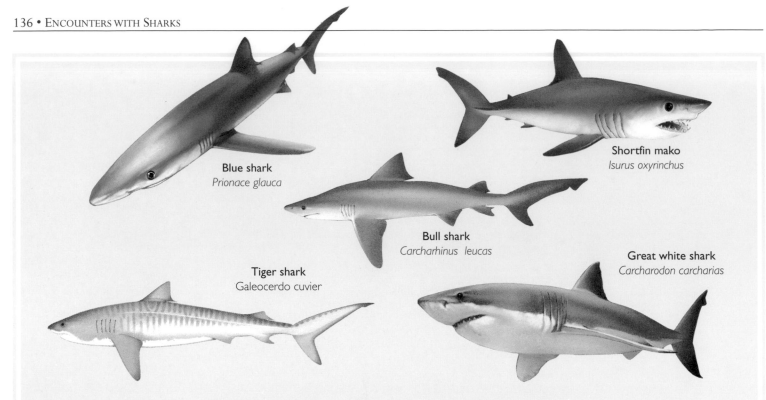

Blue shark
Prionace glauca

Shortfin mako
Isurus oxyrinchus

Bull shark
Carcharhinus leucas

Tiger shark
Galeocerdo cuvier

Great white shark
Carcharodon carcharias

POTENTIALLY DANGEROUS SHARKS IN SOUTH AFRICAN WATERS

Type	Family	Scientific Name	Common Name
sixgill and sevengill sharks	Hexanchidae	*Notorynchus cepedianus*	broadnose sevengill shark
nurse sharks	Ginglymostomatidae	*Nebrius ferrugineus*	tawny nurse
raggedtooth sharks	Odontaspididae	*Carcharias taurus*	sand tiger
mackerel sharks	Lamnidae	*Carcharodon carcharias*	great white shark
		Isurus oxyrinchus	shortfin mako
weasel sharks	Hemigaleidae	*Hemipristis elongatus*	snaggletooth shark
requiem sharks	Carcharhinidae	*Carcharhinus albimarginatus*	silvertip shark
		C. amboinensis	pigeye shark
		C. brachyurus	bronze whaler
		C. brevipinna	spinner shark
		C. leucas	bull shark
		C. limbatus	blacktip shark
		C. longimanus	oceanic whitetip shark
		C. obscurus	dusky shark
		C. wheeleri	blacktail reef shark
		Galeocerdo cuvier	tiger shark
		Negaprion acutidens	sharptooth lemon shark
		Prionace glauca	blue shark
		Triaenodon obesus	whitetip reef shark
hammerhead sharks	Sphyrnidae	*Sphyrna lewini*	scalloped hammerhead
		S. mokarran	great hammerhead
		S. zygaena	smooth hammerhead

Bay Picture Library

bathing beaches and is not a potential problem, except for offshore divers, who may be closely investigated and who may need to fend it off. It can cause difficulties (along with blue sharks) for masses of injured people in the water after rare air–sea disasters far offshore, and may have been responsible for fatalities after the troopship *Nova Scotia* was torpedoed off kwaZulu-Natal in 1942.

One or two (possibly more) injurious shark encounters in South African waters can probably be attributed to the tiger shark. This is a large, opportunistic predator that eats a variety of prey, including marine mammals, and is not averse to sampling unusual items. Tiger sharks have a traditional bad reputation in some places, but more recently they have been approached underwater by divers, and usually have not responded aggressively.

There is evidence for several injurious incidents involving both bull and great white sharks in South Africa, validated by tooth fragments, wound patterns or accounts of the victims. At least some writers have thought the bull shark was responsible for most of the injuries to, and deaths of, swimmers off bathing beaches in kwaZulu-Natal. In terms of relative abundance and habitat the bull shark is, or was, more likely to come in contact with people than the tiger

and great white sharks. Although smaller than the other two, the bull shark has large teeth, massive jaws and heavy jaw muscles for its size, feeds on a range of prey including large marine organisms, and occurs in a greater variety of inshore habitats than the other species. It has become the subject of ecotourist viewing by freeranging divers on reefs off kwaZulu-Natal, and apparently is readily approachable underwater if treated with respect by divers.

The formidable great white shark generally bites people in an inhibited fashion and often inflicts much less injury than it can. Although its injuries can be fatal, most white shark encounters are survivable. Documented cases of white sharks actually consuming people do occur, but these are rare and the sharks are far less likely to accost people than large terrestrial and freshwater predators such as the great cats, larger crocodilians and the biggest bears. Evidence from South Africa, as well as California, Australia and New Zealand, indicates that white sharks often closely approach divers underwater without contact, and are inquisitive of human activity.

The writer has interviewed several South African divers who were approached, investigated, but not injured by white sharks. In some instances these divers were spearfishing and the sharks may

ABOVE: In South Africa, as in other countries, positive identification of sharks involved in encounters with humans is rare. There may be an element of embarrassment in admitting that relatively harmless animals such as these tawny nurses *Nebrius ferrugineus* were goaded into action after harassment by divers.

have been attracted by injured fish. In other cases divers were engaged in non-fishing underwater operations, including archeological salvage, and were repeatedly approached by white sharks without aggressive displays. Recent research on the white shark has shown it to be a different animal from the fearsome and solitary eating machine featured in *Jaws*: social, inquisitive, responsive to other white sharks and to divers, complex in its behavior, and tending to focus on normal marine prey and baits rather than humans in proximity.

Of the remaining sharks listed, the tawny nurse, shortfin mako, bronze whaler, spinner shark, blacktip shark, dusky shark, blacktail reef shark, sharptooth lemon shark, blue shark, whitetip reef shark and great hammerhead have been involved in a few injurious encounters in South Africa (as they have in other areas). The snaggletooth shark, silvertip shark, pigeye shark, and the hammerheads are large species that have not been positively identified in injurious encounters anywhere.

Tawny nurses are docile tropical reef sharks that feed on small fishes and crustaceans, and are likely to defend themselves only if being harassed and provoked by foolhardy divers. Sharptooth lemon sharks occur in the same habitats as tawny nurses, but have large pointed teeth and can stoutly defend themselves when provoked or disturbed. Tawny nurses and lemon sharks are almost never caught in the kwaZulu-Natal shark nets, seldom frequent beaches used by bathers, and are rarely involved in shark encounters.

Shortfin makos are offshore sharks that eat mainly bony fishes and squid, and can cause problems primarily when hooked or otherwise provoked by sportfishermen from boats. Most mako incidents occur when fishermen hook them or are landing bony fishes that the mako then grabs, but few unprovoked injuries on swimmers and divers can be attributed to them. Small numbers of makos are taken each year in the kwaZulu-Natal shark nets, indicating occasional or regular incursions inshore from blue water close by off the narrow continental shelves.

As with oceanic whitetip sharks, blue sharks are abundant offshore and are a problem primarily to offshore divers and in air–sea disasters. Neither species figures in the kwaZulu-Natal shark net catches. Blue sharks are noticeably more timid than oceanic whitetips when interacting with divers. The whitetip reef shark is a normally timid, small-toothed, reef-loving species usually encountered by divers without incident. The spinner and blacktip sharks are fast-moving fish-eating species that rarely bite people when food is present. They have sometimes nipped spearfishing divers and swimmers or participated in so-called "feeding frenzies" involving numerous sharks feeding competitively on abundant fisheries offal.

Kevin Deacon/Auscape

The bronze whaler, silvertip and dusky sharks and the three hammerheads all grow to a total length of between 2.4 and more than 4 meters and should be treated with respect, although all have been encountered by divers without any problems. The blacktail reef shark is a moderate-size Indian Ocean shark closely related to the gray reef shark *Carcharhinus amblyrhynchos* and like that species may direct spectacular threat displays at divers who corner it or otherwise provoke it (which can end in a defensive bite if the divers do not back off). These handsome sharks are often approached on reefs by divers without incident and are popular with ecotourist shark divers.

A number of other species—sevengill sharks, sand tigers, great white sharks, blacktail reef

sharks, blacktip sharks, bronze whalers, bull sharks, tiger sharks, hammerheads, and possibly spinner sharks and dusky sharks—have often approached spearfishing divers in South African waters, and have sometimes harassed them and stolen their catches. In some cases the divers may have averted injuries by fending off the sharks with their spearguns or other objects, though the sharks generally focus on the injured fishes and are best left to carry them off.

ENCOUNTERS WITH BOATS AND SURFBOARDS
Great white and mako sharks have been responsible for several encounters with boats in South African waters, mostly off the Western Cape Province, usually but not always when fish

were being caught from the boat. From 1936 to 1977, approximately 25 boat encounters occurred in Cape waters, mostly in the Western Cape and with 13 of them in the four-year period between 1974 and 1977. Of such incidents where the shark could be identified, 14 were by white sharks and two by shortfin makos. At least 11 of these incidents, all by white sharks, have occurred in False Bay in the western Cape. On several occasions in the past white sharks and makos have severely damaged and even leapt into boats, sometimes causing injuries to the occupants.

Interestingly, the meteoric rise of cage diving for white sharks in the Western and Eastern Cape after 1992, with hundreds of different sharks repeatedly chummed and lured to within view by

ABOVE: The sand tiger *Carcharias taurus*, known as the spotted raggedtooth in South Africa, will approach spearfishing divers and on occasion steal their catches. The only "attacks" in which it has been identified occur when divers attempt to defend their catches and are injured by the shark's formidable teeth or flailing tail.

floating baits, has not resulted in any serious damage to the boats (which are usually skiboats or small cabin cruisers), though the sharks readily investigate, mouth, bite or slap the boats, motors, cages and any other artificial objects. Pulling baits away from the sharks as they attempt to feed may cause dramatic reactions reminiscent of frustration, and suggest that earlier violent white shark encounters with fishing boats could have resulted from the sharks giving chase after hooked live fish they were targeting were pulled up and out of their reach. White sharks readily jump and can even catch prey out of the water, so jumping into a boat after a fish is not surprising.

There are several recent cases of white sharks hitting surfboards in South African waters, which resemble similar cases in California and elsewhere. Although some writers have assumed that these result from "mistaken identity" when the shark mistakes a surfer for a seal or a turtle, more recent work suggests that white sharks readily investigate and sometimes gently or violently hit and grab, and then release, a wide variety of floating objects, which can be unlike either prey or surfboards, and that hits on surfboards may be independent of the surfers sitting on them. What the sharks are doing is still obscure and controversial, but apparently it is not necessarily predation.

WHERE SHARK ENCOUNTERS OCCUR

The pattern of injurious shark encounters with people off South Africa, as with the worlwide pattern, may be correlated with temperature. No injurious encounters on swimmers or divers have been recorded in the cold sector of the west coast of the Western and Northern Cape Provinces from Cape Town to the Orange River mouth, though white sharks do occur there. In the Western Cape Province and Eastern Cape Province, between the Cape Peninsula and False Bay to off the Transkei coast, shark injuries on swimmers and divers have usually occurred at a low rate, although a recent (1998) and anomalous flurry of encounters off the Eastern Cape is causing concern and speculation. Between 1940 and 1990, 78 encounters occurred off the Cape Provinces (about 1.5 per year, with a range of 0 to 6 per year), of which 10 (13 percent) were fatal. The apparent trend was for a noticeable increase in encounters from 1940 to 1960, reminiscent of a similar trend in California, and an erratic leveling off or slight increase from 1960 to 1990 and beyond.

In the past few years several shark encounters have been reported in the Eastern Cape, including sand tigers biting bathers, and several encounters between surfers and white sharks, with injuries ranging from none to fatal. Increasing shark incidents in these waters in postwar years are probably related to the growing popularity of water sports such as surfing, scuba diving and spearfishing, brought on by advances in technology that produced aqualungs, wetsuits and other dive gear as well as fiberglass surfboards. The fatality rate is lower than kwaZulu-Natal and the principal species involved in Cape waters is the white shark.

In kwaZulu-Natal the warm inshore water and splendid beaches have long enticed bathers into the shallows and exposed them to a relatively high rate of shark encounters and injuries which is, however, minuscule compared to common seaside and terrestrial accidents. Some 97 encounters were reported in kwaZulu-Natal waters between 1940 and 1990, of which 25 (26 percent) were fatal.

For the entire period encounters ranged from none to seven per year and averaged 1.9 per year, with fatalities averaging 0.5 per year. Widespread shark netting off the kwaZulu-Natal beaches began in earnest in the mid 1960s and has

BELOW: Humans may fear the great white shark *Carcharodon carcharias*, but it is the undisputed master of its own element. It has few rivals in the sea, giving way perhaps only to the orca, and embodies the intelligence and functionality of one of the world's great creatures.

Ron and Valerie Taylor

virtually eliminated shark injuries to people on netted beaches since the late 1960s.

The higher encounter, major injury and fatality rates in kwaZulu-Natal, in comparison with Cape waters, has been attributed mainly to the fact that people there use the water more for bathing and swimming. A possible additional factor is the greater diversity and abundance of large predatory sharks in warmer waters, particularly species of requiem sharks such as the bull and tiger sharks. The fatality rate between 1940 to 1990, and particularly between 1940 and 1960, when beach nets were in limited use, is strikingly higher than in the Cape provinces or in California.

Overall South Africa had 175 shark encounters between 1940 and 1990, which averaged about 3.4 per year and ranged from none to 10 per year. Fatalities were 35 over this period and averaged about 0.7 per year with a range of none to four.

ANTI-SHARK MEASURES

Protective measures against sharks in South Africa were initially centered on the popular bathing beaches of the greater Durban area and the beaches south to Margate and Port Edward in southern kwaZulu-Natal. They were expanded in the 1970s and 1980s along the entire kwaZulu-Natal coast and to one resort in the northern Transkei coast of the Eastern Cape.

In 1907 the Durban City Council constructed a semicircular enclosure 200 meters in diameter to protect bathers. This lasted 21 years, but eventually had to be demolished after corrosion and wave action had rendered it useless. The 47 shark encounters and 18 shark fatalities off

kwaZulu-Natal beaches between 1940 and 1960 generated publicity, hysteria and public clamor for protection.

Although drownings, boat accidents and the traffic accidents and other injuries connected with beachside holidays undoubtedly caused many more fatalities and injuries in kwaZulu-Natal than sharks during the 1940s and 1950s, none of these more mundane events had the same spine-chilling effect on the holiday public as did the shark encounters. Fatal or otherwise, they ruined holidaymakers' enthusiasm for the southern kwaZulu-Natal beaches, and many people cut short their beachside holidays.

Fear of sharks intensified to a fever pitch during the summer of 1957–58. In five months there were seven encounters, five of them fatal. Four occurred during the "Black December" Christmas holiday season of 1957. These incidents, and the publicity they generated, resulted in wholesale desertion of beaches. The

ABOVE: The first sharkproof enclosure in South Africa was constructed by the Durban City Council in 1907. It was demolished in 1928 and never replaced.

LEFT: Netting of Durban beaches began in 1952 under the auspices of the Durban City Council and in response to public concern about the presence of sharks close to popular beaches. The program has to date successfully eliminated shark encounters at the netted beaches.

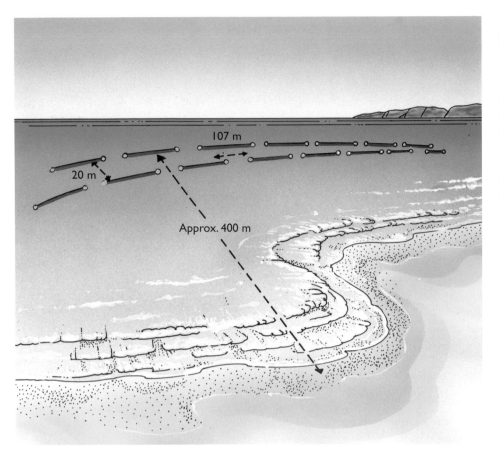

ABOVE: Shark netting in Natal. The Natal Sharks Board is responsible for installing and maintaining shark nets at 60 beaches along 325 kilometers of coastline. The nets are set in two staggered rows beyond the surfline and are serviced regularly by meshing teams working from skiboats. (After Wallett 1983)

RIGHT: A net in position. While the nets provide effective protection, they are expensive to install and maintain, and their effectiveness is diminished by tangling and tearing in bad weather and rough seas. (After Wallett 1983)

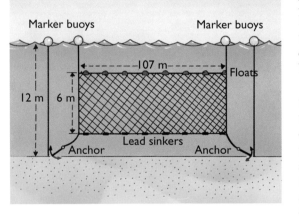

organized and local police were authorized to drop hand grenades on sharks when they were sighted!

The City Council of Durban had earlier responded to public concern about shark encounters off Durban and elsewhere in kwaZulu-Natal; in 1948 it proposed the construction of a beach enclosure to replace the one built in 1907. This was delayed for a few years due to its cost, but meanwhile the council was evaluating other, more aggressive methods of protecting its beaches. It was greatly impressed by the successes of the shark meshing program at Sydney beaches in New South Wales, Australia, and proposed a similar program for South Africa. This would use offshore wide-mesh gillnets to reduce the number of large sharks off Durban's beaches. The program was initiated in 1952 and has so far completely eliminated shark injuries and fatalities at beaches where the nets were installed.

Four municipalities in popular holiday areas copied Durban in the early 1960s by installing anti-shark nets off their beaches. In 1964, local anti-shark activities coalesced into a centralized kwaZulu-Natal-wide organization, created by the provincial administration and analogous to the military and police and fire departments. This unique entity was for many years titled the Natal Anti-Shark Measures Board but was renamed the Natal Sharks Board in the late 1980s. The Sharks Board is a kind of "shark police" that maintains the kwaZulu-Natal netting program as well as extensive public relations activities that make for broad community and media recognition.

The Sharks Board uses a fleet of skiboats with twin outboard motors, towed by four-wheel drive vehicles and launched directly from the beaches or from nearby launch sites, to tend the nets. Six-man shark meshing teams operate these boats and some 180 people set, retrieve, repair and rebuild the nets, which are set in a staggered double row offshore just beyond the surfline. The nets do not form an absolute barrier for the protected beaches and 35 percent of the sharks are caught on the landward side of the nets.

Except where weather prohibits it, nets are serviced daily through the year and are replaced every two to three weeks for cleaning. Bad weather and rough seas can tangle and damage the nets, and bathing may be banned temporarily while the nets are repaired and repositioned. Every year during the annual sardine run, the nets are removed for a few days to avoid excess catches of migratory sharks, game fish, dolphins and rays that follow the run, and to prevent the damage these could cause to the expensive nets.

At present about 60 beaches are netted and more than 40 kilometers of nets have been deployed along 325 kilometers of coastline. Large resorts and municipalities pay for the cost of the nets, while the expenses of smaller entities are subsidized by the kwaZulu-Natal authorities. Nets

panic climaxed in April 1958 when two fatal encounters off Uvongo, just north of Margate, caused a mass evacuation of the beaches. One of the results of the shark panic was economic disaster for hotels, resorts, businesses and municipalities dependent on holiday patronage.

To help recoup their losses from the 1957 Christmas disaster, some of the hotels and municipalities built anti-shark enclosures in early 1958. These gave protection from sharks while they remained intact, but they were unsightly and proved expensive and difficult to maintain. After "Black December" and its aftermath, the South African Navy dispatched a frigate to drop depth charges off Margate and Uvongo in the hope of killing sharks. The results were unexpected. While few sharks were killed, many were attracted by the bony fishes stunned and killed by the blasts. At Margate small boat patrols were are built and repaired at the headquarters of the Natal Sharks Board at Umhlanga Rocks, in an impressive, ultramodern installation that features exhibits on sharks and the operations of the Board, and houses maintenance and research facilities. In the 1980s the facilities of the Board were greatly expanded; they now include a lecture theater and a dissection amphitheater. About 60,000 visitors view the displays each year.

The Natal Sharks Board conducts research, based on field data collected by meshing teams and laboratory data taken by dissecting teams, on sharks and other marine animals captured in the nets. The Board also supplies shark specimens, parasites and tissue samples to researchers in South Africa, maintains the South African section of the International Shark Attack File, and provides advice worldwide for shark-related problems, including ongoing protection of beaches in Hong Kong with small-mesh barrier nets that exclude rather than capture sharks.

THE FUTURE OF NETTING

The activities of the Sharks Board have at times generated controversy in kwaZulu-Natal and nationwide. Anglers, conservationists and some scientists are concerned about the ecological effects of long-term shark netting. Big-game shark

anglers have been affected as much by the cessation of whaling off Durban as they have by netting, and have either abandoned their sport, converted to light tackle angling, or gone farther afield to northern kwaZulu-Natal or Transkei in the Eastern Cape in search of large sharks.

In the 1980s anglers and scientists suggested that there seemed to be a marked increase in numbers of juvenile dusky sharks, milk sharks and possibly other small sharks, and attributed this to the shark nets. According to this view, which is not supported by Sharks Board researchers, the nets have depressed the number of larger sharks that feed in part on smaller sharks. The supposed result is an apparent decline in bony fishes targeted for sport, which may at least in part be an effect of increased numbers of small sharks as well as of greatly increased angling and commercial fishing pressure and localized habitat modification and destruction. The Sharks Board has denied that such an increase in sharks, if correct, was occurring as a result of shark netting alone, but that other environmental factors must be considered.

The small sharks controversy was largely overshadowed in the late 1980s by the emotive conservation issue of catches of coastal dolphins in the nets and possible declines in their numbers,

Bill Wood

ABOVE: Warning signs are posted on Durban beaches. Shark meshing has been so effective in reducing the numbers of shark attacks in South Africa that nearly all encounters now occur either at beaches where nets are not deployed or at times when usually netted beaches are without protection.

BELOW: The netting of potential killers, such as this tiger shark, is seen by many as justification for wholesale meshing programs, though some argue that there have been adverse effects on other marine animals.

Ron & Valerie Taylor

ENCOUNTERS WITH SHARKS AT AMANZIMTOTI

The resort beach of Amanzimtoti, 27 kilometers south of Durban, has had more shark encounters recorded than any other beach in the world. Since 1940, 11 attacks—three of them fatal—have been documented. All took place close to a rocky headland called Inyoni Rocks.

There have been six encounters since 1962 when offshore shark nets were laid; five of these occurred between January 1974 and February 1975. The 1974–75 attacks seem to have been linked with the presence close to the beach of larger than usual numbers of fish. It has been suggested that temporary increases in food supply may well stimulate increased predatory activity by sharks and thus explain such an abnormal number of encounters in a short period.

DAMON KENDRICK, FEBRUARY 13, 1974

Fourteen-year-old Kendrick had been training for the lifesaving championships when he was bitten by a shark in water 1.5 meters deep. Swimming had been banned because shark nets had not been serviced for several days and the sea was murky, with visibility less than a meter. Water temperature was 24.5° Celsius.

Kendrick and a friend, Joe Kool, reached the Inyoni Rocks after their training session and decided to wash the sand from their bodies in the shorebreak. They moved exuberantly through the shorebreak into the channel and then body surfed to the sand.

"Joe was about five meters away from me when he suddenly shouted. As I turned a shark bit my leg and I heard a growl as its powerful jaws shook me viciously … Everything took place so fast that I really didn't know what was happening. The shark shook me for about two seconds and as it let me go I was pushed into the shorebreak, which washed me on to the sand. I pushed myself backwards up the sloping beach holding my injured leg up in front of me. Only then did I know what had happened and my mind did not want to accept what I was seeing. Great strips of skin and muscle hung like old rags from where my calf muscle used to be. Blood spurted and dripped from my leg and formed a river of blood in the sand."

Kendrick's serious injury was caused by three bites: the first severed the fibula above the ankle; the second cut partly through the fibula near the knee; and the third took away the calf muscle and fibula. His calf muscle was so severely damaged that the right leg was amputated below the knee.

JAMES GURR, MARCH 21, 1974

James Gurr, 21 years old, encountered a shark 50 meters south of Inyoni Rocks. Water visibility was 2 meters and the water temperature was 25° Celsius. Swimming had been banned because conditions were thought to be conducive to the presence of sharks.

Large waves were breaking over a sandbank 150 meters offshore. They were then reforming and breaking about 50 meters from the shore. A strong current had created a deep channel at the water's edge. Gurr was riding a surfboard when he saw a shark's fin coming straight for him. Murky water obscured its form.

"Sitting on my surfboard I felt helpless, there was nothing I could do. I lifted my legs and the shark hit the board, tumbling me into the water. A feeling of terror took my breath away but I made a conscious effort to remain calm. My surfboard was about two meters away. I swam to it and turned it the right way up. As I was about to pull myself aboard, a violent shove pushed me sideways and simultaneously I felt the shark against my chest and under my arm.

"This was the last straw—panic swept through me—and I began paddling for shore … I had unbelievable strength and was surging through the water. Without warning, there was a terrific jolt and next thing I was upside down in the sea again … In a frenzy I remounted my surfboard and in desperation began paddling shorewards again. The shark zigzagged in front of me and, if it was possible, my fear increased as a broken wave overtook me and pushed me over the shark. I paddled into the shorebreak, which dumped me on to the sand."

Gurr miraculously escaped the encounter without injury. When the shark pushed him sideways, it bit into his surfboard. A clear semicircular imprint, 19 centimeters in diameter, of its teeth was left in the fiberglass.

ANTHONY BAKER, APRIL 4, 1974

Seventeen-year-old Anthony Baker was bitten while surfing about 50 meters offshore just south of Inyoni Rocks. His brother Raymond was about 10 meters farther out. Swimming had been banned because conditions were believed to be similar to those of earlier shark encounters.

Waves were breaking on a sandbank 150 meters offshore, then reforming and breaking about 50 meters from the beach. The sea temperature was 24.5° Celsius. Baker had a white sock tied to his right foot, to which a surfboard leash was attached.

"I was facing shore when there was a tug at my foot and it felt warm. Because of the other attack I knew instantly that a shark had bitten me. I felt no pain but I had heard that shark bites were painless so I turned around to make sure both my legs were still there.

"There was a lot of blood in the water and the sock tied around my ankle was stained red. Only when I saw the blood did I begin to feel frightened. I shouted a warning to Raymond and began paddling shorewards … On the beach I checked my foot and saw a gaping cut to my right heel which was bleeding badly. I remember feeling thankful that it didn't look so serious."

Baker was taken to a local doctor by his brother and two holidaymakers. He received 19 stitches to a 10-centimeter laceration on the outer side of his right heel. A number of punctures were visible along the outer edge of the foot for another 8 centimeters.

The shark may have been attracted to the white sock around Baker's ankle; ironically the bite was cushioned by several layers of sock material.

and by concerns about shark conservation after the white shark was protected in 1991. Although the catch of the shark nets is small compared to national commercial fisheries for cartilaginous fishes, with an average of about 1,400 sharks being taken each year for the past 18 years, anti-shark measures are an unselective and costly way of preventing small numbers of shark encounters. By the early 1990s the Sharks Board was trying to reduce or eliminate the dolphin catch and had begun to release and tag sharks, rays and other marine animals caught in the nets.

Alternatives and supplements to the shark netting program have been and are currently being tested by the Sharks Board, including more selective heavy longlines to supplement nets, different mesh sizes of nets, and netting for only part of each month rather than for most of the year. The effective, if expensive, use of enclosures or barrier nets in the past off kwaZulu-Natal has not been followed up recently in South Africa, although a new set of wading pools built on the

Ben Cropp

LEFT: Bronze whalers *Carcharhinus brachyurus* have been implicated in injurious encounters in South African waters. They grow to between 2.4 and 4 meters and should be treated with respect and caution.

BELOW: The blacktip reef shark *Carcharhinus melanopterus* is common in shallow water near reefs and islands, and will often approach divers out of curiosity. Spearfishing, however, will excite blacktips and cause them to rush in to take wounded fish. This species has been identified in several encounters, mainly on divers' legs and feet.

AF Photographic Library

Durban marina are in effect sheltered bathing enclosures that are assuredly free of sharks. Enclosures, and for that matter shark nets, are expensive to maintain because of fouling and the heavy seas and strong currents off the beaches, but new materials and building techniques may make for more durable enclosures and barrier nets. The rather theatrical use of explosives on sharks has already been mentioned, and apparently was a non-starter for shark protection although it was suitably militant for the times.

Chemical shark repellents were investigated for a long time in the United States under the

ABOVE: A netting team aboard a Natal Sharks Board skiboat. The South African meshing program began in Durban in 1952 and has been considerably expanded since the early 1960s. More than 170 nets are set and regularly monitored by the Board's netting crews.

sponsorship of the US Navy, but although effective repellents were eventually found, they were not suitable for beach protection and have therefore not been adopted.

Dr. E.D. Smith of the National Physics Research Laboratory, Council for Scientific and Industrial Research, Pretoria, developed a pulsed-current cable system in the 1980s that forms an electromagnetic barrier to repel sharks. This was tested successfully in the shark tank at the Oceanographic Research Institute, Durban, and in the field at St. Lucia. This "eddy current electrode system" has the interesting effect of working in direct proportion to the mass of the animal that enters its field. Large sharks are repelled but small ones are not. The advantage of this system is that it has the potential to rid bathing areas of large sharks without killing them. A pilot cable installed at Margate ran into problems and experienced delays in operation, particularly as a result of sea damage and burying with sand. After several years of attempts to solve the problems, the cable was due to become fully operational in 1988, but was abandoned after further problems, including bathers being shocked on the beach.

Subsequently, the Sharks Board began researching electronic barriers and announced the development of its own electronic shark repellent in 1991. Testing of electronic barriers has continued since then, and the Board has developed and marketed a personal electronic barrier termed Shark POD (Protective Oceanic Device) for use by scuba and hookah divers. This is apparently quite effective in repelling white sharks and other large species when used according to directions. Progress on beach protection using electronic barriers has been slower due to operational problems. Pending development of effective electronic barriers, the Sharks Board has various initiatives to reduce net mortality. These include continuing to remove the nets during the sardine run; permanent removal of nets from little-used beaches; reduction of net numbers and possible replacement of some of them with longlines; regular maintenance of the nets to release all live animals; and making the nets more readily detectable by dolphins.

Because of history and lingering shark fear, beach protection and anti-shark measures will undoubtedly persist in kwaZulu-Natal into the next century. Once instituted and integrated into communities, anti-shark measures become extremely difficult to remove because of shark fear, which is, in part, reinforced by their continued presence. However, beach protection could evolve from unselective anti-shark measures to policies of keeping sharks and bathers apart in selected areas through the use of passive or active barriers, and in realistically defining the risks of shark encounters for swimmers and divers utilizing unprotected areas.

CHANGING ATTITUDES

The Sharks Board has grown steadily over the years and is undeniably expensive to operate. It should be seen, however, in the context of the strong public demand for action against sharks after the 1957–58 panics. The support for aggressive meshing techniques (analogous to predator control on land), rather than passive devices such as enclosures and barriers, grew in the fertile soil of shark fear and fostered a reactive "shark war" approach to shark encounters. Sharks were little understood biologically and behaviorally: the only good shark was a dead one, and all large sharks were perceived to be dangerous maneaters. In an atmosphere of isolation, ignorance, fear and panic, it is not hard to understand why a few shark injuries and a handful of fatalities caused crowds to desert the beaches and rush like lemmings back home, while risking many more injuries and deaths from vehicular accidents. During such shark-induced panics people tended to forget that the sea is an alien environment, that people always enter or travel on it at risk, and that the sea itself is far

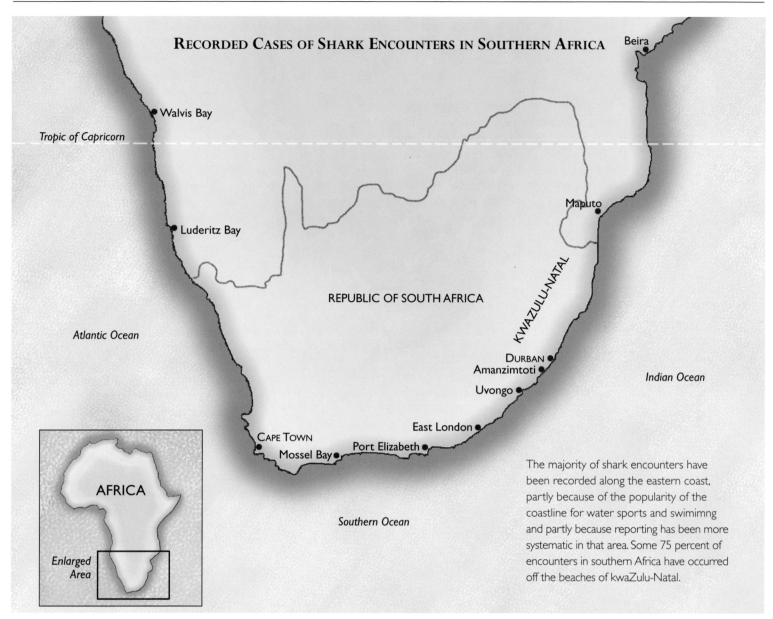

RECORDED CASES OF SHARK ENCOUNTERS IN SOUTHERN AFRICA

Beira

Walvis Bay

Tropic of Capricorn

Luderitz Bay

Maputo

KWAZULU-NATAL

REPUBLIC OF SOUTH AFRICA

Atlantic Ocean

DURBAN
Amanzimtoti

Indian Ocean

Uvongo

East London

CAPE TOWN

Port Elizabeth

Mossel Bay

AFRICA

Enlarged
Area

Southern Ocean

The majority of shark encounters have been recorded along the eastern coast, partly because of the popularity of the coastline for water sports and swimimng and partly because reporting has been more systematic in that area. Some 75 percent of encounters in southern Africa have occurred off the beaches of kwaZulu-Natal.

more dangerous than sharks. In the Port Alfred area in the Christmas holiday of 1983–84, one person was bitten by a shark on one weekend without serious results; on the same weekend 14 people drowned, but the shark encounter attracted far greater attention.

Shark "attack" is primarily a problem of fear and education, as sharks are minor contributors to human problems. In 1986 nearly 160,000 people died of all causes in South Africa, of which one was a shark fatality (out of three shark incidents that year), while 166 were killed by lightning and nearly 1,300 by drowning. The maximum number of shark fatalities per calendar year has been four to date. However, the old anti-shark mentality is demonstrably if gradually changing, and many people now support shark conservation, including protection of the ultimate *Jaws* bogeyman, the great white shark, which South Africa pioneered in 1991.

The need for shark conservation and rational management of sharks is now widely accepted internationally, and South African regulatory

agencies are moving to develop a plan for management of local sharks including endemics. Anglers generally take a less hostile attitude to sharks than before and have been tagging and releasing them for many years, while macho "shark-hunting" for large white sharks is now history. The future of anti-shark measures in South Africa remains to be seen, but as the public perception of sharks changes measures are evolving and show signs of being transformed into a policy analogous to game park management, where predators are regarded as valuable assets. Similarly, sharks are increasingly viewed as positive assets that are more valuable alive than dead and are a potent drawcard for expanding international tourism.

With the political, economic and perceptual changes in South Africa, and with burgeoning problems with conservation of sharks worldwide, perhaps South Africa can become a place famed for its wide variety of sharks that are being actively conserved, rather than where they were being hunted and despised as in the not so distant past.

ENCOUNTERS WITH SHARKS IN NEW ZEALAND

LARRY J. PAUL

*S*ummertime. Long, warm days beside, on, or in the sea. New Zealanders flock to their favorite beaches to indulge in a variety of recreational activities: boating, fishing, swimming, surfing, diving. Local radio stations report on weather, beach and traffic conditions, sometimes aided by spotter aircraft. A few shark sightings are reported, nearby beaches are cleared and the media begins running shark stories. Apparent "experts" are consulted, tragedies are retold and questions and speculation begin. What kind of sharks are they, and are they dangerous? Where have they come from? Are water temperatures rising? Have fishermen so depleted the sharks' natural food that they are forced inshore to seek other prey? Is there a clear detectable pattern to shark attacks? How does one avoid becoming the next shark attack statistic? And, more generally, what else is known about New Zealand sharks?

FACING PAGE: More than 60 species of sharks have been recorded from New Zealand waters, though most are small, inoffensive and deepwater varieties. There has never been a verified attack by a tiger shark in New Zealand, but its reputation and its capture off the North Island indicate that the potential exists for a fatal attack on a human.

KINDS OF SHARKS

This is one of the easier questions, at least in a general sense. However, the actual species involved in each sighting or attack is less easily determined. There are more than 60 species of sharks in New Zealand waters. About 40 live in deep water and are encountered only by commercial fishermen and scientists. Most are smallish, about a meter or less in length, dark in color and, though they are clearly efficient little predators, not dangerous to humans unless handled carelessly when caught. A few of these are at least semi-pelagic, roving into mid or surface waters to feed.

A second group of six species is found in shallow coastal waters. Four of them—the smoothhound, catshark and two spiny dogfishes—are smallish, bottom-dwelling, and essentially harmless unless provoked. The tope shark, though larger, is also harmless. The broadnose sevengill, however, is larger again and is powerful and aggressive when caught.

The third group comprises more than a dozen species of large, open-water pelagic sharks. Most range widely through the world's oceans, and many have been implicated in shark attacks. The white shark and tiger shark are the most dangerous, while the mako, blue shark and bronze whaler must also be regarded as dangerous. The thresher and hammerhead are suspected of attacks elsewhere and must be treated with caution, while the porbeagle, though uncommon locally, is a potential danger. The large basking shark, not uncommon seasonally in some localities, is an inoffensive plankton feeder but, because of its sheer size, strength and abrasive skin, can become dangerous when trapped. The other species are quite rare. Further notes on the identity and New Zealand distribution and

RECORDED SHARK ATTACKS IN NEW ZEALAND WATERS

Hauraki Gulf

AUCKLAND

Bay of Plenty

New Plymouth

Napier

40°S

Castlepoint

Wellington

Cape Foulwind

Christchurch

Oamaru

Dunedin

• Fatal attacks
· Non-fatal attacks

ABOVE: The great white shark has been blamed for several attacks in New Zealand waters, but this may owe more to publicity than to positive identification.

abundance of these potential attackers are given in the box below. It is, however, important to remember that in terms of aggression, humans clearly have the upper hand.

WHERE HAVE THEY COME FROM?

There is undoubtedly a general real increase in shark numbers in coastal waters in warmer months. This is partly due to the seasonal southward movement of wideranging Indo-Pacific, Australian or Pacific Ocean sharks, either actively migrating or simply following the currents to New Zealand's coastal feeding grounds. Several tuna and marlin species also arrive this way. These movements continue along the coastline, with northern species becoming more common in southern localities. Some species occur in southern waters only during summer. Then there are inshore movements, generally by pregnant females to give birth in the warm water of sheltered bays, but probably also by males and immature fish to feed on the burgeoning summer increase in small fishes and bottom life.

Sharks are more clearly visible during summer and people are, therefore, more aware of them. Surface water warms up more rapidly than that near the seafloor, attracting several kinds of sharks and bringing others to the surface. Calmer weather makes cruising fins much easier to see, and there are simply more people at the beach, in boats, or watching from spotter aircraft.

DANGEROUS SHARKS OF NEW ZEALAND WATERS

The sharks described below are widely distributed in other oceans and seas; only their New Zealand distribution is noted here. They all tolerate a wide range of environmental conditions and, though most are typically open-water fishes, they may at times be found close inshore, where they may encounter swimmers or surfers. Most are influenced but not controlled by the currents around New Zealand, and an understanding of the origins and movements of these explains some aspects of their distribution.

Most of the surface water surrounding New Zealand derives from the Tasman Sea and moves eastward, around North Cape, through Cook Strait and around southern New Zealand. It moves south and east past the North Island, and northward up the east coast of the South Island to flow eastward along the Chatham Rise. Some South Pacific Ocean water appears to come more directly from the north.

The entire coastline, and much of the continental shelf, are influenced by this subtropical water. The warmest water is in the northeast but, particularly in summer, there is still reasonably warm water in the southwest. Coolest surface temperatures are found in the subantarctic water that moves northeastward across the Campbell Plateau south of New Zealand. The boundary between these two water masses, the Subtropical Convergence, lies a short distance off the southeast coast and swings eastward across the Chatham Rise; this mixed zone provides some of the country's richest fishing grounds.

Tropical species such as the tiger shark are more or less confined to the northeast. Species that can tolerate cooler water, such as the white shark, are found both in the northeast and along the southern coasts. Most New Zealand sharks are warm temperate species and range widely, particularly during summer.

WHITE SHARK *Carcharodon carcharias* Heavy but streamlined body; crescentic tail; short conical snout; long gill slits; large triangular serrated teeth; color grayish, white below, often with dark blotch at the base of the pectoral fin. Widely distributed around New Zealand but not common. More usually encountered in shallow water than in the open sea, typically around islands and reefs, in bays, and sometimes even harbors and estuaries.

TIGER SHARK *Galeocerdo cuvier* Large head and short blunt snout; tapering body; broad serrated teeth; color brownish with the tiger markings most prominent in small fish. Present, but not common, off northern (mainly northeastern) New Zealand in summer, both offshore and in shallow coastal waters.

MAKO *Isurus oxyrinchus* Sturdy but streamlined body; conical head and snout; crescentic tail with prominent lateral keels; large smooth-edged teeth, the anterior few curved; color gray to bluish above, white below. Present around much of New Zealand but more common in the northeast, usually in open to offshore waters but on occasion may be encountered close inshore.

HAVE WATER TEMPERATURES CHANGED?

Although the evidence is rather meager, NewZealand's seawater temperatures appear to have risen slightly this century, most strongly since about 1970. This, presumably, has allowed some increase in shark numbers, and a southward extension of the range of warm water shark species. Complementing this gradual temperature increase is an irregular cycle, from warmer to cooler and linked to the meteorological outer oscillation, that recurs every few years. The El Niño/La Niña weather cycle is closely linked to sea temperatures. There are also shorter term and more localized coastal temperature variations and current shifts caused by changes in prevailing wind patterns. The difficulty of monitoring all these factors means that shark distribution and behavior remain unpredictable.

HAS THEIR FOOD SUPPLY CHANGED?

The popular theory that overfishing by foreigners or by New Zealand commercial fishermen has so altered the sea's food chain that top predators such as sharks are forced to scavenge inshore is, at best, highly dubious. Although detailed feeding patterns are not well known, most large sharks appear to be opportunistic carnivores, or even omnivores, taking whatever is locally and seasonally most abundant; they seem well adapted to a changing food supply. Throughout the world, shark attacks seldom appear to be motivated by hunger; aggressively feeding sharks

BLUE SHARK *Prionace glauca* Slender body; long pointed head and snout; long upper tail lobe with small lateral keels; long pectoral fins; finely serrated teeth; color bright blue above, white below. Present around much of New Zealand but more common in the north. One of the most strongly oceanic sharks but may also occur inshore, particularly as juveniles.

BRONZE WHALER *Carcharhinus brachyurus* Fairly slender body; pointed head and snout; upper tail lobe longer; finely serrated teeth; color brownish gray, often with a bronze sheen. Present around the North Island, moderately common in some northern areas; a coastal species typically occurring close inshore and entering estuaries, but may also be encountered in the open sea.

THRESHER SHARK *Alopias vulpinus* Easily recognized by the tail length. Present around the North Island and northern South Island, both in offshore waters and, particularly as juveniles and small adults, in closer inshore waters.

BROADNOSE SEVENGILL SHARK *Notorynchus cepedianus* Large head and short blunt snout; tapering body and long upper tail lobe; single dorsal fin; seven gill slits; lower teeth comb-shaped and serrated; color brownish with small dark spots. Present around much of New Zealand, usually in shallow coastal waters, including estuaries; quite common in some areas, particularly in the north.

SMOOTH HAMMERHEAD *Sphyrna zygaena* Easily recognized by the head shape. Present around the North Island, particularly in the north. Generally inhabits open coastal to offshore waters, but juveniles are very abundant in some shallow bays.

OTHER SHARKS The porbeagle is not common in New Zealand coastal waters, and elsewhere is regarded as only potentially dangerous. The tope shark *Galeorhinus galeus* is probably New Zealand's most common moderate-size shark (it reaches 2 meters) and because of its schooling behavior at or near the surface, may be responsible for many of the shark sightings off beaches; however, it is quite harmless unless directly provoked or mishandled during capture. The "gray nurse" so often mentioned in newspaper accounts does not occur in New Zealand, though a related species is occasionally caught in deep water.

RIGHT: The Subtropical Convergence, where subtropical and subantarctic water masses meet, provides rich feeding grounds for sharks and other marine creatures.

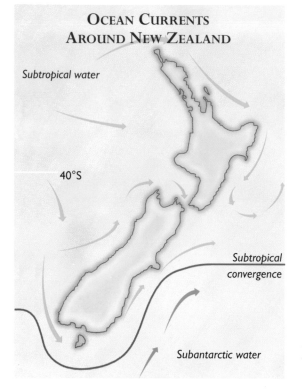

OCEAN CURRENTS
AROUND NEW ZEALAND

Subtropical water

40°S

Subtropical
convergence

Subantarctic water

FACING PAGE: The oceanic blue shark has been indicted in attacks in the open ocean and in deep coastal waters. It is regarded as especially dangerous to survivors of plane crashes or ship sinkings, but to date has not been verified as responsible for attacks in New Zealand waters.

with as many in the cooler and less populated south as in the north. Only a few of the sharks involved have been tentatively identified and suspicion generally falls on the white shark, a cool-water species. The three Dunedin fatalities in 1964, 1967 and 1968 might have resulted from a single shark, but most New Zealand attacks appear to have been unlucky encounters with particularly aggressive individual sharks.

Two possible explanations of shark attack (as shown by overseas studies) seem relevant in at least the more recent New Zealand incidents: a defensive retaliation by the shark for inadvertent intrusion into its individual territory; or an investigatory slash at supposed food, either (with people spearfishing) stimulated by the smell and vibration of wounded fish, or (with boardriders and wetsuited divers) because of a visual similarity to seals.

HOW DOES ONE AVOID BECOMING A SHARK STATISTIC?

Only by never going into the water, for sharks are unpredictable and no measures give total security. However, in New Zealand the risks are low, and can be reduced further by using commonsense and some knowledge of what may invite or provoke an attack. In particular, avoid areas where large sharks have been reported, particularly if they show erratic behavior. If an attack has occurred in an area, there is some chance there may be more.

Seen underwater, territorially threatened sharks often hunch their backs and swim jerkily. Do not trail wounded fish when spearfishing, or remain overlong in an area where many fish have been speared, or where animal waste and offal have been dumped.

could be expected to do far more damage than occurs in most attacks. It is actually more likely that commercial fishermen are reducing some shark populations more rapidly than those of other species of fishes.

IS THERE A PATTERN OF ATTACKS?

No. Despite the large number of people who use the water and the fact that potentially dangerous shark species are quite regularly in their vicinity, shark attacks in New Zealand are extremely rare. There are too few to detect any common features. They are distributed right around the coastline,

FATAL SHARK ATTACKS IN NEW ZEALAND

YEAR	MONTH	LOCALITY	ACTIVITY
1852	Jan	Wellington Harbor	Swimming; a soldier, attacked 300 meters off Te Aro Beach
1886	Dec	Kumara, Westland	Probably swimming near a river mouth but details not known
1886	Dec	Napier	Not known
1907		Moeraki, Otago	Swimming; leg stripped to bone as swimmer came ashore
1911?		Manukau Harbor, Auckland	Not known
1964	Feb	Dunedin	Surfing 250 meters offshore; leg taken and body severely mauled; probably a white shark
1966	Jan	New Plymouth	Swimming and surfing 100 meters offshore; probably a white shark
1967	Mar	Dunedin	A surf lifesaver, swimming out through surf during a competition
1968	Sept	Dunedin	Spearfishing in a wetsuit; identified as a white shark from tooth fragments
1976	Jan	Te Kaha, eastern Bay of Plenty	Spearfishing in a wetsuit

Kevin Deacon/Auscape

Avoid diving near seals; not only may a white shark be waiting for stragglers, but in certain situations the seals themselves can become aggressive. And never provoke a shark; a few sharks that look small and harmless are so, but the majority will defend themselves.

IS THERE A "HUMAN ATTACK" PROBLEM?

Yes. In New Zealand, as in most parts of the world, the conflict between humans and sharks is very one-sided. While there have been only 10 fatal shark attacks in more than 130 years, the number of sharks killed during the same period is enormous. Tope sharks and smoothhounds amounting to more than a million fish are caught annually by commercial fishermen. Thousands of large sharks (mako, blue, requiem, tiger, and others) are caught on tuna longlines in the vicinity of New Zealand, and recreational fishermen catch, and usually kill, thousands of sharks each year. Most shark species are slow-growing and long-lived, with a low reproductive rate. They are therefore vulnerable, and are hence highly susceptible to overfishing. Although none is yet endangered, the numbers of some species are declining.

ABOVE: The basking shark *Cetorhinus maximus* is an inoffensive filter feeder seasonally common in the colder waters of New Zealand. It does not attack humans but its size (up to 10 meters in length), its strength and abrasive skin have caused injury and damage to people who have been trying to harpoon or trap it for its flesh and oil-rich liver.

FACING PAGE: Despite the number of potentially dangerous species found around its coastline and the popularity of swimming and surfing, shark attacks are rare in New Zealand. Nevertheless, too many recreational fishermen believe that "the only good shark is a dead shark" and kill whatever they catch regardless of its size or species.

NON-FATAL SHARK ATTACKS IN NEW ZEALAND

YEAR	MONTH	LOCALITY	ACTIVITY
1868?		Auckland Harbor	Not known
1880		Auckland Harbor	Not known
1914		Oamaru	Not known
1920		Auckland Harbor	Not known
1927	Feb	Banks Peninsula	Not known
1928		Firth of Thames	Two women involved
1956	Dec	Not known	Provoked attack on a fisherman
1960	Feb	Mangawhai, Hauraki Gulf	Not known
1962	Jan	Westport, Westland	Not known
1962		Oreti Beach, Southland	Not known
1962	Jan	Slipper Island, Bay of Plenty	Spearfishing, holding speared fish
1962	Mar	Aldermen Islands, Bay of Plenty	Provoked attack
1962	Feb	Longbeach, Canterbury	Provoked attack
1964	Feb	Pukerua Bay	Spearfishing, holding speared fish
1968	Dec	Dunedin	Surfing
1971	Mar	Dunedin	Surfing
1973	Mar	Moeraki, Otago	Swimming
1977	Jan	Castlepoint, Wairarapa	Underwater diving in wetsuit

The list is almost certainly incomplete. There must have been many more close but non-fatal encounters not reported to authorities or mentioned in the newspapers. Most of the activities listed here as "not known" would probably have been swimming.

Bay Picture Library

ABOVE: The indigenous peoples of the Pacific have an intimate relationship with the sea and interact with sharks regularly. They have therefore come to regard the danger of shark attack in a far more realistic way than their continental counterparts.

ENCOUNTERS WITH SHARKS IN THE TROPICAL PACIFIC

LEIGHTON R. TAYLOR JR.

*A*ny review of shark attack in the Pacific Ocean is burdened by at least three factors: the huge geographic expanse of the area; the remoteness and isolation of many islands; and the lack or incompleteness of written records. In remote areas, many shark attacks may go entirely unrecorded. Others are noted only in the files of local medical clinics or dispensaries. Attacks may be documented in small, unindexed regional magazines or newspapers of very limited circulation. The shark attacks accounted for in the scientific literature probably represent only a small fraction of those that occur.

However, as marine scientists and sport divers travel widely in the Pacific area and have excellent communication networks, the proportion of attacks reported is probably higher than one might expect. With the revitalization of the International Shark Attack File and the Hawaiian Shark Attack File (curated by George Balazs and based in Honolulu, Hawaii), and the increasing ease of Internet correspondence, the likelihood a of a shark attack being recorded has increased significantly in the past decade.

STUDYING THE PACIFIC

Students of shark behavior owe a debt to the Shark Research Panel of the American Institute of Biological Sciences (AIBS), formed in 1958, ably chaired by Dr. Perry Gilbert, and active until 1970. The US Navy (probably for obvious reasons) supported this program for more than 30 years. The panel established the Shark Attack File, which maintained worldwide records of shark accidents for a number of years. Subsequently, the file was maintained by Mote Marine Laboratory (Sarasota, Florida) and later by the National Underwater Accident Data Center (University of Rhode Island). In 1988, the files (and reporting center) moved to the Florida Natural History Museum. Under the auspices of the American Elasmobranch Society it is now actively curated by George H. Burgess and Matthew Callahan. This data set and its excellent curation makes it much easier to report and retrieve data about shark attacks worldwide.

Because of the vastness of the Pacific area it has been possible to cover only part of it in this chapter. The survey is limited to selected major island groups in the tropical Pacific between 140°E and 130°W and between the tropics. Island groups included are Hawaii (including Johnston Island), the Line Islands, French Polynesia, Western Samoa, American Samoa, Fiji, the Phoenix Islands, the Marshall Islands, the eastern and western Carolines, the Cook Islands, the Solomon Islands, Tonga and New Caledonia. The Philippines, Papua New Guinea and southern Japan are excluded.

INTERACTING WITH SHARKS

The indigenous people of these areas have a long cultural history that has been strongly influenced by the ocean and its living creatures. In most Pacific cultures, sharks are viewed from a variety of perspectives. They play central roles in religion, culture, fishing techniques, folklore, and

BELOW: A shark in shallow water will cause panic among swimmers in most countries, even if it is an inoffensive species such as this zebra shark *Stegostoma fasciatum*, common off reefs and atolls of the western Pacific Ocean.

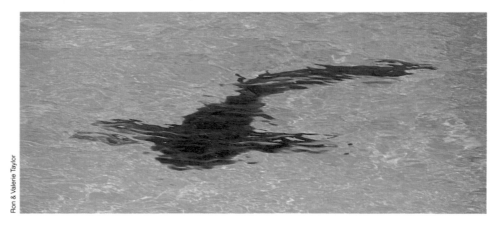

Ron & Valerie Taylor

A SUMMARY OF SHARK ATTACK RECORDS
FROM SELECTED AREAS OF THE TROPICAL PACIFIC OCEAN

Some cases are recorded by more than one author; therefore a total of cases reported for a given area cannot be calculated by summing all reported cases. Where detailed reports have been published in books, scientific journals or periodicals I have merely listed the reference. More detailed information is included here if the reporting source is ephemeral—such as a personal interview or local newspaper. The bibliographic sources referred to in the table are cited at the end of this publication.

NUMBER OF CASES AND/OR DATE	SPECIES	LOCALE AND RESULT (F = FATAL)	SOURCE
HAWAII			
52; 1886–1980	various	various	Balazs & Kam (1981)
9; 1981–83	various	various	Lipman, V. (1983)
35; 1941–68	various	various, including Midway Island	Baldridge, H.D. (1973)
25;1886–1960	various	various	Schultz & Malin (1963)
June 13, 1982	Carcharhinus sp.(?)	Ho'okipa, Maui. Windsurfer; 120 stitches in upper thigh	Schweitzer, D. (1982)
June 5, 1984	Sphyrna lewini(?)	Kaneohe Bay, Oahu. 13-year-old girl swimmer bitten on right foot	Personal communication with victim's mother
May 24, 1985	Galeocerdo cuvier(?)	Makaweli, Kauai, Board surfer severely bumped	Cook, C. (1985)
October 13, 1985	Carcharhinus sp.	Barber's Point, Oahu. Lobster diver's arm gashed	Anonymous (1985)
October 18, 1985	Galeocerdo cuvier	Solitary adult male boogieboarder lost right hand; board bitten in two	Personal communication with victim; and Taylor and Thompson (in prep.)
April 22, 1986	Galeocerdo cuvier(?)	Only fragments of shoreside drowning victim recovered	Personal communication with George Balazs
101; 1779–1992	various	various	Balazs in Taylor 1993
17; 1992–98	various	various	Balazs, pers. comm 9/98
JOHNSTON ISLAND			
December 19, 1965	Carcharhinus amblyrhynchos	Lagoon	Fellows & Murchison (1967)
October 1, 1960	unnamed `	Lagoon	Schultz & Malin (1963)
FRENCH POLYNESIA			
16	various	Tahiti, Tuamotus (some F)	Fouques et al (1972)
10; August 1962–June 1966	Carcharhinus amblyrhynchos and others	Tahiti, Tuamotus	Bagnis (1968)
14; 1942–February 1972	Carcharhinus amblyrhynchos in 10 cases	(some F)	Lagraulet et al (1972)
3; 1975	Triaenodon obesus	various	Randall (1977)
2; 1951	unnamed	Tuamotus	Schultz & Malin (1963)
MARSHALL ISLANDS			
3; September 1957–September 1960	Carcharhinus amblyrhynchos	Enewetak	Schultz & Malin (1963)
1; March 1976	Triaenodon obesus	Enewetak	Randall (1977)
	unnamed	Enewatak	Baldridge (1973)
1; April 1978	Carcharhinus amblyrhynchos	Enewetak	De Gruy, pers. comm.
2; August 1968–January 1972	Carcharhinus melanopterus	Enewetak	Randall & Helfman (1973)
TRUK			
2; July–September 1910	Carcharhinus albimarginatus	Truk, Namonuito	Jones (1972)
PALAU			
September 15, 1970	Carcharhinus sp.	Western Babelthuap	Read (1971)
April–May 1970	Carcharhinus melanopterus	Babelthuap, Ngerobelobang	Randall & Helfman (1973)
PHOENIX ISLANDS			
February 6 , 1972	Carcharhinus melanopterus	Canton	Randall & Helfman (1973)
LINE ISLANDS			
2; November 1959–June 1965	Carcharhinus melanopterus	Palmyra	Randall & Helfman (1973) and Baldridge
AMERICAN SAMOA			
2; August 1955–December 1963	unnamed	Tutuila (F)	Schultz & Malin (1963)
WESTERN SAMOA			
1; February 1972	Galeocerdo cuvier	Nu'u'lua	Balazs, pers. comm.
TONGA			
1; 1930	unnamed	Niua Fo'oa Island (F)	Schultz & Malin (1963)
FIJI			
5; 1925–61	unnamed	various (F)	Schultz & Malin (1963)
5; 1988–98	various	various	Burgess Int Shark Att. Files 1998
SOLOMON ISLANDS			
11; 1880–1957	unnamed	insufficient data	Schultz & Malin (1963)
1; 1992	various (some F)	insufficient data	Burgess Int Shark Att. Files 1998
NEW CALEDONIA			
2; 1950–6?	unnamed	various	Schultz & Malin (1963)
1; 1994	insufficient data	Noumea	Burgess Int Shark Att. Files 1998

may provide important resources for tools and weapons. Most Pacific Islanders literally grow up with sharks and, while recognizing their danger, have attitudes toward them quite different from those from Western, continental cultures.

Late arrivals to the Pacific, the European-derived peoples tend to look on sharks very negatively; they will react significantly to the mere sighting of a shark. It is not surprising, therefore, that an attack or incident in an area such as Hawaii will be more widely reported than one that occurs in an outlying island of the eastern Carolines. However, a recent trend of sport divers to seek out scheduled opportunities to dive with and observe feeding sharks suggests that a more balanced view is developing in Western minds. Perhaps the outlook of sea-wise Westerners is approaching the traditional view of the cultures of the tropical Pacific.

Shark biologists warn that it is far better to observe only natural behaviors and avoid unnatural feeding. Although such feeding by experienced dive guides attracts a large and exciting number of sharks, it has its risks. The reported attacks on the dive guides (who are nearest the food) have been slashes and lacerations. We can expect more, perhaps increasingly severe, bites as sharks and divers become bolder. Biologist George Burgess has

reported that hand-fed sharks are learning to associate the sound of boat engines with feeding. In some areas, they gather when any boat approaches.

Even in areas where shark attacks are likely to be well reported and widely publicized there are ambiguities. For example, occasionally shore fishermen will be washed offshore or fishermen will fall from boats; their remains are seldom recovered. Although these are reported as accidental drownings by medical authorities, the deaths could equally be the result of shark attack.

SHARK ATTACK DATA
The nature and result of shark attacks and the circumstances surrounding each incident vary widely. Captain David Baldridge has made a

ABOVE: The Pacific may be an attractive recreational destination, but it has several records of shark attacks on boardriders and windsurfers. Most of these are blamed on tiger and great white sharks.

BELOW: Great whites are among the very few species of sharks that appear actually to eat humans, perhaps mistaking divers and surfers for seals and sea lions.

RIGHT: Several attacks on divers in the Pacific have apparently been motivated by confusion with turtles or by spearfishing, when blood in the water has excited reef sharks. On some occasions, however, a diver's intrusion into a shark's hunting grounds will stimulate attack as the shark defends its territory.

detailed review and statistical analysis of 1,165 shark attacks that occurred worldwide between 1941 and 1968 and were carefully recorded in the AIBS Shark Attack File. Of these, 127 were in the tropical Pacific area.

While Baldridge reported some interesting and suggestive correlations, he was unable to state any definite principles of cause and effect. This is of course due to the accidental nature of shark attack. Certainly no careful experiments have been conducted in which variables have been scientifically controlled. Such experiments are (let us hope) unlikely ever to be performed and therefore, any suggested patterns, beyond very general ones, are impossible to verify.

Baldridge's analysis includes the following cases from the Pacific Islands. (The number of documented attacks is in parentheses.) Admiralty Island (4); Bismarck Archipelago (28); Caroline Islands (4); Fiji Islands (22); Galapagos Islands, Ecuador (2); Guam (1); Hawaii, United States (including Midway) (33); Johnston Island (2); Line Islands (2); Marshall Islands (5); New Caledonia (3); Samoa (3); Society Islands (3); Solomon Islands (19); Tonga Islands (2); Wake Island (3).

Gunther Deichmann/Wekton Trannies

ABOVE: Spearfishing is a popular Pacific sport, but one that increases the possibility of shark attack through the struggles and bleeding of a speared fish. Like all predators, sharks are sensitive to signs of a potential meal and have been known to injure divers while stealing speared fish.

FEEDING AND AGGRESSION

In simple terms most shark attacks can be classified as either "feed stimulated" or "aggression stimulated." Attacks on humans by large species such as tiger sharks, which commonly feed on large prey such as sea turtles, and great white sharks, which commonly feed on seals, are almost certainly related to feeding. Attacks by most other species are probably due to responses other than feeding. Exceptions occur where other stimuli relating to feeding—such as speared and bleeding fish, injured victims or an abundance of the shark's normal prey—are in the water.

Until fairly recently, scientists believed shark attack was always motivated by stimuli relating to food and feeding. Starkly stated, this hypothesis held that sharks attacked humans because they

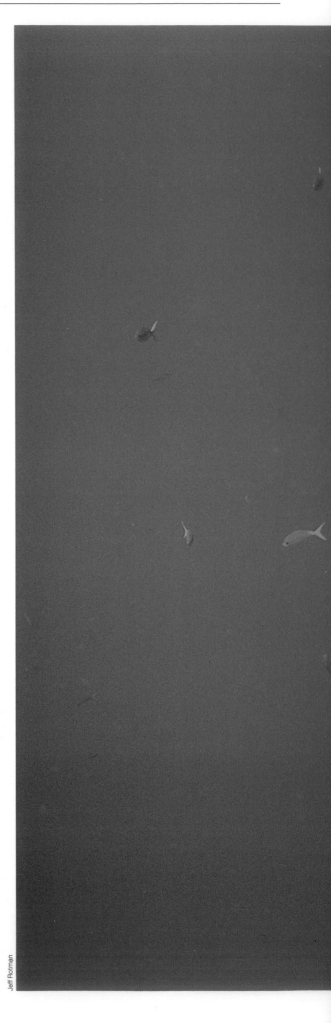

Jeff Rotman

Yves Lanceau/Auscape

ABOVE: The tawny nurse *Nebrius ferrugineus* is common throughout the Pacific and Indian oceans. It is normally docile and will usually react to harassment by grunting and spitting water at its tormenter. However, the tawny nurse has been implicated in attacks.

wanted to eat them. A booklet prepared by the US Navy in 1944 for the information of naval personnel who might encounter sharks in tropical waters stated that "The truth about sharks biting people seems to be this: like most fish the shark is a carnivorous or meat-eating animal . . . " Since the publication of this booklet there has been substantial research on the behavior of sharks, much of it supported by the same Office of Naval Research that prepared the original edition.

Some attacks in the Pacific, such as open-ocean attacks following accidents, have clearly been the result of feeding behavior. The 1945

tragedy of the USS *Indianapolis* is an example. Four hundred sailors went under when the heavy cruiser was torpedoed; nearly 800 jumped clear and were adrift in the equatorial Pacific, 300 kilometers from the Philippines. During the next four days and five nights nearly 500 perished. It has been estimated between 60 and 80 of them were killed by sharks, many fewer than the 600 that were counted by the fictional Captain Quint in Peter Benchley's *Jaws*.

Feeding was also the most likely motivation in at least three other documented shark attacks in the Pacific. In February 1972 Alan Banner, a marine biologist studying sea turtle biology in Western Samoa, was taken by a large tiger shark while snorkeling off a beach known to be a turtle hatchery. Sea turtles are a common prey for large tigers. Banner's snorkeling partner looked on in shock as the large tiger dragged him away.

On October 18, 1985, boogieboarder Joe Thomson was attacked off Princeville, Kauai, by a tiger shark, also presumably motivated by turtle feeding. The yellow-contoured bottom of Thomson's boogieboard closely resembled the plastron (the underside of the shell) of a large green sea turtle. Thomson had sighted several turtles in the area, where on the day of the attack the normally clear water was very murky. Thomson survived the attack with the loss of his right hand and a severely injured left wrist.

SHARK ATTACK: ANOTHER PERIL OF WAR

CARSON CREAGH

Before World War II, shark attack was an accepted hazard of life in Pacific waters. Sharks were certainly treated with caution by native fishermen and European settlers, but they were regarded as an everyday risk. Fatal traffic accidents—barely reported today—were given front-page attention. An objective view of the risks of shark attack in the Pacific was provided by George Llano in *Sharks and Survival* in 1963: "Concern about the shark menace was noted in a study of some 2,500 aviation survival accounts from World War II archives, particularly from men who flew over tropical waters . Analysis of these records revealed only 38 shark sightings, of which only 12 resulted in casualties or injuries."

Those statistics translated as a 1.5 percent chance of seeing a shark, and a risk of around 0.5 percent—one in 200—of attack. Given the number of servicemen in the Pacific theater, and the chance of shipwreck or airplane crash, the risk could hardly be called a major one.

Llano's interviews reveal a surprising number of wartime shark "contacts" that were no more than sightings. From one interview, we learn that: "I saw a large fin come toward the little raft . . . It rolled over and reappeared on the other side . . . The shark repeated the behavior several times at varied

intervals but at no time seemed concerned with us or touched the raft . . ." From another, "The raft was followed for a great part of the time [10 days] by sharks . . . each time, the shark sounded and did not bother us again. Aside from the nuisance, they did not bother the raft."

Many personnel found that the fish that sheltered beneath their rafts, and not themselves, were the focus of attention: "From practically the first day," said one pilot, "sharks were continually hitting up against the boat trying to get the small fish under it. I was quite scared at first, but soon got accustomed to it when I learned what they were after." That this was a common attitude is borne out by remarks such as "Sharks around all the time—no bother," and "He never came very close and did not constitute a problem." Even aggressive behavior was regarded as normal; one pilot laconically recalled dealing with a shark that, excited by its companions feeding on fish, repeatedly attacked the pilot's life raft: "One large one . . . came to the surface and started to bump the boat with his nose. This had become a rather commonplace procedure with me by this time and I put the .45 about six inches [15 centimeters] from his head . . . to give him his iron for the day . . ."

Attacks involving great white sharks are almost always related to feeding behavior. In the tropical Pacific records of attack by this species are limited to Hawaii. John McCosker of the California Academy of Science has suggested that a growing number of attacks by great white sharks on surfers off the west coast of the United States may be due to similarities both in appearance and behavior between surfers and seals, sea lions and elephant seals—the normal prey of coastal white sharks. With the exception of the northwest Hawaiian islands, seals are not found in the tropical Pacific. However, there seems little doubt that the fatal attack by a white shark on William J. Groins while he was swimming near Haleiwa, Oahu, Hawaii on May 18, 1926 was due to feeding behavior. According to a report, Groins gave a sudden shriek and then disappeared; his remains were found in a 3.5-meter great white shark that was caught nearby two days later.

These incidents indicate that feeding has certainly been an important motivation in some attacks in the Pacific, particularly in those involving large species such as tiger sharks and great white sharks and in incidents where bleeding, either by an injured victim or speared fish, had occurred. However, it is now widely believed that behavior relating to a "territorial imperative" is also significant. This "aggression" of certain perhaps territorial species may be

Yves Lanceau/Auscape

responsible for most non-fatal shark attacks. Simply put, some sharks bite some people for the same reason that dogs bite mail deliverers. A well-fed spaniel will sink its teeth into the calf of an intruder into its yard with no thought of eating the visitor; the dog is simply defending its territory against an interloper.

A similar explanation probably holds for many Pacific shark attacks. For example, in 1982, a windsurfer was attacked off Ho'okipa Beach, Maui, after rapidly sailing into a turbulent area and falling from his board. The two bites to his right thigh resulted in little tissue loss and were

ABOVE: Tawny nurses are usually found resting on the bottom of reefs or in coral caves, where they also search for their prey of crabs, lobsters, squid and sea urchins. This species employs its muscular pharynx to inhale prey from crevices, and may respond to being disturbed by using its powerful jaws on a diver's arm or leg.

Even where survivors were harassed or attacked, few succumbed to the sort of panic that would today be regarded as almost mandatory. Eleven survivors of a 1944 plane ditching were approached and occasionally harassed by sharks. The men drove the sharks away by shooting and kicking: one man was "bitten slightly," became frightened and died during the second night of the 42-hour ordeal.

At five o'clock on the third morning, the remaining six men were rescued. Their rescuers were "greatly agitated" by the presence of sharks and one survivor remarked that, "We got a kick out of it."

A US Navy officer named Kabat, whose ship had been sunk and who was floating in the water, felt a "scratching, tickling sensation" in his left foot. "Slightly startled, I held it up. It was gushing blood . . . not ten feet [3 meters] away was the glistening, brown back of a great fish . . . swimming away. The real fear did not hit me until I saw him turn and head back towards me. I thrashed out . . . brought my fist down on his nose again and again. I discovered that he had torn off a piece of my left hand . . ." Kabat's matter-of-fact account continues with details of further attacks: "The big toe on my left foot was dangling. A piece of my right heel was gone. My left elbow, hand and calf were torn . . ." In the excitement of trying to attract the attention of a passing ship, Kabat forgot the shark, which struck again and bit him on the thigh, exposing the bone. Several sailors began firing at the shark:

"A terrible fear of being shot to death in the water . . . swept over me. I screamed and pleaded and cried for them to stop . . ."

An impression of calmness and resignation, due no doubt to shock, is common to many of the reports. A US Navy pilot reported the death of his radio operator: "A said he felt something strike his right foot and that it hurt. I told him to get on my back and keep his right foot out of the water, but before he could the sharks struck again and we were both jerked underwater . . . I knew that we were in for it as there were more than five sharks around. He showed me his leg . . . not only did he have bites all over his right leg, but his left thigh was badly mauled. He wasn't in any particular pain except every time they struck I knew it and felt the jerk."

Although interviews and research revealed a surprisingly low incidence of shark sightings, much less attacks, the fact remains that a great number of servicemen were injured or lost their lives from shark attacks in Pacific waters during World War II. The presence of hundreds of thousands of people in the area, the obviously increased risk of shipwreck or airplane crash and the likelihood of blood in the water made investigation by predatory and aggressive sharks inevitable.

The total number of attacks and fatalities will never be known. Allied war records did not list shark attacks as such, referring merely to "unspecified animal bites." And as Llano himself succinctly notes, "When sharks are successful they leave no evidence."

RIGHT: Marine turtles are important in the diet of tiger sharks and attacks have been reported from areas where turtles are common. In one case, a surfer whose board resembled the shell of a green turtle was attacked and injured by a positively identified tiger shark.

BELOW: At least 12 species of requiem sharks have been identified or implicated in attacks in the Pacific region. Several species are especially active at night or around dawn and dusk on tropical reefs, when divers' visibility is more than usually limited and the risk of an attack unconnected with feeding is greatest.

probably caused by a frightened and threatened shark rather than a hungry maneater. Attacks by smaller species are undoubtedly motivated by factors other than feeding, except in those cases where dead or injured fish were present before the incident.

Although many shark incidents are now attributed to territorial defence, there is little formal experimental evidence that this is the cause. Johnson and Nelson (1972) first described agonistic display in the gray reef shark and suggested in subsequent writings that this was warning behavior that preceded attack. Although this hypothesis has been questioned by other biologists, no rigorous testing has disproved it. Indeed the attack on Michael deGruy by a gray reef shark in Enewetak Atoll, Marshall Islands, in April 1978, provides empirical evidence that supports the hypothesis.

SPECIES IMPLICATED IN ATTACK

At least 19 species in five families and 10 genera, have been implicated in attacks on humans in the tropical Pacific Ocean. Only in a minority of cases have attacking sharks been confidently identified. In many cases, the specific identity of the shark has been guessed at.

While the tiny cookiecutter shark *Isistius brasiliensis*, at around 35 centimeters, is unlikely to be described as "dangerous," it has been implicated in at least two recent attacks on humans in Hawaii. In July 1992, off Waianae Oahu, the dead victim of a boating accident was recovered from the sea with two wounds (probably posthumous) likely caused by a cookiecutter shark. The victim (non-fatal) of an attack in 1995 was surfing in cloudy water in mid-afternoon off the island of Kauai. A fragment recovered from the leg wound appeared to be from *Isistius*.

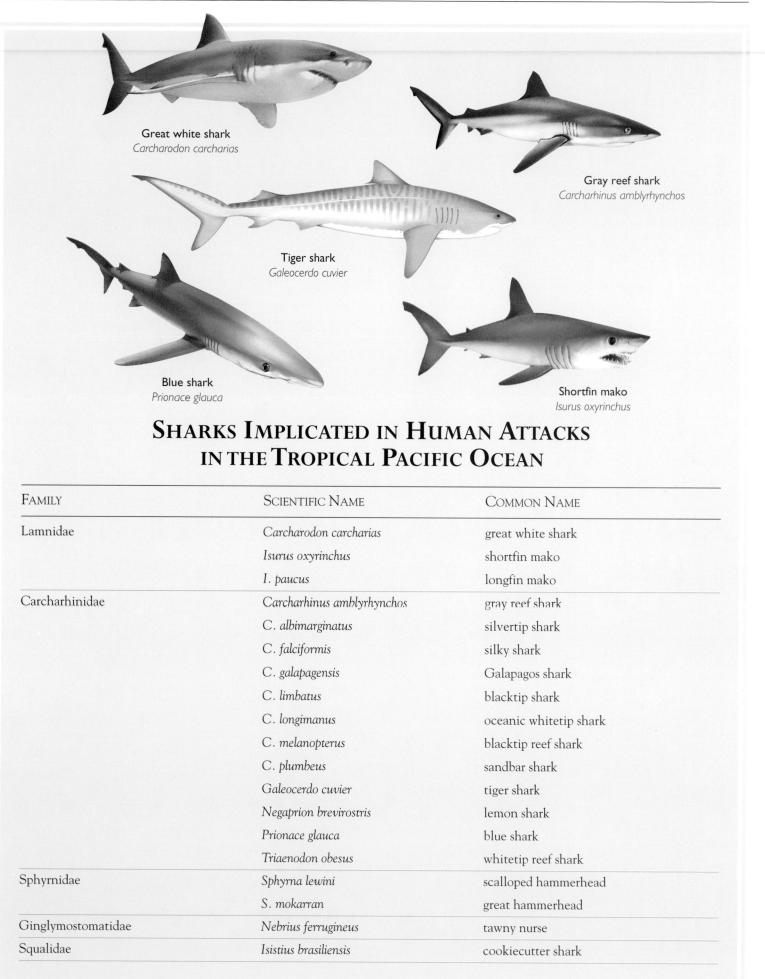

Great white shark
Carcharodon carcharias

Gray reef shark
Carcharhinus amblyrhynchos

Tiger shark
Galeocerdo cuvier

Blue shark
Prionace glauca

Shortfin mako
Isurus oxyrinchus

SHARKS IMPLICATED IN HUMAN ATTACKS
IN THE TROPICAL PACIFIC OCEAN

FAMILY	SCIENTIFIC NAME	COMMON NAME
Lamnidae	*Carcharodon carcharias*	great white shark
	Isurus oxyrinchus	shortfin mako
	I. paucus	longfin mako
Carcharhinidae	*Carcharhinus amblyrhynchos*	gray reef shark
	C. albimarginatus	silvertip shark
	C. falciformis	silky shark
	C. galapagensis	Galapagos shark
	C. limbatus	blacktip shark
	C. longimanus	oceanic whitetip shark
	C. melanopterus	blacktip reef shark
	C. plumbeus	sandbar shark
	Galeocerdo cuvier	tiger shark
	Negaprion brevirostris	lemon shark
	Prionace glauca	blue shark
	Triaenodon obesus	whitetip reef shark
Sphyrnidae	*Sphyrna lewini*	scalloped hammerhead
	S. mokarran	great hammerhead
Ginglymostomatidae	*Nebrius ferrugineus*	tawny nurse
Squalidae	*Isistius brasiliensis*	cookiecutter shark

SHARK ATTACK IN OTHER PARTS OF THE WORLD

CARSON CREAGH

In 1958, at the instigation of the US Navy, a panel of scientists began to compile a worldwide historic database of shark attacks. Now known as the International Shark Attack File, the database by 1996 contained more than 1,800 confirmed sharks attacks. However, there is no accurate information available on the number of people killed by sharks during World War II, and more than 90 percent of attacks were recorded from English-speaking nations.

The real total may be closer to 4,000 attacks—an average of 20 to 30 per year. In contrast, at least 12 million sharks were killed by humans in 1991 alone, making the shark fatality rate from human "attack" many thousands of times higher than for shark attacks on humans. It may seem a specious distinction, but it is important to remember that we run a far greater risk of death by drowning than of even seeing a shark. A significant number of so-called attacks occur when fishermen (most of them professional fishermen) are bitten, hit or scratched by one of those millions of sharks caught each year.

In fact, the most northerly shark attack on a human occurred when fisherman Hans Joachim Schapper was bitten on the arm by a small shark near Wick, Scotland, (58°26'N) on June 27, 1960. Similar incidents, misleadingly termed "provoked attacks," have taken place around the world and a number have occurred off both Ireland and Scotland, where basking sharks harpooned for their oil-rich livers have retaliated by smashing boats and occasionally injuring their hunters.

The world's highest risk areas are Australia, where 50 people drown each year for every person attacked by a shark; South Africa, where the ratio is 600 to one; and the United States (1,000 to one). Although statistics for the rest of the world are sketchy (due, in part, to language differences and a decreased likelihood of extensive media attention), the Shark Attack File lists the most dangerous areas as: eastern Asia, from Singapore to the China Sea and Japan; the Mediterranean; the east coast of India, especially the Ganges delta and the mouth of the Hooghly in Bengal; and the Arabian Gulf and the Red Sea.

Apart from the Schapper "attack" in 1960, the only other attacks in European waters took place in 1937, when two sailing boats were attacked (possibly by the same shark) off Scotland; and on August 4, 1960, when William Capel was injured by an unidentified shark off the coast of Devon, England.

Three rather doubtful attacks are recorded from Canada. The first allegedly took place in 1948, when an Indian family crossing the Gulf of St. Lawrence by canoe escaped attack by throwing a baby overboard; a warden was "menaced" by a shark as he crossed ice floes near Basque Island in 1940; and a 4-meter dory was capsized by a shark off Cape Breton Island, Nova Scotia, in 1953.

In eastern Asia most attacks have, unsurprisingly, been recorded from densely populated areas such as Singapore, Hong

ABOVE: In a melodramatic illustration, Tunisian boatmen watch in horror as a sponge diver's leg is bitten off during a shark attack. *Le Petit Parisien*, 1909.

Kong, China and Japan. The most northerly fatal attack in the eastern Pacific took place in 1938 at Tsingtao, in northern China (36°3'N).

The east coast of the Indian subcontinent (in particular Bengal and Bangladesh) has a bad record for fatal attacks. The Ganges shark *Glyphis gangeticus* was once regarded as a ferocious maneater responsible for innumerable attacks, mainly in the Hooghly River at Calcutta. A sixteenth-century traveler claimed that, "They which are weary of this world, and desire … a quick passage to Paradise, cast in themselves here to be devoured of these Fishes."

Recent research, however, indicates that the widely distributed and aggressive bull shark *Carcharhinus leucas*, a confirmed maneater that has been identified in fatal attacks as far from the sea as Lake Nicaragua, is responsible for attacks in India—not on those "weary of this world" as the ancient traveler suggested, but on pilgrims performing ritual ablutions at the numerous bathing ghats on the banks of the Hooghly. Partially cremated bodies dumped into the Hooghly at Calcutta are also a source of food for sharks, and may have predisposed them to attack living humans.

ABOVE: Convicts escaping from Devil's Island are surrounded by sharks off the coast of Guyana; the outcome is unknown. *Le Petit Parisien*, 1906.

Although there are few confirmed attacks from the warm waters of Sri Lanka, western India and Pakistan, the Arabian Gulf and Red Sea feature heavily. The Shark Attack File lists one mass attack in 1949, when 27 people were attacked (14 fatally) near Ahwaz in the Persian Gulf. Fishermen, pearl divers and boatmen are in greatest danger of attack, though the file mentions non-fatal attacks on a British constable near Tel Aviv (1945) and a Gurkha soldier at the junction of the Tigris and Euphrates rivers(1941).

Given the long history of civilization on its shores, its dense population, heavy water traffic and the recorded presence of many dangerous species, it is surprising that the Mediterranean does not have a worse shark attack record. It was from here that sharks—and shark attacks—were first described. Herodotus wrote of the destruction of a Persian war fleet in 492 BC when thousands of soldiers and sailors were "seized and devoured" by "monsters." Caius Plinius Secundus (Pliny the Elder) told in AD 77 of divers involved in "fierce fights with the dog-fish; these attack their loins and heels and all the white parts of the body."

Our understanding of sharks made little progress from those times until the nineteenth century, when oceanographic research institutes in France and Italy began scientific investigations of sharks and their behavior.

The Shark Attack File lists 18 attacks in the Mediterranean, from 1863 to the death of Sabit Plana at Opatija, Slovenia, in 1961. No attacks since that date have been reported in scientific journals. Italy has the highest number of attacks (five), followed by Greece (four), Egypt and former Yugoslavia (three each) and one each

from Malta, France, an unspecified location and one off the African coast. The northernmost attack in the Mediterranean occurred on September 4, 1934, when Agnes Novak lost her life at Sisak, Croatia (45°29'N).

All three Egyptian attacks took place at Port Said on August 8, 1899; none was fatal. The pattern of attacks throughout the Mediterranean shows a predictable bias toward the Northern Hemisphere summer months. Three attacks on unknown dates, four in July, five in August, five in September and one in December (the December attack occurred in warmer waters off the coast of Africa), reflect the usual increase during warm holiday months when people are in the water more often. This pattern has, predictably enough, also been reported from other areas where sharks attack humans.

The most interesting feature of shark attack in the Mediterranean is the unusually high proportion of fatal attacks—two-thirds of the attacks listed were fatal, which is twice the world average—and the absence of both the bull *Carcharhinus leucas* and tiger *Galeocerdo cuvier* sharks from Mediterranean waters. Although the Shark Attack File does not seek to identify species responsible for attacks in the Mediterranean, the great white *Carcharodon carcharias*, shortfin mako *Isurus oxyrinchus*, bronze whaler *Carcharhinus brachyurus*, blue shark *Prionace glauca* and great hammerhead *Sphyrna mokarran* have all been collected from the region. All have been confirmed or implicated in unprovoked attacks on humans. Recent research suggests that most attacks in the Mediterranean are from great whites.

Mary Evans Picture Library

ABOVE: The whale shark is the largest living fish in the world but hunts only small fish, tiny plankton and krill.

MYTH AND REALITY

THE LEGENDARY SHARK

RICHARD ELLIS

FACING PAGE: A shark-god from the Pacific, depicted in human form. Carved in wood, the statue is 39 centimeters high.

The Polynesians told of the shark-god Kauhuhu who lived inside a great cavern from which no one who entered over emerged. In Australian Aboriginal mythology, the tiger shark Bangudja attacked a dolphin-man in the Gulf of Carpentaria, leaving a large red stain that can still be seen on the rocks of Chasm Island. The Solomon Islanders, whose religious life consists of ghosts, spirits and other manifestations of the supernatural, believed that the bodies of sharks were inhabited by the ghosts of the departed. In the art of the Northwest Coast Indians of North America, the dogfish was often used decoratively as a reminder of the woman who was carried off by a shark and then became one herself.

But, except by the peoples of the Pacific, the shark was generally ignored as a symbol. European legends contain few references to the shark. Sharks generally appear only in natural histories or seafarers' journals, where it was common to write about and occasionally identify these often large, always mysterious, creatures. It was not until fairly recently that the shark insinuated itself, figuratively and literally, into our collective consciousness.

RIGHT: Olaus Magnus gave the world the first illustration of a man being attacked by sharks in Historia de Gentibus Septentrionalibus, published in Rome in 1555. Australian shark researcher Gilbert Whitley felt the bather was about to be rescued by the "benevolent" ray on the right, but its teeth and fierce expression may mean it is about to join the feast.

Icones Animalium

BELOW: Although many Polynesian societies regarded sharks as gods or demigods, the Australian Aboriginal perspective was principally economic. This bark painting of a shark from eastern Arnhem Land, in the Northern Territory, uses the Aboriginal "x-ray" technique to illustrate the shark's large and nutritionally important liver.

THE ORIGINS OF MYTH

We "advanced" folk of the late twentieth century probably think of ourselves as beyond pagan mysticism; in fact we are in the grip of an even stronger mythology. In our pantheon, we have elevated the shark to a position that transcends that of any other animal. Only the whale has achieved a comparable mythification; but there we have fabricated a benevolent spirit, a spirit contrasted with the shark as the embodiment of evil, the representative of the underworld.

Perhaps it is the mysterious nature of the shark that has been responsible for its enthronement. After all, we know very little about this animal and we tend to fear that which we do not understand. Elsewhere in this volume, the reader will encounter discussions of shark biology, the shark's senses and shark behavior but, even in these relatively well-researched areas, our knowledge is sadly deficient. When it comes to discussions of shark attacks around the world, writers can do little more than inventory the attacks and hypothesize on their causes.

There are many creatures in the oceans that we know little about, but none fascinates us or holds us in thrall as does the shark. From the 30-centimeter dogfishes to the 14-meter whale shark (the largest fish in the world), all the 350-odd species have succeeded in withholding some of their secrets from the prying eyes of the scientists. Consider the great white shark, surely the most fearsome of all. We know almost nothing about its breeding habits (only a few white shark embryos have ever been examined), its swimming speed in the wild, its food preferences, its abundance, range or ancestry.

For all our ignorance about this fish, perhaps the most disturbing aspect of its behavior is its seeming predilection for attacking people and

Jennifer Isaacs

Brian Brake/Otago Museum

Brian Brake/Otago Museum

ABOVE: Detail of a wooden carving of Menalo, one of the chief shark-gods of the Pacific.

Brian Brake/Auckland Institute & Museum

ABOVE: A shark spirit, carved into a cuttlefish shell c.1930.

SHARKS ARE HUMAN

About three years ago I was fishing for barracuda. I was catching them in the night, and a shark took my line. I drew in the line close to the canoe and tied it round my waist and paddled ashore pulling the shark behind me. I pulled the shark onto the beach and took the hook out, I did not cut the line. I cut the hook away at the mouth. Then I helped the shark back into the sea. He was not biting me.

Frightened. What was there to be frightened of?

I wanted to save the shark, yes. But I wanted to save my line too. I saved the line and the hook.

All the fish that are in the sea here we can eat—sailor fish and boar fish and sea slugs and bonito and trevally and barracuda. Dolphins, too. But not sharks. Sharks are human. To us a dolphin is like another fish. A dolphin is not a shark.

If an outside man comes here and catches a shark we do not harm the man but we keep away from him. We do not have anything to do with him. We never fish for sharks. He is a person with us. We are related. The other ones we do not eat are rays and crocodiles because they are related to us, too.

Oh sharks can save people, yes. I know of two cases. In one case a cutter boat broke in two and was smashed out there in the open sea. There were four people in the boat, two were salt water people like us and two were bush people. The two bush people were lost.

The other two people were taken—guided, yes—by the sharks to Florida Island and were safe. The sharks did not touch them, they only guided them. They helped them swim to the island. The sharks do not help the bush people because the bush people don't believe in the spirit. They are not related.

Is it safe for you to swim in the sea? On the other side, on Guadalcanal, the sharks attack people, but not here. Here you are protected. What happened was that a long time ago a shark, the one that my tribe followed, came out of a woman. The woman gave birth to that shark, yes.

We say "came out of." Ever since then my people worship the shark, and the sharks stop attacking people in the lagoon. The spirit of that woman entered into the shark, therefore when we worship the shark we are worshiping the old people. It is a belief that was in us before. We can talk to the sharks. We can call them. We don't call them by name, we talk to the spirit as a human on land and transfer the spirit to the shark. We talk to them when there is a sacrifice.

The priest makes the sacrifice, he sacrifices a pig. The shark priest, yes. He is the one who controls the area. The sharks can come in but they can't attack anybody. The priest makes it safe. He strangles the pig. No, not strangle. He ties a string round the snout and the pig cannot breathe. He prays as the pig is dying.

On the island there is a channel where the sharks come and a stone where he makes the sacrifice over the channel. First he kills the pig, cooks it, cuts it up and divides it for eating. There are no women there. We eat the meat and the priest calls the sharks with an offering of the same meat—so we share the same spirit.

Oh, the sharks come in! They come right in, almost onto the beach. The last time we called the sharks—my brother was there, everyone was there, women, children, everybody, we were all in the water with the sharks, talking to them and patting them on the back. Nobody was harmed.

Nobody has ever been harmed by a shark in this lagoon. I never heard of a case of injury except one—a man came down who was not from here and he went fishing and got lost. He was a man from the bush.

Yes, the priest still makes the sacrifice. He sacrifices to all the sharks. To us, the shark is known as the shark. We call to all the sharks that come here. The white shark, the blacktip shark, the gray reef shark, the shark-like-the-whale, the hammerhead shark, the tiger shark, the shark-with-no-proper teeth. They are familiar to us and we never eat them. We adore them.

Moses,
Malaita, Solomon Islands

occasionally devouring them. This inclination might prove to be nothing more complex than the attempt of a big, carnivorous fish to eat what appear to be edible objects, but the simplicity of this interpretation does not diminish the terror—it may even intensify it.

Similar gaps exist in our knowledge of other species. We can only guess about the function of the whiplike tail of the thresher or the pattern of spots, stripes and ridges that decorate the whale shark. Our paucity of hard knowledge has contributed substantially to our mythification of the shark. Here let me acknowledge that there is no such thing as "the shark," any more than there is one bird that fulfills all avian criteria. Just as all birds have feathers and lay eggs, so do all sharks have multiple gill slits, cartilaginous skeletons and denticular skin. But there are as many differences between a mako and a nurse shark as there are between an eagle and a sparrow. Nevertheless, legends do not differentiate on specific grounds, so unless I want to make a point about a particular species, I will continue to refer to "the shark."

Since the cartilaginous skeletons of sharks lend themselves poorly to fossilization, we have only fragmented evidence regarding their evolution. (Only the teeth and the vertebral centra have been preserved and, as we shall see, these often cause more problems than they resolve.) There is no question that sharks are among the oldest of the vertebrates, and we can trace their lineage back some 450 million years. (At best, *Homo sapiens* can claim only a 4-million-year-old ancestor.)

If the origins of the sharks themselves are lost in the mists of elapsed time, so too are the origins of the legends. We can easily identify some of the early folktales, but I wish to address the position that the shark currently holds in our culture.

THE SHARK IN LITERATURE AND ART

From the time people first put to sea in dugouts, canoes, dhows or coracles, they were probably aware of the sharks around them. Pliny the Elder, who lived from AD 23 to 79, wrote of sharks in his *Historia Naturalis*. Sharks appear in many whaling journals, since they appeared to many whalers, especially when the bloody whale carcases were brought alongside the ships for the flensing. In *Moby Dick*, Melville wrote about the sharks around the *Pequod* this way:

Ben Cropp

FACING PAGE: Carved from a single piece of wood and using genuine sharks' teeth, this sculpture from Wuvulu Island in the Bismarck Sea celebrates the beauty, power and grace of the shark and expresses an attitude of respect.

ABOVE AND BELOW: Western attitudes to sharks are so colored by emotion that it is often difficult to reconcile the docility of the gigantic whale shark with the images of mindless ferocity conjured by the word "shark."

Neville Coleman

THE LITERARY SHARK

From the witches' curse in *Macbeth* to the graphic description of *Jaws*, the shark has featured in literature.

> *Scale of dragon, tooth of wolf,*
> *Witches' mummy, maw and gulf*
> *Of the ravined salt-sea shark,*
> *Root of hemlock digged i' th' dark …*

Macbeth, Act four, Scene one

At the height of the slave trade, dead and dying slaves were thrown overboard to the sharks:

> *… here dwells the direful Shark, lured by the scent*
> *Of reeking crowds, of rank disease and death.*
> *Behold! he rushing cuts the briny flood,*
> *Swift as the gale can bear the ship along;*
> *And from the partners of that cruel trade*
> *Which spoils unhappy Guinea of her sons,*
> *Demands his share of prey …*

The Book of Fishes, 1835

In 1952 Ernest Hemingway wrote brilliantly about the mako:

> He was built as a sword fish, except for his huge jaws which were tight shut now as he swam fast, just under the surface with his high dorsal fin knifing through the water without wavering. Inside the closed double lip of his jaws all of his eight rows of teeth were slanted inwards. They were not like the ordinary pyramid-shaped teeth of most sharks. They were shaped like a man's fingers when they are crisped like claws.

The Old Man and the Sea, 1952

And then, in 1974, came Peter Benchley's *Jaws*:

The fish slid backward out of the cage and turned sharply to the right in a tight circle. Hooper reached behind his head, found the regulator tube, and followed it with his hand until he located the mouthpiece. He put it in his mouth and, forgetting to exhale first, sucked for air. He got water, and he gagged and choked until at last the mouthpiece cleared and he drew an agonised breath. It was then that he saw the wide gap in the bars and saw the giant head lunging through it. He raised his hands above his head, grasping at the escape hatch.

The fish rammed through the space between the bars, spreading them still farther with each thrust of its tail. Hooper, flattened against the back of the cage, saw the mouth reaching, straining for him. He remembered the power head, and he tried to lower his right arm and grab it. The fish thrust again, and Hooper saw with the terror of doom that the mouth was going to reach him.

The jaws closed around his torso. Hooper felt a terrible pressure as if his guts were compacted. He jabbed his fist into the black eye. The fish bit down, and the last thing Hooper saw before he died was the eye gazing at him through a cloud of his own blood.

Richard Ellis

RICHARD ELLIS – 1974

"The mako has more deadly beauty and fighting spirit than any other shark." *Peter Goadby*

They viciously snapped, not only at each other's disembowelments, but like flexible bows, bent round, and bit their own; till those entrails seemed swallowed over and over by the same mouth, to be oppositely voided by the same wound … It was unsafe to meddle with the corpses and ghosts of these creatures.

A sort of generic or Pantheistic vitality seemed to lurk in their very joints and bones, after what might be called their individual vitality had departed.

Many books have been written about sharks. Probably the first that dealt exclusively with them was Horace Mazet's *Shark! Shark!* This 1934 chronicle told of Captain William Young's obsessive hunt for sharks that began in Honolulu and took him around the world, killing sharks for sport, for the safety of swimmers and for sharkskin leather. At one point, Young refers to the sharks as "savage, armored sea tigers which had become my totem, my fetish." Then there were books about shark fishing (including *Tigers of the Sea*, by C. Hugh Wise in 1937, and Zane Grey's accounts of his big-game fishing exploits in California and New Zealand) and also about shark attacks: Victor Coppleson, an Australian surgeon, wrote *Shark Attack* in 1958; David Davies, a South African scientist, wrote *About Sharks and Shark Attack* in 1964; and other, less rational, discussions of the "shark menace" followed to fuel popular misconceptions.

Nor has the shark been a particularly popular subject for artists. In almost all pictorial representations of sharks the shark is depicted as a menace to swimmers or sailors. Think of Copley's *Watson and the Shark*, where a host of boatmen try to save Brook Watson, who seems to have been swimming naked in Havana harbor. One of Watson's rescuers is poised on the bow of the skiff with a boathook raised, about to drive it into the head of a huge but unrecognizable species of shark with a Moorish arch for an upper lip. (Watson, who commissioned the painting, actually lost a foot to the shark, but survived to become the Lord Mayor of London.)

The other celebrated appearance of the shark in art is Winslow Homer's *The Gulf Stream*, where a sailor gazes listlessly over the stem of his dismasted sloop as several sharks circle hungrily, waiting for whatever happens next in this permanently arrested drama. There is a waterspout visible on the horizon, and also a fully rigged ship.

Does the hurricane come and dump the hapless sailor, or is this the very hurricane that wrecked his boat in the first place? There seems to be plenty of blood in the water, so I think the sharks have already eaten the other crew members and are awaiting their next meal.

When the painting was first exhibited in 1900, so many people found the subject

BELOW: Winslow Homer's 1899 oil painting, *The Gulf Stream*, brings together drama, fear and the improbable hope of salvation in a graphic interpretation of human versus shark.

The Gulf Stream; Winslow Homer; Metropolitan Museum of Art, New York; Wolfe Fund, 1906; Catherine Lorillard Wolfe Collection

depressing that Homer wrote a letter to his gallery in which he explained, probably facetiously: "You can tell these ladies that the unfortunate negro, who is now so dazed and parboiled, will be rescued & returned to his friends and home, & ever after live happily." Neither Copley's nor Homer's painting glorified the shark; rather they embellished its already nefarious character.

THE SHARK'S MODERN STATUS

It was not until 1974 that the reputation of the shark took a quantum leap forward—or backward, if you will. In that year, Peter Benchley wrote *Jaws*, a novel that has as its main character not a man, but a fish—and not just any fish, but a great white shark.

Benchley was not the first person to contribute to the white shark's elevation to totemic status. As early as 1916, reports of a series of shark attacks in New Jersey vied for newspaper space with the Battle of the Somme in France.

Four people died in the New Jersey surf within a period of three weeks and another lost a leg. Although these attacks were attributed to the great white, the identity of the attacking shark (or more likely, sharks) was never proved. Later interpretations favor the bull shark as the culprit, but the white shark got the credit at the time.

In the development of *Jaws*, Benchley incorporated the "rogue shark" theory, where a single hungry shark cruised the beaches of a particular area, seeking to satisfy its craving for human flesh. This was Victor Coppleson's explanation for many shark attacks in Australian waters, but I do not believe it is correct. Nor do I think that sharks develop a taste for people. If they did, there would be no beach on earth that was safe for swimming.

Later in the century, shark attacks became front-page news, especially in South Africa and Australia. In 1959, the American Institute of Biological Sciences convened the Shark Research Panel, which collected data on shark attacks

ABOVE: John Singleton Copley's *Watson and the Shark*, first exhibited in 1778, is one of the most famous of all shark paintings. At a time when few people believed that sharks would attack humans, Copley's painting and the questionable claims of its hero, Brook Watson (later Lord Mayor of London), were advanced as graphic evidence.

RIGHT: The manufacture of a legend. Valerie Taylor poses beside one of the three 7.3-meter mechanical sharks, collectively named Bruce, created by movie special effects expert Bob Mattey for *Jaws*. Weighing about 1.5 tonnes, the three Bruces were operated by 13 technicians.

RIGHT CENTER: Bruce is 90 centimeters longer than the maximum recorded real great white, though there are probably individuals 8 meters long. It is unlikely that even an 8-meter great white would sport teeth as large as Bruce's, which were deliberately oversized to add to the impact of the shark's appearance on screen.

BELOW AND BELOW RIGHT: Australian underwater filmmakers Ron and Valerie Taylor spent weeks training live great white sharks near Port Lincoln, in South Australia, to attack on cue for action sequences in *Jaws*. The local talent, said Valerie Taylor, responded superbly, though a 1.5-meter stuntman was hired to make a 4.8-meter great white's attack on a diving cage look more like that of the movie's 7.3-meter star.

around the world. The Shark Attack File, then maintained at the Mote Marine Laboratory in Sarasota, Florida, was reviewed by H. David Baldridge, who first compiled a report on the data contained in the file and then wrote a popular book called *Shark Attack*. Published in 1975, it contained this message on the jacket: "True tales of shark attacks on man—facts more terrifying than the fiction of *Jaws*." Other books were written, but the sharks did not have to rely on published material to get themselves noticed. They were doing very nicely on their own.

In South Australia, three divers were attacked by white sharks: in 1961, Brian Rodger was bitten; the next year Geoff Corner was killed; and in 1963, Rodney Fox was attacked by a great white. It took 462 stitches to sew Fox together again. In 1967 Rodney Fox went to Spencer Gulf to look for the fish that nearly killed him. With him were Henri Bource, another victim, who had lost a leg to a white shark in 1964, Ron Taylor and Alf Dean, the fisherman who holds the record for the largest fish ever caught on rod and reel—a 1200-kilogram white shark.

The photos of great whites that Ron Taylor took on this expedition are among the best ever shot and they have probably been used more often than any other pictures of the shark some Australians call "white death." One of Taylor's photos of a shark approaching the camera with its jaws agape was used on the poster advertising Peter Gimbel's 1968 film of his search for the great white shark, *Blue Water, White Death*. It was the first time the white shark had been filmed underwater, but it was not going to be the last.

The novel *Jaws* was a smashing success, selling hundreds of thousands of copies around the world, and the movie made from the book was a blockbuster; for a while it was the highest grossing film in Hollywood history. *Jaws II* followed with less box-office and critical success, and then *Jaws III* limped into the theaters, an ineffectual shadow of its predecessors.

In a 1979 article in *Skin Diver* magazine, underwater cameraman Stan Waterman wrote: "Something there is about the shark that continues to tickle the macabre fancy of man. And it is, of course, both simple and profitable to exploit." There were now shark movies, shark novels, shark television specials. On the cover of its June 23, 1975, issue, *Time* magazine featured a shark bursting out of the water accompanied by the headline "Super Shark." We have indeed elevated the shark to mythic proportions; it has now become one of our own culture's abiding legends. Like the Hawaiians, we too have a shark-god.

GREAT WHITES, MODERN AND ANCIENT

Much of the shark's status is based on misinformation, but it is nowhere written that legends must have a foundation in fact. (Was the Hawaiian shark-god really a man with a set of shark jaws in his back?) In this new mythology, there is an emphasis on one species, *Carcharodon carcharias*, the great white shark. Forget that there are another 350 species of sharks, most of which are harmless to humans. Forget also that there are no authenticated reports of white sharks over 6.5 meters in length. (The shark in *Jaws* was never measured, but the ichthyologist suggests that is might be more than 7.5 meters long.)

There continue to be reports of monster sharks, ranging from 9 to 35 meters in length. In a 1963 edition of *Sharks and Rays of Australian Seas*, David G. Stead recounts a tale of a monster shark, that fishers knew "was not a whale," seen in 1918 off Broughton Island off the coast of Queensland. Stead writes that "in this occurrence we had one of those very rare occasions when humans have been vouchsafed a glimpse of one of those enormous sharks of the White Death type, which we know to exist, or to have existed in the recent past, in the depths of the sea."

In 1982, I went to the Azores to track down reports of a 9-meter shark that was supposed to have been harpooned by sperm whalers. I spent the better part of two weeks in these islands, interviewing scientists, fishers, journalists and administrators. I found no evidence at all that a white shark of such a size had ever been seen in the Azores. Of course, that does not conclusively prove that such a fish does not exist, but it does suggest that it is myth, not reality

A similar situation exists with *Carcharodon megalodon*, an extinct relative of the white shark.

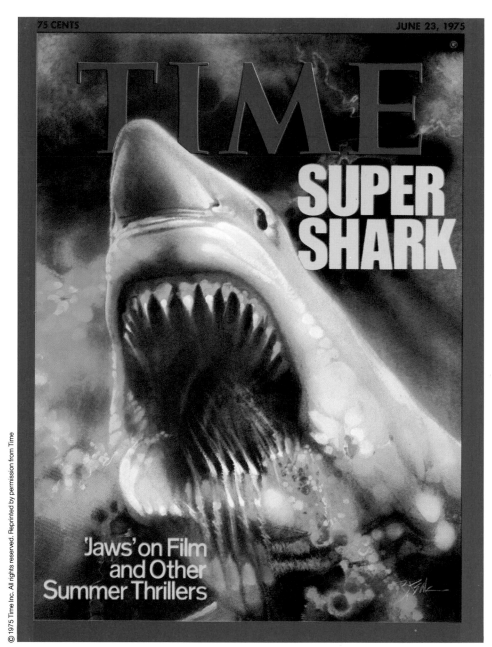

75 CENTS   JUNE 23, 1975

TIME

SUPER SHARK

'Jaws' on Film and Other Summer Thrillers

With teeth that measured 15 centimeters or more along their serrated edges, these monsters probably reached lengths of between 12 and 15 meters—large enough to swallow a horse. The only evidence for the existence of these terrifying creatures is their huge fossil teeth, but quite often in the popular literature these teeth mysteriously lose their fossil character and are used to prove that *megalodon* still exists.

In Peter Matthiessen's otherwise excellent book *Blue Meridian*, the chronicle of the *Blue Water, White Death* expedition, the author incorrectly assumes that *C. carcharias* and *C. megalodon* are the same species and that, therefore, there could be 15-meter white sharks cruising the seas today. Then there is Robin Brown's novel *Megalodon*, which concerns itself with 600-meter, barnacle-encrusted sharks that lie on the bottom, waiting to gobble up nuclear submarines like so many peanuts. Like *Jaws*, *Megalodon* is fiction, but in our search for

ABOVE: *Time* magazine's edition of June 23, 1975, capitalized on the popular image of the great white as "one of nature's most efficient killing machines," to quote the edition's story on the making of *Jaws*. The movie's box-office success also sparked a wave of shark attack hysteria in Australian, American and South African newspapers.

© RICHARD ELLIS-1975

Richard Ellis

symbols, we are often willing to allow novelists to contribute to our fears and thus to our legends.

The white shark has come to represent all sharks because in a sense, it is all sharks. It is big, powerful, extremely dangerous and frightening to behold. It has all the features that characterize the voracious shark: razor-sharp, serrated teeth; the soulless black eye (Matthiessen wrote that it was "impenetrable and empty as the eye of God"); and of course, that all-important triangular dorsal fin, always "knifing" through the water.

Of all large, predatory animals, the white shark is probably the most dangerous to humans. Cobras in India kill many more people than sharks around the world, but as they don't eat their victims, they do not, at least in Western countries, have the same reputation.

Lions, tigers, polar bears and grizzlies also attack people on occasion, but their attacks are rare, probably because the carnivores themselves are rare. We don't often hear about big cats or bears as a threat to our existence or even our safety; in fact, we tend nowadays to regard these animals as relatively harmless inhabitants of zoos and circuses.

While some species of large sharks, such as nurses, lemons and sand tigers, are successfully kept in aquariums, all attempts to keep whites or their relatives, the makos and the porbeagles, have met with unqualified failure. Therefore, we can see the shark only as an offshore menace, unreachable even by those who only want to learn a little more about it.

The shark occupies a habitat that is not of our terrestrial understanding. Despite the technological advances that have enabled us to enter the water, we do so as trespassers in an alien and decidedly hostile world. Even the medium is hostile—unlike the fishes, we cannot breathe it; without a face mask we can barely see through it. In its thick, liquid environment, the shark evidently reigns supreme.

What are the elements that make up this love–hate relationship? Are we jealous of the ease with which sharks move, breathe, feed and reproduce in the water? Is it that these big fish have circumvented our every effort to control or even understand them? Do we admire these hunter-killers because we have lost these natural abilities ourselves? Or do we admire their lethal graceful form, their spare economy of line and motion, their smooth, sleek and overwhelmingly ancient efficiency? Is it something that goes even deeper into our collective psyche? Perhaps it is our atavistic fear of being eaten that simultaneously lends distance and a disturbing proximity to our relationship with the shark. It is, after all, the only animal on earth that we fear can—or worse, will—eat us, and that is the stuff of which legends are made.

LEFT: "The most terrible monster that the seas of Mother Earth have produced," wrote David Stead in *Sharks and Rays of Australian Seas*, referring to the shark he preferred to call "white death." Richard Ellis's painting seeks to illustrate the predatory grace and undeniable power of the animal behind the image.

SHARKS AT CLOSE QUARTERS

VALERIE TAYLOR

For more than 35 years my husband Ron and I have mingled at close quarters with a great variety of sharks in our quest for ever more spectacular film footage. The vast majority of our experiences have been exciting, often exhilarating, and only occasionally have we felt threatened by a shark's unwanted attention.

Marty Snyderman

RIGHT: Most close encounters with sharks are accidental and in the majority of cases the shark, more startled than the diver (and with more to fear), will flee. All sharks, however, should be treated with caution and respect. Even this angelshark could deliver a nasty, if non-fatal, bite with its small teeth.

DIVING WITH SHARKS

Because underwater visibility is poor, divers are generally unaware of sharks until they are fairly close. In the case of wobbegongs, sand tigers and the like, this never causes any alarm but the sudden appearance of tigers, bronze whalers and great whites can give the heart a nasty jolt. In fact, I know of divers who have given the sport away after such a frightening encounter. Fortunately, people are now far better educated about sharks than they were when I started diving, 42 years ago. Then almost every shark was a potential killer and the "get it before it gets me" syndrome prevailed. Thousands of innocent sharks were blasted into eternity before experience replaced ignorant fear. Take the sand tiger. Once killed indiscriminately as so-called attackers of humans, these gentle fishes have been proven innocent and are, I am delighted to say, now totally protected in New South Wales. Areas populated by these sharks have become popular dive-sites.

In places such as the Maldives and Caribbean, divers pay to go down and see

Ron & Valerie Taylor

Marty Snyderman

RIGHT: Even experienced divers and scientists must approach sharks with caution. At right, Herwarth Voigtmann feeds gray reef sharks from his mouth on a reef in the Maldives. At far right, Dr. Samuel Gruber and colleagues inject a lemon shark during a growth study experiment at Bimini in the Bahamas.

ABOVE: Filmmakers have come from many countries to work with Australian great whites, setting out from Port Lincoln in South Australia to obtain spectacular footage for box-office successes.

reef sharks being fed by the dive master. Herwarth Voigtmann from Bandos Island in the Maldives, feeds his group of gray reef sharks from his mouth. They are all nicely trained to come in one at a time for a fish—not a bad effort considering the mad frenzies usually associated with large numbers of feeding gray reefs. In Australia, several charter boats organize shark feeds. A good feeding frenzy is often the high spot of the visit of the diving tourist. Generally the baits are taken down by the vessel's dive master and fastened to the seafloor. The guest divers are positioned against the reef. If the area is frequently used by feeding sharks the predators

will be waiting and the action starts immediately the baits are in place, but in a new area where sharks are not conditioned to being fed it can take up to 40 minutes before they appear.

The best shark display in Australia is called Scuba Zoo. A 23-meter and a 7-meter cage have been permanently positioned on the sandy bottom 12 meters down near Flinders Reef out from Townsville, Queensland. Even before any baits are in the water up to 35 sharks of several species can be patrolling around the cage. Once divers are in the cage a drum of fish is attached to a pulley which drags it through the water. A swirling horde of hungry sharks follows the drum, pushing and shoving, all trying for the closest position. After 15 minutes, which gives all the watchers plenty of time to get their pictures, the drum is opened and the sharks go into a mad frenzy right in front of the divers. Once the bait is gone the action calms down and everyone leaves the cage to swim with the sharks in the open water. The entire show is manipulated to give the viewer an exciting but safe experience.

FACE TO FACE WITH A GREAT WHITE
The drama of meeting a shark at close quarters is enhanced by the potential danger presented by some species. Of them all, there is no doubt the

great white shark, or white pointer as it is sometimes called, tops the danger list. It is not that these sharks are responsible for most attacks on humans—the open-water oceanic sharks that hunt their victims among shipwreck survivors claim that unpopular title. But ever since the feature films *Blue Water, White Death* and *Jaws*, great whites have been not only the world's best-known sharks, but also the most feared. Since 1965, when Ron became the first person to film a white shark in its natural element, these awesome fish have held a special place in the public consciousness. Unlike some other sharks, whites do not survive in captivity, no matter how large the aquarium. Because of this the great white remains very much a mystery—the big, unknown danger out there silently controlling the world's oceans.

Viewing white sharks at close quarters is either accidental and terrifying (if not fatal) or contrived and expensive. With only two exceptions all our meetings have been planned and executed with experience and expense. First, huge quantities of meat, minced tuna and blood are needed to attract the marauder. It is impossible to go out and simply find a white; we must lure him to us. Next we need steel cages

LEFT: Jeremiah Sullivan, codeveloper of the Neptunic anti-shark suit, seems to be sharing a good joke with a juvenile mako *Isurus oxyrinchus*.

and a boat capable of supporting us and our equipment for weeks at a time. Once the expedition is organized, we move to offshore locations, preferably near a sea lion colony, and wait for the food slick to work. Sometimes it takes days, and occasionally weeks, for the shark to come and investigate.

Seeing a great white underwater swimming toward you smiling his sawtooth smile—beautiful, deadly, the epitome of grace—has to be one of life's greatest experiences. Game

BELOW: Meeting a great white underwater is a thrill divers from around the world will pay to experience. Their power and silent grace are certainly impressive, but the possibility of being attacked (accidentally or otherwise) by even a relatively small great white makes any encounter a matter for caution.

Ron & Valerie Taylor

ABOVE: Diver Mark Heighes has trained this whitetip reef shark *Triaenodon obesus* to take food from his hand, demonstrating not only the shark's intelligence and learning ability but its essentially unaggressive nature. On reefs where spearfishing is common, whitetips will gather around divers and take food that is offered to them.

fishers boast of the thrill they get sitting safely on the deck of a game boat watching some wretched creature fighting hopelessly for survival on the end of a line. Personally I find that type of thrill rather distasteful; it certainly cannot compare with confronting the same marauder free, at home in his natural element.

In 1965, when Ron had his first encounter with a great white, he was working from a tuna boat. On board was Alf Dean, probably the greatest shark fisher in the world. Alf had attracted the sharks near Dangerous Reef, South Australia. Here is what Ron wrote about seeing his first great white:

"Embedded in my mind is the 'grin of death' as a 12-foot [3.7-meter] great white came toward me. Hair prickled my neck, my heart pounded. At a distance of 2 feet [60 centimeters] the mouth started to open. White triangular teeth filled the viewing frame. With a violent lunge, I heaved my body from the water. No one had ever filmed a white shark in its natural element before. I could well understand why. It was dangerous to the point of stupidity."

Nowadays, thrill-seeking divers come from all over the world to experience visual contact with a great white shark. It is considered to be the ultimate diving trip. They pay, not only in money but in mental and physical endurance, to stand in a cage waiting for a glimpse. It may not be a fun experience, but it is one of the greatest, and it is attracting increasing numbers of people.

Most white shark trips leave from Port Lincoln, South Australia. *Blue Water, White Death, Jaws, Jaws II, Orca*: all used live shark footage shot out from Port Lincoln. Filmmakers come from all over the world to work with Australian sharks. It is not that they don't have great whites elsewhere; they do. The northwest coast of America, if the reports are to be believed, is practically swarming with them. It is just that the Australian ones are the best performers and also, I guess, the most famous.

WORKING WITH SHARKS

While great whites may not be the easiest sharks to find and work with, there are several species that, with a little tasty encouragement and once they know you, will give guaranteed performances year after year on cue. We used to work with a group that lived near the Marion Reef, off the coast of Queensland. Because of their wild behavior and willingness to swim close to the camera they have appeared in many of our shark specials. Unfortunately the Asian taste for sharkfin soup and the huge price that will be paid for this so-called delicacy has seen a dramatic worldwide decline in these marvelous predators. Sadly our Marion Reef actors have now been caught and killed for their fins. This extract from my diary tells how we first met; the location is Coralita Pass in the Marion Reef, the date December 28, 1975.

"Well, John and I nearly cashed in our chips this morning. I can still hardly believe it. This afternoon we had the worst shark experience imaginable without actually being bitten. It was terrifying. Ron, John, Alex and myself decided to stir up some sharks for filming. I planning to use the 35 mm Eymo movie camera because we had been having such good shark action, so fast that I could not take still photographs quickly enough. I thought using the 35 mm movie film would be like having a motor drive on a still camera containing a 30-meter load of film.

Wally, our skipper, pointed out an area near the main entrance into Marion Lagoon. Wally reckoned it would be a really hairy place to work. His exact words were, 'I think a lot of big tough sharks live down there.' Well! I considered myself to be a big tough shark photographer; fighting off sharks was a daily occurrence. After lunch, Alex, John, myself and Ron loaded our dinghy with fish skeletons and diving gear. We anchored our aluminum dinghy over a big sandy hole on the edge of the pass about 9 meters in from the drop-off. I took my fish carcases down. It was a very unusual looking area. The sand patch was around 45 meters across and curved in a big half-circle back into the coral reef. The front of the half-circle opened into deep purple nothingness. It was a very strange and eerie, like a marine colosseum. Beautiful, but unfriendly.

Alex vanished behind some yellow coral. He is an enthusiastic spearfisherman, full of energy and a great help to us. All was still in my warm pale blue world. I stuffed my baits into the coral where I planned to work. Blood and gore drifted gently up from the hard yellow coral, staining green trails in the water. We had been down around ten minutes when I heard or perhaps felt a thump. I was told later that Alex had speared a fish. My eyes strained toward the distant purple. I thought if monsters could live anywhere, they could live out there, and from out there they came—a squadron in ragged formation, eight or nine sharks swimming high, their smiling maws black semicircles against their white undercarriages. I felt a twinge of fear. These were different sharks from the usual: bigger, fatter, less nervous, in fact, not nervous at all. They cruised around in midwater sniffing the current, oozing confidence, eyeing us with cold yellow eyes. This was their world and it showed. Alex, however,

had (luckily for him) lost the fish. The current must have told the marauders this, for one by one they slipped away, vanishing like wraiths into the deeps until the great purple void hung empty over the white edge of sand.

A coral trout appeared. John followed the fish, trying to get in a good shot. I heard a thump, then a flapping. John rose from the obscuring coral with the trout struggling on his spear and began to swim toward me. What I saw behind John chilled me to the bone. I surfaced and yelled at Ron, who was sitting half asleep in the dinghy, 'Get Alex out of the water quick.' I descended

ABOVE: A gray reef shark trails behind a spearfisherman.

BELOW: Feeding frenzies are well documented in gray reef sharks and are not—despite popular belief—directed at divers. They are, however, frightening experiences and there is a danger of a diver or underwater photographer being bitten by sharks that are apparently totally unaware of their surroundings.

fast. John had not looked behind. He waved his fish at me, appearing very pleased with himself. I pointed frantically behind him. One over-the-shoulder look and John picked up considerable speed. The lead sharks swimming midwater were only meters away. He began trying to shake the fish off the spear, sending up tantalizing puffs of blood. As he drew alongside he gave me a very worried look. The fish had dropped on to the sand, where it struggled feebly. No sharks approached it. I was somewhat amazed by this unusual attitude so I left my camera on the coral, swam down and cut the trout's throat. Green blood drifted up. 'Now for some action,' I thought with anticipation.

Back on the coral ledge, John was waiting, his spear gun loaded, eyes round and worried inside his face mask. The sharks were big and fast, bigger and faster than any we had seen on the trip. I sensed trouble in those moving torpedo shapes. One of the larger sharks circled only a few meters away. I noticed it was a female—fat, arrogant and without fear. I was puzzled that these sharks showed no interest in the baits. John and I, by now sitting back to back high on the coral, were the sole recipients of their attention. It was very nerve-racking. 'Why don't they eat the baits? Why don't they behave normally?' was all I could think.

The female shark circling closest dropped to the bottom of our coral patch. Almost out of sight behind the outcrop, she began to swim back and forth, back and forth, gathering speed with each pass, the turns lightning quick, yellow eyes

BLUE SHARKS ARE REAL SHARKS, TOO

MARTY SNYDERMAN

Ninety kilometers out to sea, in water several thousand meters deep, and everywhere I looked I saw sharks. There were at least 35, perhaps as many as 50, and all were at least two meters long. I had seen two makos earlier in the day, but at that moment all the sharks within my field of vision were blue sharks, the most common of the open-ocean sharks in southern California.

Although I had been in similar situations on literally dozens of dives, there was something noticeably different about the sharks this day. Usually blue sharks will swim away quite readily if you hit or push them. Although they will turn and come right back toward you after they have been struck, especially if you are filming from a position that is downstream from a bait, they will almost always retreat when a diver tries to fend them off. Not so this day.

I was working as a safety diver behind cameraman Howard Hall, who was filming a sequence for the television show "Animals, Animals." My job was to keep Howard from getting bitten while his eye was glued to the viewfinder of his camera. Howard and I were filming some sequences of the blue sharks; later in the day we were going to make another dive with Ron and Valerie Taylor from Australia. Ron and Val are world-renowned shark experts and filmmakers, and they have worked with many species of sharks in a diversity of settings. For this particular episode, Val was to be the on-camera talent, a job for which she is well qualified.

During my dive with Howard it was all I could do to keep the sharks away from us. I have no idea how many times I hit, poked, pushed and shoved the sharks. Exactly why they were so excited I don't know, but the action never slowed down. By the end of our dive I was both physically exhausted and emotionally drained. The prospect of making a second dive gave me a knot in the pit of my stomach, especially

C.S. Johnson

watching. I stared, horrified. I knew what was coming, but felt helpless to alter the situation.

Suddenly she shot away some 10 meters, spun in her own length, then sped like a bullet, jaws distended, straight for me. As she hit I rammed the big 35 mm movie camera housing into her maw. The impact pushed the housing up into my face and I went rolling over backward into the coral. She turned and struck at my legs. Again the camera housing held her off. John came in between my legs and poked hard with his gun to her belly. Mouth still open, teeth showing, she struck once more. I landed a futile unfelt blow to the top of her head, but it was John who really saved me as he beat her with his gun in a fury of fear and desperation. The water foamed. I couldn't get enough air from my tank, my lungs strained to suck more than the regulator would allow. Never leaving our immediate vicinity, she flicked around to John. He kicked with his flippers, hit with his gun. 'Shoot it, shoot it, shoot it!' I screamed over and over, but though John heard his hands were stilled by horror. 'Shoot, Shoot!' I screamed, and became furious that he hesitated. I thought John was mad not to try and save himself.

Together we twisted in a foamy, sharky mess, hacking, kicking, punching. I was becoming exhausted. I hardly knew what I was doing any more. I felt breathless, faint. Then, like a blessed miracle, John fired, the headless shaft ramming deep into the shark's gills. It shot away, John swam to the surface and yelled to Ron, 'Bring the boat quick!'"

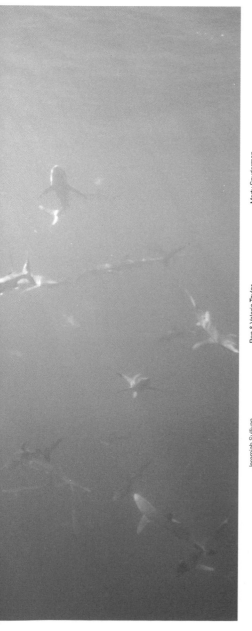

Marty Snyderman

Ron & Valerie Taylor

Jeremiah Sullivan

ABOVE: After being bitten on the leg by an oceanic blue shark *Prionace glauca*, apparently frustrated in its attempts to take fish from her hand, Valerie Taylor is winched aboard the helicopter that will take her to the hospital.

considering the fact that Valerie was going to be working without the benefit of having a safety diver behind her. Sitting on the boat between dives we discussed the plan for the coming dive. I strongly suggested that Valerie have a safety diver, but Ron, Val and the show's producers thought it unnecessary. They were convinced that Valerie could handle the situation. Having worked with Valerie on several previous occasions, I was also convinced that on most days she could have protected herself. In fact, on the previous dive I had believed that I would have no trouble fending the sharks away from Howard and me. But now I had the advantage of having made one dive on the day in question and I knew it was an unusual day. That day we all made a mistake. The sharks were unusually aggressive, but from a vantage point aboard the boat it was impossible to detect their mood.

I insisted that Fred Fischer join me and that we work in tandem to protect Howard. Rarely before in my work with sharks had I suggested the need for two safety divers to protect one cameraman. Valerie entered the water with a string of fish, with which she could attract the sharks, attached to her weight belt. The fish were not necessary. Within a matter of minutes she was badly bitten on the shin and calf by a blue shark. It had her leg in its mouth for only a few seconds but the damage was done.

I got a real education in documentary filmmaking that day. Immediately after being hit, Val surfaced and yelled out to the topside cameraman, "Roll the cameras. I have been hit. I think it is bad." Then she descended, placed her regulator in her mouth and allowed herself to be towed back to the boat. The topside crew was able to film the action from that point on. Valerie's wound was severe enough that we called a coastguard helicopter to fly her to a hospital. The doctors did a remarkable job and she was back in the water filming sharks only a few weeks later.

I know that many experts consider blue sharks to be pussy cats, more closely related to housepets than to maneaters such as white sharks and tiger sharks. But the lesson learned from Valerie's misfortune is never to take blue sharks—or any sharks for that matter—for granted.

We worked with the Marion Reef sharks for many years. They always remembered us. We trained them to understand that a certain pattern of behavior brought a rich reward, while aggressive behavior resulted in a sharp whack on the nose.

In 1982, we were there with filmmaker Dick Dennison shooting a segment for a television special, when our usual reef marauders were joined by a beautiful female tiger. I know tiger sharks supposedly eat people, but in our experience they have always been slow, gentle and obliging. This tiger took her first piece of fish from my hand. For the rest of the dive she swam around us—pure magic for the film. Several times she actually bumped me, so close did she come. The other, smaller sharks gave her space. Big means a great deal in the marine world, but she accepted us and in return we respected her. I was sorry when the film ran out and can remember seeing her circling around as I climbed into the dinghy. All the tiger sharks we have met have behaved in a similar fashion. To achieve the same compatibility with a wide and dangerous land animal would be impossible.

A FRIENDLY GREAT WHITE

Perhaps the most amazing example of working with a shark at close quarters took place during a white shark filming expedition on the charter boat *Tradewind*. There were two whites around, but one was more willing to perform. We were throwing out small baits tied to a rope. As the shark reached for the fish we would pull it away, drawing the predator closer. Eventually the shark, realizing he would only receive his reward close to the stern, started popping up next to the little swim platform, almost like a dog begging for food. The great white has one trait not found in other fish: it will lift its head above the surface to get a better view of what is happening—a rather disconcerting habit until you become used to it.

This shark was doing just that—lifting his head out of the water and looking at us. Ron suggested I try hand-feeding him from the swim platform. Great whites have been known to rise above the surface and take a bait or a seal lying near the water's edge, so the idea was not without danger. The shark watched as I climbed down, my weight causing the platform to submerge a little. I offered a fish by leaning down and dangling it under the surface. Whitey cruised over. He seemed a rather clumsy eater, raising his pointy head up next to the fish rather than under it. I had to put the fish into his mouth. He took it nicely—no snapping about, just one big splashy bite. It was exciting, it was easy, it was fun. I gave him five more fish with a little pat on the nose each time while Ron filmed. There was no doubt the shark knew how the game was being played. I was totally vulnerable; he could have taken me at any time, but he didn't. He took only the fish. In about 20 minutes this giant marine predator had learnt a little trick; no punishment was needed, just a small reward. Ron and I knew that one day we will swim with a white. We expect him to behave like his cousin the tiger, slow and polite, but we are going to have to choose the conditions, place and shark very carefully.

A NOTE OF CAUTION

The excitement of mixing at close quarters with sharks in their own environment is something that can only be enjoyed after years of experience in dealing safely with these fascinating but often dangerous creatures of the deep. Ron and I, after more than 35 years of working professionally with sharks, still don't profess to be experts, though we can claim to know and understand the species we have worked with a little better than do most people.

What we do may seem crazy, and perhaps it is. But patting great whites and hand-feeding tigers are skills that have been acquired only after years of patient observation and discipline. To try and copy us would very likely mean becoming another statistic in the shark attack files. Sharks can be dangerous and are far smarter than they are often given credit for. They should always be treated with caution and respect.

ABOVE: The great white is the only shark—indeed, the only fish—that lifts its head out of the water. This behavior is believed to be analogous to the "spy-hopping" of orcas. Both species include seals and sea lions in their diets and may lift their heads to look for prey on rocks or to scare potential prey into the water.

FACING PAGE: The tiger shark *Galeocerdo cuvier* has a justly infamous reputation. However, as Valerie Taylor found at Marion Reef in Queensland, even these fearsome creatures can be "slow, gentle and obliging."

BELOW: A mature and potentially lethal male great white shark demonstrates his intelligence and apparent willingness to cooperate by taking fish from Valerie Taylor's hand.

Marty Snyderman

HOLD YOUR BREATH OR YOU'LL SCARE THE SHARKS

MARTY SNYDERMAN

The sight before me was enough to make my knees shake and my mouth go dry. I was looking up at a minimum of 200 hammerhead sharks between 2 and 3 meters long. I was approximately 18 meters deep at the now famous El Bajo seamount in Mexico's Sea of Cortez, and there was no shark cage in the water. The seamount is well known among the diving community that visits the Sea of Cortez for frequent encounters with manta rays, whale sharks and large gatherings of scalloped hammerheads *Sphyrna lewini*.

The hammerheads were swimming in a large circle as they cruised around the seamount. The scene above me was truly spectacular and I felt fortunate to have the chance to film it. My pounding heart seemed to be in my throat. Although I had heard about the large gatherings of hammerhead sharks at the seamount, this was my first encounter of the kind. I watched for a moment and then tried to approach the sharks so that I could photograph the scene.

I was on scuba, and as soon as I began to approach I exhaled—and the sharks bolted away. The noise from my exhaust bubbles scared every one of the 200 or more sharks; they simply vanished beyond the 30-meter range of visibility. When I first broke into the business of underwater filming I never thought I would have to worry about scaring the sharks.

Over time I have learned that the only way successfully to film these large groups of scalloped hammerheads is while free diving, without the use of scuba. Skilled free divers have acquired some awesome photographs by breath-hold diving into the schools at depths of 25 meters or more, but the sharks almost always bolt as soon as they hear the unfamiliar noise from scuba systems.

The most interesting question as far as the scientific community is concerned is why these sharks gather in large groups or schools. (In strict scientific terms these gatherings are not true schools because there is no one leader, the swimming is not synchronized and the sharks mill about instead of all swimming in the same direction.) Schooling is a rare behavior for apex predators—animals at the top of the food chain. Scalloped hammerheads have few, if any, natural predators, so what advantage can they possibly gain by schooling? Surely it takes a lot more small fish to feed 200 hammerheads than to feed one. After years of study, no one in the scientific community is prepared to make the definitive statement. Perhaps migration or mating is at the heart of the issue, but no one is sure.

One thing is certain, however. Anyone who wants to study or film scalloped hammerheads must be a good free diver. The schools are almost impossible to get close to on scuba.

REPELLING SHARKS

C. SCOTT JOHNSON

T he first recorded shark attack was reported by Herodotus in 492 BC. Jonah, of course, was swallowed by a "big fish" that may have been a shark, but he survived uninjured. Since their earliest encounters with sharks, people have been trying to devise ways of protecting themselves from them. Hawaiian women tattooed their ankles as a means of protection; Hawaiians also paid homage to shark-gods who used "good" sharks to protect them from "bad" sharks. Solomon Islanders offered human sacrifices to shark-gods.

In keeping sharks at bay there are times when almost anything works and there are times when nothing seems to. Fortunately, shark attacks on humans are not common. Human attacks on sharks are much more frequent, for over 700,000 tonnes of sharks are caught each year by fishermen throughout the world. Sharks would have to eat more than 10 million people a year to equal this amount. In fact, other people are by far the most dangerous animals humans have to encounter. Of the more than 260 million people in the United States, about 24,000 are murdered each year and another 4 million are wounded in acts of violence. Another 50,000 die in automobile crashes. In the United States each year a million people are bitten by pet dogs and several die as a result. In an average year sharks injure only a dozen or so people and only a handful of the attacks are fatal. Despite this we have a morbid foreboding about shark attack. Even though we know the problem is more psychological than actual, it is none the less real to us.

Perry W. Gilbert

ABOVE: The best way to keep sharks away from people is to provide a sharkproof barrier like a steel-fenced swimming enclosure. Unfortunately, even this is inefficient as enclosures are difficult to construct and expensive to maintain. In addition, they protect only very small portions of shoreline such as this harbor beach in Sydney, Australia.

PROTECTING BEACHES

Although the chances of being attacked are greater offshore, in deep water where there are likely to be more sharks, most shark attacks occur at bathing beaches. This is simply because of the large number of people there.

The most effective way to protect beaches is to fence or wall in the bathing area and so physically prevent sharks from entering. This technique has been used effectively in Australia, South Africa, South America and many other

parts of the world. The reason this method is not used more is because it is expensive. Initial construction costs are high and, because the sea is a relentless destroyer, so are maintenance costs. In reviewing the various methods of keeping sharks at bay, it becomes evident that economic considerations are almost always the limiting factor in their use.

Since the possibility of attack depends on there being a person and a shark in the same place at the same time, an effective method of lowering the chances of attack is simply to reduce the number of sharks present by catching them. The most common method of shark fishing for this purpose is called meshing and it has been used quite successfully in both Australia and South Africa.

Meshing consists of setting large-mesh gillnets at distances of between 400 and 500 meters from beaches. The nets are not continuous; usually there are two parallel rows of nets between 100 and 150 meters long with one being 50 to 75 meters closer to shore than the other. While swimming to and from the beach sharks become entangled in the nets and suffocate. Most of the sharks are caught at night when they swim closer to shore in search of food. The nets are usually checked every other day to make repairs and remove dead sharks. In areas not on shark migration routes the population of sharks, and

Ben Cropp

LEFT: Nothing short of keeping people out of the water will totally eliminate the risk of shark attack, but the most successful practicable method seems to be offshore meshing of swimming beaches. Popular in Australia and South Africa, the method's limitations are cost of installation and maintenance and the impossibility of netting the entire length of every beach.

BELOW: An Australian invention, the bubble curtain was developed in 1960 and sold to several resort owners in the United States before testing revealed that it was quite ineffective in preventing sharks from approaching beaches. Of 12 large tiger sharks tested at the Lerner Marine Laboratory in the Bahamas, only one was repelled by the bubble curtain.

hence the chance of shark attack, in a given area can be greatly reduced. At certain times of the year large numbers of migrating sharks invade South Africa's beaches. When this happens the nets quickly fill with sharks and are rendered useless. During these periods the nets are not set and bathers are warned not to swim. Because meshing is expensive it can be used to protect only a limited number of beaches. An unfortunate side effect of meshing is that many harmless species of sharks, along with large fish and marine mammals, are caught and killed.

THE BUBBLE CURTAIN

New methods of protection are continually being devised and tested. Unfortunately some inventors, in their quest for quick returns, begin selling their "brainchild" before it has been thoroughly tested. One example of inadequate testing was the bubble curtain or bubble fence.

Perry W. Gilbert

ABOVE: A diver with a 3-meter tiger shark that was killed by a "bangstick" or powerhead, a hand-held spear whose head is fitted with a shotgun cartridge.

ABOVE: The electric harpoon paralyzes the shark by passing a large current at a relatively low voltage through the shark's body.

BELOW: The Shark Shield has shown promising results in laboratory and field tests. Consisting of two electrodes with a pulsed electric current flowing between them, it is ignored by a lemon shark (below) when the current is turned off, but when the current is on (right) the shark will turn abruptly and retreat from the invisible barrier.

This idea, which originated in Australia in 1960, consisted of an ordinary garden hose in which many holes had been drilled. The hose was laid on the seafloor and attached to an air compressor to create a "fence" of bubbles. Sharks, it was advertised, would not cross the bubble fence. Several of these devices were sold to hotel owners in the United States for the protection of their beaches. The bubble curtain wasn't actually tested until the spring of 1961, when Dr. Perry Gilbert, working at the Lerner Marine Laboratory in the Bahamas, tested it against 12 large tiger sharks. Only one shark was repelled by the bubbles; the other 11 swam back and forth at will through the curtain.

The importance of adequate testing cannot be overemphasized. Not only should many different species of dangerous sharks be used. Until it has been tested on many members of each of the species, no shark deterrent should be adopted.

ELECTRIC FIELDS

The fact that sharks, and all other species of fish, are affected by electric fields has been exploited in South Africa to develop a beach protection system. When an electric field above a certain minimum value is produced between two wires, a shark located between the wires will feel a shock and swim away rapidly. This is called a startle response. If the voltage between the two wires is raised, the shark will involuntarily turn and swim toward the wire that is positive. This is called an electrotaxis reaction. If the voltage is high enough, the shark will be paralyzed and in several minutes will suffocate because it cannot swim or move its gills to take in oxygen from the water. This state is called electronarcosis.

Many years of research and testing have gone into the development of this South African system. The basic idea is to anchor a pattern of electrical cables around bathing beaches, outside the surf zone. If the voltages are large enough to produce electrotaxis, sharks swimming toward the beach are forced to turn around and swim away.

There were many problems to be solved in developing this system. Because sea water is a very good conductor of electric current, continuous or direct current generators could not be used. The scientists had to produce a pulsed voltage of just the right character; otherwise too much current would be needed, operating costs would rise and the electrical cables would be destroyed through electrolysis. A successful system was eventually developed but the costs of construction and operation were still too high. The system is not being used, but research is continuing and, in time, the economic problem may be overcome.

PROTECTION FOR DIVERS

Skindivers and scuba divers run the greatest risk of being attacked. This is because their activities increase the possibility of encounters with sharks. Several weapons have been developed for divers to use against sharks. Many divers carry knives, but most are made of stainless steel to prevent saltwater corrosion and neither their edges nor their points are sharp enough to provide adequate protection. Most sharks have tough hides that only the sharpest knives can penetrate and then only with effort.

Sharks are also difficult to kill outright. A shark whose spinal cord has been severed near the brain can continue to swim. Neural signals to the swimming muscles are not controlled by the brain; only signals to speed up or slow down come from the brain. Even spearguns with enough power to penetrate the shark's skin are not very effective unless a hit to the brain is scored.

However, a speargun can be made into an effective weapon with the addition to the spear top of a "powerhead." Powerheads, sometimes called bangsticks, are in reality nothing more than short-barreled single shotguns, designed to discharge on contact with the shark. These can be obtained in almost any caliber from .22 to 12 bore. One potent version of the powerhead has a small explosive charge in the barrel instead of a cartridge case.

Another weapon that has been widely used is the carbon dioxide anti-shark dart. This device consists of a small carbon dioxide cylinder attached to a large hollow needle. When shot into the side of the shark, the cylinder is punctured and carbon dioxide flows through the needle into the shark's body cavity, causing a large bubble to form. The shark, which is almost weightless in water, becomes buoyant and is forced to the surface. If large amounts of gas are injected, the internal pressure caused by the gas can paralyze the shark or force its internal organs out of its mouth. A limitation of carbon dioxide darts is that they can be used only from the side or bottom; these are the only directions from which the needle can effectively penetrate the body cavity. As a precaution, US Navy frogmen carried carbon dioxide darts when they aided in the recovery of the astronauts following the splashdowns of Apollo missions 15 and 16.

All these devices are dangerous weapons both in and out of water and must be treated with great care and respect. At least one careless diver has been severely injured in his own garage by the accidental discharge of a powerhead. Many divers are more afraid of these weapons than of the sharks themselves. A cardinal rule for all anti-shark measures is that they present a negligible danger to the user.

An electric anti-shark harpoon was developed several years ago. This device featured two electrodes supplied with a large current from a power supply. One of the electrodes had a sharp, thick point and when it was thrust into the shark, a current was turned on between the inside and the outside of the shark. As long as the current was on, the shark was paralyzed and unable to move or breathe. Because of the high cost of manufacture this weapon has never been produced commercially. However, because it only kills the shark if left on long enough for the fish to suffocate—usually more than 30 minutes—it could be a useful aid to researchers who want to capture sharks.

US Navy scientists have developed a non-lethal device that interferes with the shark's ability to swim. Called a drogue dart, it consists simply of a sharp, barbed point to which is attached a small parachute. When the barbed point is shot into the shark the parachute opens, causing an unbalanced drag force that the shark fights against much as it would if it were hooked by a fisherman. The shark is thus distracted from harming the diver. Drogue darts are not presently being manufactured.

Another way of fending off sharks is through the use of a "shark billy," which was developed by Jacques-Yves Cousteau, coinventor of the aqualung, and his divers. It is nothing more than a stout wooden club, about 2 meters long, that is used to push away curious sharks. The "shark" end of the club has nails driven into it to help prevent sharks from slipping off. Some years ago, an electrified version of the shark billy found its way on to the market. Called a Shark Tazer, it resembles an underwater cattle prod. It is held near or against the shark and when switched on, the shark receives a jolt of electric current.

Weapons, no matter how effective they are or how skillfully they are used, are of no value if the shark cannot be seen. This restricts their use to relatively clear water—and records show that only half the divers attacked saw the shark beforehand. Several efforts have been made to protect divers from shark that cannot be sighted. One of these is an electric repeller that pulses an

BELOW: Although they have unnecessarily killed many harmless sharks, powerheads can protect divers from potential threat from dangerous species such as these bronze whalers *Carcharhinus brachyurus*.

Ron & Valerie Taylor

RIGHT: In the belief that sharks do not eat their attendant pilotfish because they have black and white stripes, striped "shark repellent" wetsuits have been marketed, despite the fact that they have no repellent effect at all. Sharks do not eat pilotfish because if they are strong and healthy, they are simply too difficult to catch!

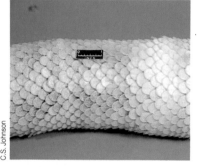

ABOVE: A wetsuit covered with tough overlapping scales made of plastic was tested by US Navy scientists. It was resistant to shark bites but restricted divers' movements.

ABOVE: The first practicable sharkproof suit was the Neptunic, which consists of approximately 400,000 small stainless steel rings interlocked to form chain mail.

electric current in the water around the diver about once a second. Several similar designs have been patented and it is not clear who was the first to develop the idea. One version that has been successfully tested is the Shark Shield. The Shark Shield was originally built to protect the cod ends of shrimp fishermen's trawl nets from damage by sharks. A smaller version was designed to be worn by divers. A rechargeable power supply, attached to the diver's belt, delivers 120-volt pulses to electrodes on the arms and legs of the diver's wetsuit. It is designed to work for 12 hours without recharging.

While Shark Shield has been shown to repel several species of dangerous sharks, some divers complain that the large electric pulses generated make their teeth fillings ache. If the power is on and the electrodes are touched while out of water a nasty but non-lethal shock is administered to the careless person. Unfortunately, an electrical measuring instrument of some kind is necessary to verify that the device is on and working properly—that is, unless you don't mind getting shocked in order to test its operation. Shark Shields are currently being used only by shrimp fishermen; a market has not developed for the divers' version.

In Japan, women divers, called *amas*, have collected abalone and seaweed for centuries. Some of them wear a *fundoshi* as shark protection. This abbreviated garment consists of a G-string-size loincloth with a piece of red cloth, 15 centimeters wide and 2 meters long, attached. While diving, the red tail flutters behind the *ama*. The idea here is twofold: first the fluttering tail

may frighten the shark away; failing that, if the shark attacks, it is much more likely to bite the cloth tail than the *ama*. Finding the tail not good to eat, the shark will leave.

The validity of the *fundoshi* as a protection from attack has never been tested scientifically, but there is no record of an *ama* being attacked while wearing one. In fact, *amas* not wearing *fundoshi* have never been attacked either, which may only mean that dangerous sharks are not found where the *amas* swim.

PROTECTIVE SUITS

Some open-sea, or pelagic, sharks are frequently seen swimming with small, black and white striped fish. These are called pilotfish because they usually swim in front of the sharks. Some think that the pilotfish are not eaten by the sharks because of their black and white stripes. In fact, the pilotfish would be safe no matter what

their color just as long as they were strong and healthy. Like all predators, sharks seek out the weak and sick; the strong and healthy are too difficult to catch.

Nevertheless, a black and white striped suit has been advertised as successfully repelling sharks. In tests conducted by US Navy scientists with several species of known dangerous sharks, no such repelling effect was found. In fact, in one test with blue sharks two man-size dummies, one in a black wetsuit and one in a black and white striped wetsuit, were placed in the sea with the sharks. Only the striped-suited dummy was bitten. Ron and Valerie Taylor, the well-known underwater filmmakers, also tested the striped suit design. After exhaustive testing they found the suits to have no effect on sharks at all. *Caveat emptor*—let the buyer beware—the ancient Roman caution, is especially apt when it comes to shark deterrents.

Developing a suit that is proof against shark bite is probably the most logical way of protecting divers against shark attack. While providing adequate protection, the suit must allow the user complete mobility and must not be too heavy. In order to accomplish this, compromises must be made. The worst injuries inflicted during attacks consist of cuts caused by the shark's sharp teeth. A bad bruise or even a broken limb can more easily be survived. For this reason the designer's main aim must be to produce a suit that will reduce the cutting effect of the shark's teeth.

US Navy scientists have tested two designs. The first model was basically a neoprene wetsuit covered with overlapping plastic scales much like the scales of a fish. A tough plastic was used in the scales. The idea was to distribute the force of the bites over an area of a square centimeter or so and negate the cutting action of the teeth. Tests indicated that the suit was resistant to shark

ABOVE: Valerie Taylor tests the Neptunic in the field, allowing herself to be bitten by a 2-meter blue shark in deep water off the coast of California. Extensive testing has found the Neptunic to be effective against sharks of this size.

RIGHT: A graphic demonstration of how the Neptunic works. Even the large, sharp and pointed tooth of a great white cannot penetrate the steel mesh, though a bite from a large shark would cause at least severe bruising and crushing of tissues, possibly broken bones and, if the wearer were bitten on the torso, internal bleeding.

Ron & Valerie Taylor

BELOW: If divers have to enter the water to observe or photograph sharks in their own environment, the best form of protection is undoubtedly the shark cage. Sharks cannot reach the diver if the cage's bars are sufficiently close together and the cage—and diver—can be winched out of the water in the event of damage.

bites, but that it restricted the movement of the diver too much. The second design was simply a pair of coveralls made of several layers of a new, very strong material called Kevlar. Kevlar caught the scientists' attention because of its use in making lightweight bulletproof vests. This time the suits, while they gave the divers plenty of freedom of motion, were not sufficiently resistant to shark bites.

A practical sharkproof suit has now been produced. Ron and Valerie Taylor, along with American Jeremiah Sullivan, have developed a garment composed of approximately 400,000 interlocking stainless steel rings. The suit looks

exactly like the chain mail worn by medieval warriors, except the stainless steel rings are so small that the shark's teeth cannot reach through them. The suit—commercially named Neptunic—has been shown to be effective against the species of sharks responsible for most shark attacks.

CHEMICAL REPELLENTS

Just after midnight on July 30, 1945, Lieutenant Commander Mochitsura Hashimoto, captain of the Japanese submarine I-58, sighted a large unescorted enemy warship steaming in a straight line instead of zigzagging to avoid submarine attack. He fired two torpedoes and 12 minutes later the heavy cruiser uss Indianapolis, flagship of the Fifth Fleet, disappeared from sight forever. It was steaming under radio silence and no SOS was sent. The highly classified mission it had just completed had been to deliver the first two nuclear bombs to Guam.

For four long days and nights the survivors of one of the greatest tragedies in United States naval history waited for rescue. Of the 1,196 on board that night only 316 would come home. It will never be known how many were taken by sharks. Guesses range from 50 to 100, certainly far less than the 600 that Quint, the character

Ron & Valerie Taylor

from *Jaws*, claimed. Sharks were present for most of the four days between sinking and rescue. The survivors have a reunion every five years, and many are still bothered by the memory of those horrifying days more than 50 years ago. The tragedy so haunted the skipper of the *Indianapolis* that he took his own life in 1977.

While naval disasters of this magnitude did not happen often during World War II, many lesser ones did occur. Early in the war the need for some kind of shark protection for the members of the Allied Forces was clearly recognized. A crash program was instituted in the United States and a few months later a chemical shark repellent, called Shark Chaser, was produced. The scientists involved knew that shark fishermen believed (they still believe to this day) that sharks are repelled by the presence of decaying shark flesh. So they created a repellent that combined the chemical they believed to be the significant one from decaying sharks, with a black dye and a wax binder. The dye was designed to spread out around the users to provide further protection by hiding them from the sharks' view.

The final package, which needed to be compact, was only 2 centimeters thick, 10 centimeters long and 7.5 centimeters wide. The packet contained about 170 grams of the active ingredients and would dissolve at a fairly uniform rate over around three and a half hours. A similar compound was developed by the British Admiralty. It was called Admiralty Pattern 0471/1399 and was made with the same chemicals—copper acetate and a nigrosine dye— as Shark Chaser. Hastily conducted tests seemed to show that the compound was effective in repelling sharks.

While Shark Chaser and Pattern 1399 undoubtedly provided comfort to those forced to use them, tests since World War II have shown them to be of little or no value as shark repellents and the US Navy stopped procuring Shark Chaser in 1976. No search for a replacement has ever been started. The main reason for this is that since World War II only one US military person has been injured by a shark while on active duty.

On September 23, 1961, a US Navy aircraft ditched in the mid-Atlantic. The three crew members drifted, bothered by sharks, for many hours before rescue. As he was trying to climb aboard a rescue craft one of the three fell back into the sea and was attacked by a shark. Fortunately, his wounds were not serious. In the intervening period, hundreds of United States airmen have had to parachute into the sea. None who survived suffered a shark attack and the recovered remains of those who did not survive have shown no sign of shark bite.

High-performance fighter pilots carry a one-man liferaft in case they are forced to eject over

Marty Snyderman

the ocean and these certainly provide adequate protection against sharks.

RECENT RESEARCH
Even though the US Navy is not officially searching for a replacement for Shark Chaser, it does provide some funding for shark research. Most of the research is basic in character and is done at various universities and at one Navy laboratory, the Naval Ocean Systems Center (NOSC) in San Diego, California. The basic aim of the work at NOSC is to translate the available knowledge about sharks into ways of solving problems that sharks cause for the Navy. Sharks may not injure people very often but they can, and occasionally do, damage important and

ABOVE: The design of most shark cages is a compromise between optimum protection for the diver and optimum opportunity for underwater photography. Sufficient space for cameras often means that a small shark can enter the cage and could possibly injure a trapped diver. Most sharks, however, are simply anxious to escape.

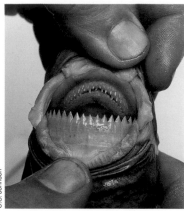

ABOVE: Mystifying damage to the rubber coating of underwater cables in US Navy hydrophones was identified as being due to a small deepwater dogfish, the cookiecutter shark *Isistius brasiliensis*, which attaches itself by suction to whales, tuna, marlins or megamouth sharks and cuts out a neat circular plug of flesh. A layer of fiberglass frustrated the shark's bizarre feeding method and eliminated damage to vital naval equipment.

valuable equipment. Dozens of towed arrays—long pieces of hose filled with underwater listening devices—have been damaged by sharks. The Navy tows these devices behind submarines and surface ships in order to locate enemy submarines. Companies prospecting acoustically for oil use them to collect information from echoes produced in sub-bottom structures by small explosions set off at the sea surface.

Damage to rubber covers on submarine hydrophones (underwater microphones) was a cause for concern to the US Navy until a scientist at NOSC identified the cause as the cookiecutter shark. This small species of shark, *Isistius brasiliensis*, grows to a maximum length of only around 50 centimeters. It feeds by attaching itself to the sides of large fish, dolphins, whales and other sea creatures with its suction-cup lips. Then with its lower sawlike set of teeth it carves out hemispherical chunks of flesh up to 5 centimeters in diameter. Once the cause of the damage was identified, a protective layer of fiberglass was applied to the rubber coverings and the problem was solved.

Chemical repellents continue to be developed and tested. Several years ago Dr. Eugenie Clark discovered a small fish in the Red Sea that sharks were reluctant to bite. She found that when in danger this fish, the Moses sole *Pardachirus*

marmoratus, excreted a milky white fluid that worked extremely rapidly on the sharks she tested. Other scientists studying the sole's fluid found that it chemically resembled a group of chemicals called surfactants (the ingredients that cause the foaming action in many soaps and detergents). While surfactants have been shown to repel sharks, they are not as effective as other chemicals that have been tested. The basic problem with all the chemicals tested to date is that far too great quantities are needed to produce the desired repelling effect. The Moses sole's strategy is to inject its fluid into the shark's mouth, thus producing a very high local concentration of repelling material.

One promising idea involves sharks' ability to detect extremely weak electrical fields: indeed, sharks attracted to the electrical field generated by transoceanic telephone cables have caused expensive damage by attacking the cables, perhaps in the belief the cables were prey. We know that sharks are more sensitive to electrical fields than any other marine animal. All living things in the sea generate tiny electrical fields around their bodies. As in a battery, these fields are produced by the chemical interaction of various body fluids. Nerve impulses are not detected by sharks because they occur at frequencies too high for them to sense. Instead,

SAFETY IN A PLASTIC BAG

While the United States Navy is not actively trying to develop shark deterrent devices, it does test some of the better ideas that come along. One device developed by scientists is called the Johnson Shark Bag. The Johnson Shark Bag is simply a large cylindrical plastic bag that is closed at the bottom and has inflatable rings around the open top. It folds into a small package weighing about half a kilogram. If it becomes necessary to use a Johnson Shark Bag the package is unfolded, one or more of the three inflatable rings is inflated, and the user climbs inside. The user then scoops in water to extend the bag fully.

The idea for the Johnson Shark Bag originated in the knowledge that most shark bites are to the arms and legs. It was known, too, that swimmers had often been bitten on their legs when they stopped swimming and stood up to wade ashore. The logical thing to do was to cover up the arms and legs and present only one shapeless object to the surrounding water. There are no protruding areas that might invite an exploratory bite and, with the bottom closed, blood or other

chemicals that might provoke an attack are kept inside. Tests of the Johnson Shark Bag on many species of dangerous sharks have been extremely successful. When devices are made of dark-colored materials, sharks have been found to be reluctant to make close approaches, even when fresh fish are attached to the sides. On land, Johnson Shark Bags can be used as tents, solar stills or sleeping bags. They are potentially valuable pieces of general survival gear. Although the Navy has not adopted the Johnson Shark Bag for use, it is being sold by private manufacturers.

PRACTICAL GUIDELINES

RICHARD MARTIN

Most shark cages are relatively lightweight and employed at or near the surface, where water movement is greatest. When diving in a cage, do not wear fins and keep at least one hand free—if the cage is jostled by an unexpected swell or the ponderous bulk of a highly stimulated great white, you may need to stabilize yourself quickly to avoid being knocked about inside the cage. Such collisions can result in surprisingly painful, long-lasting bruises. Smaller, faster sharks—such as blues and makos—colliding with a cage tend to ricochet off rather than slam it about. Since many dive operators attach baits directly to or very near the cage, take care that your extremities remain inside the protective structure—an excited shark may unwittingly take a nip of a favorite body part you wanted to keep.

When spearfishing, remove speared fish from the water as quickly as possible, as their death throes often attract sharks. Reef sharks can move with astonishing swiftness and deceptively slow-moving offshore sharks, such as the oceanic whitetip, are often dangerously persistent. If you must retain your catch underwater, do not attach speared fishes directly to your body; instead, use a long lanyard or stringer. If a shark contests ownership of a speared fish, prudence dictates unequivocal surrender of your catch—in its natural habitat, a shark has every advantage over a diver: speed, agility, striking range, exquisite senses and sharp teeth.

Underwater photographers should be aware that their craft poses special risks. The optical properties of seawater demand close proximity to a shark to ensure crisp, clear images. This often causes inadvertent intrusion into the animal's kinosphere (or "personal space")—a roughly spherical region with a radius of about two body lengths that it may defend violently if persistently broached. The localized electromagnetic flux of a recharging strobe may elicit investigatory nipping or determined biting on the part of a shark; in at least one well-documented case, the firing of an underwater strobe while photographing a gray reef shark in agonistic display provoked a rapid, slashing attack resulting in serious injuries to the photographer and his dive buddy.

they use their electrical sensors to find prey buried in the sand and in complete darkness. With their electrical sensory system they can also detect the earth's magnetic field, which they may use to determine directions for migrations.

A recent breakthrough in repellents using electrical impulses has been the shark POD (Protective Oceanic Device), which has been tested by the Natal Sharks Board and Ron and Valerie Taylor. This compact piece of equipment can fit onto a scuba diver's gas cylinder and, when activated, creates an electrical field that disorients the shark by disrupting the signals detected by its ampullae of Lorenzini, the detectors used to locate prey. Tests suggest that the POD is not only effective in repelling sharks but also non-injurious, either to sharks or to other marine animals.

As we learn more about sharks, new ideas for repellents will undoubtedly be forthcoming. Some may be successful in protecting people cast away at sea. To date, though, the best advice to anyone floating in the water is to keep calm. Erratic movements may attract sharks. Do not remove shoes or any other clothing. Clothing helps conserve body heat, thereby reducing the onset of exposure.

Do not swim unless necessary. Again, swimming uses up vital energy reserves and can hasten the onset of exposure. Use the Heat Escape Lessening Procedure (HELP), developed by Canadian scientist J. D. Hayward to lessen the effects of exposure. To conserve body heat and reduce the possibility of exposure, tuck the legs up into a crouch as tightly as possible, and hug the body with the arms. If more than one person is present everyone should huddle together to conserve energy. HELP and huddling not only conserve energy, they change the outlines of those floating into shapes less likely to be bitten by sharks.

ABOVE: During World War II the possibility of shipwrecked sailors or downed airmen being attacked by sharks inspired a search for a chemical shark repellent. Shark Chaser, a package of copper acetate and nigrosine dye, was issued to Allied personnel but proved ineffective; some sharks even ate the packages!

LEFT: The battery-powered shark POD is the most effective deterrent yet devised. It generates an electrical field around the diver, disturbing the shark's sensitivity to electrical stimuli. It has proved effective up to 7 meters.

USING SHARKS

A.M. OLSEN

To many people, inspired by hysterical newspaper headlines or sensational movies, sharks symbolize terror: they are portrayed as sinister, silent killing machines, ceaselessly patrolling the oceans in search of human prey. The reality is very different. Sharks are far less dangerous than humans or their inventions and, in fact, provide a host of benefits. Their meat is eaten or used for fertilizer and their fins are made into soup. Oils rich in Vitamin A are extracted from their livers, and anticoagulants from their blood. Their eyes provide corneas for transplants; their cartilage has a number of medical applications. Chances are a shark has provided meat for your table, lubricants for your machines, oil for your plants—even squalene for your cosmetics.

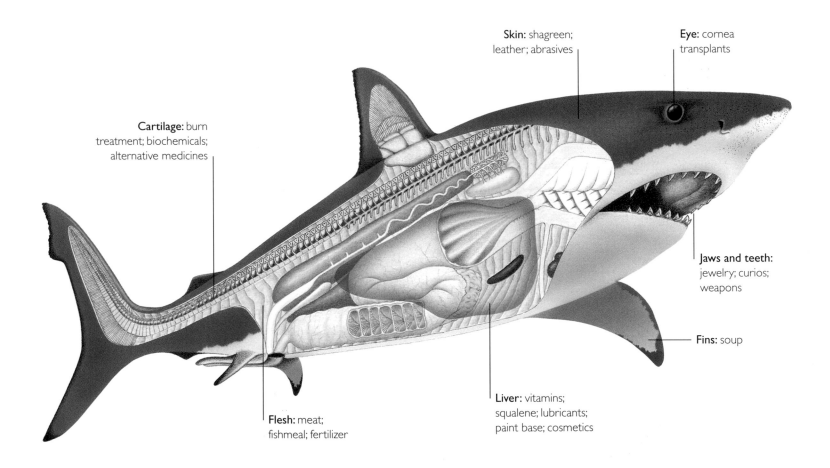

Skin: shagreen; leather; abrasives

Eye: cornea transplants

Cartilage: burn treatment; biochemicals; alternative medicines

Jaws and teeth: jewelry; curios; weapons

Fins: soup

Flesh: meat; fishmeal; fertilizer

Liver: vitamins; squalene; lubricants; paint base; cosmetics

ABOVE: The usable shark. Sharks provide a remarkable array of products useful to humans.

SHARK FISHING: AN AUSTRALIAN CASE STUDY

When the first white settlers arrived at Sydney Cove in New South Wales in 1788 they depended, at least in the short term, on food they had brought with them. They supplemented these scanty resources by fishing. It is known that sharks were caught and eaten, and oil extracted from their livers was used for lighting and other purposes. Liver oil from the sand tiger *Carcharias taurus* was sold in 1794 for one shilling a quart.

As late as 1857 the oil from this same shark was still being used for lighting the tower at the government station on the northern entrance to Botany Bay and in the homes of the nearby villages. At that time imported candles were too costly for general use. The fins of sharks were also used for the sharkfin soup trade. Samuel Lord, merchant of Sydney Cove, advertised in 1804 "for a contractor to supply a quantity of shark fins, properly dried and preserved," presumably for the Chinese market.

In 1851, gold fever gripped the colony and men deserted the coastal settlements in droves to try their luck as gold diggers. Thus there was a dearth of maritime fishing activity and the industry languished for some time. Furthermore,

LEFT: Until World War II sharks were never a significant part of popular mythology. They were known to attack and eat humans but were seen as "chinless cowards" in the words of one naturalist. Their major importance was as competitors for food or as food themselves. This 1881 etching shows a shark being harpooned off the Australian coast.

BELOW: Netting, harpooning and shore-based fishing for sharks were of fluctuating economic importance in the nineteenth century. Shark meat was used for human consumption, skin—or shagreen—for sandpaper, liver oil for lighting and lubrication, and undressed carcases were sold to farmers as fertilizer for their orchards.

ABOVE: The discovery of squalene in 1916 gave fresh impetus to shark hunting, as industry became aware of its value for lubrication in high-technology applications, pharmaceuticals and cosmetics.

BELOW: Near Santa Rosalia on the Baja Peninsula in western Mexico, hammerheads are captured by hook and line and by netting, and are a significant resource in the region's subsistence economy. As well as providing food, sharks caught in this area are utilized for their skins, which are tanned for the manufacture of wallets, belts and other leathergoods.

the discovery of mineral oil reserves in Pennsylvania in the United States in 1859 and aggressive merchandising of this new lighting oil slackened the demand for shark liver oil.

In 1875, when the Reverend Tenison Woods visited the fishing establishment at Recherche Bay, southern Tasmania, he found a depressed situation with the men of the 10 families catching tope sharks *Galeorhinus galeus* for their fins and drying abalone or muttonfish for the Chinese market. Vessels trading between England and China called regularly at both Hobart and Sydney and could pick up consignments of abalone and shark fins to trade in China.

There are few records of the use of elasmobranch resources in Australia between 1875 and the early 1920s. Some fishermen in Tasmania, however, found they could use burley

to attract tope sharks around their vessels. The sharks were gaffed and hauled aboard. This operation took place during the run of gravid females in October–December toward the pupping grounds in protected and sheltered bays and inlets. As much as three or four tonnes of tope shark could be landed by this arduous method in a single day. The undressed carcases were sold to farmers as fertilizers for their orchards and buried around the bases of the trees.

To provide flesh for human consumption a tope shark fishery was established in 1927 at Port Albert in Victoria. A small shipment of 2 tonnes of shark fillets was sent to Melbourne to test market reaction. The response was cautious but further small orders were forthcoming to encourage the fishermen. Within two years other Victorian ports were forwarding small consignments of tope shark to Melbourne markets. Twenty-six tonnes passed through the market in 1929 but the demand was reduced in the Depression years. However in 1934, 115 tonnes were marketed and by 1939 this had risen to 514 tonnes.

The demand for livers, rich in Vitamin A, gave impetus to the fishery. This demand intensified during World War II when the Vitamin A-rich oil was used to fortify rations for Australian troops. In 1942 the catch comprised about 80 percent tope shark, with the remaining 20 percent made up from gummy sharks *Mustelus antarcticus*, whiskery sharks *Furgaleus macki* and sawsharks *Pristiophorus* spp.

Within a decade, however, the demand for livers had disappeared. In 1946 Japanese interests flooded the world's markets with high potency Vitamin A fish liver oil, and in 1950 the marketing of synthetic Vitamin A made shark livers redundant. The Victorian shark fishery continued to operate only for the flesh it supplied to the local markets.

Between 1942 and 1970 the annual shark catch remained around 80 percent tope shark and

20 percent gummy shark, but thereafter the composition changed gradually. By 1993, the year of the peak catch of 4,179 tonnes carcase weight in southeastern Australian waters, gummies represented 65 percent, tope sharks 29.5 percent and other elasmobranchs 5.5 percent. Scientists estimated that the stock of tope sharks had been depleted to 10–25 percent of its original biomass. Measures were taken to peg the annual catch of tope sharks to 550 tonnes. In 1997 further measures were introduced to reduce fishing's effect on the unsustainable stock of tope sharks.

Tope sharks have a low fecundity and a longevity span of more than 60 years. The longevity span was determined from recaptures of a 1948–54 tagging program. Nine tagged tope sharks of both sexes have been recaptured after 33 to 42.5 years of freedom. During a freedom of 42.5 years, the male tope shark increased in length only by 16 centimeters and another male free for 41 years and 9 months increased only 17 centimeters. The remaining recaptured sharks had similar or lower length increments. The period of freedom of 42.5 years represents a world record for any fish or elasmobranch species. The gummy shark is a slightly more fecund species and has a longevity span of 16 years. Under the present management regime, the gummy shark supports a sustainable elasmobranch fishery.

USING THE SKIN

The most characteristic feature of the skin of sharks is its roughness, due to the placoid scales embedded in the skin itself. The scales are variously called "skin teeth" or dermal denticles. Each scale has a flat base and one or more backward-pointed spines—cored with dentine and tipped with ivory or enamel—rising from its upper surface. These scales or denticles are arranged in various patterns over the whole or parts of the body surface. The dried skin is called

shagreen because it is thought to resemble the granular, untanned leather of the same name made from the backs and rumps of horses. The distribution, shape and height of the spines of the denticles determine the purpose for which a particular shagreen is used.

Shagreen was once used for polishing wood. Today, however, glasspaper or carborundum sheets have supplanted it as a smoothing agent. In Sumatra the stretched and dried skin of stingrays *Himantura* spp. is used for the tympanums of drums and tambourines; in certain Pacific Islands shagreen from another stringray is said to be preferred for this purpose. Shagreen from stingrays was used also by traditional swordmakers in Japan for binding onto the hilts of their swords—the surface provided a non-slip grip for the hand.

Certain Moroccan sharks provide shagreen for so-called Boroso leather, which is in great demand in the specialties market. The denticles are not removed but are lightly polished to make an extremely tough and beautiful covering. In the seventeenth century shagreen-covered articles from Asia created immense interest and were in great demand. European artisans soon learned the art of using this treated shagreen to cover such personal articles as jewelry boxes, spectacle cases and cases for silverware as well as for book bindings. However, despite the beauty and durability of the shagreen covering, the fashion for such articles waned and now the "galuchat"— polished shagreen—covered articles are in demand only as antique collectors' items.

People have known for centuries how to tan the hides of mammals but it was not until after World War I that two teams of research chemists working independently in the United States found a successful method for tanning the skins of large sharks without denticles. The breakthrough was made by the discovery of a chemical process that could remove the denticles without adversely affecting the tanning properties of the shark hides.

Shark leather has a higher tensile strength than leather made from cattle hides. The

LEFT: Shark liver oil has long been popular in Asia for its medicinal qualities. It is becoming increasingly common in Western societies.

LEFT: Shark skin with its denticles intact is still used as fine sandpaper by craftspeople. With the denticles removed by a special chemical process, sharkskin leather is in demand for applications where, paradoxically, both great tensile strength and flexibility are needed.

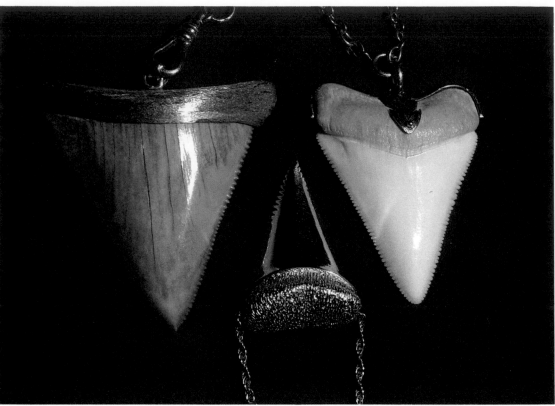

ABOVE AND RIGHT: Not all parts of a shark are used for practical purposes. Shark teeth have traditionally been used for weapons, decoration or ritual, though today they are more likely to be employed in the design of jewelry or curios. A selection of large and expensive "fossil," modern and gold-plated great white shark pendants (right); and a fanciful shell shark (above) manufactured in Taiwan.

intermeshing connective fibers within the skin of sharks are much longer than the fibers in mammal hides. The high collagen content of sharks' connective fibers also facilitates the tanning process.

CORNEAS AND CARTILAGE

Sharks' corneas have been used as successful substitutes for human corneas. It is a peculiar characteristic of shark corneas that they do not swell when placed in varying concentrations of salt solutions. On the other hand, the corneas of bony fish do swell when placed in salt solutions and hence have no value as transplants.

There is an international industry producing powdered shark cartilage of varying quality and price to meet the demands of users of alternative medicine for an anti-inflammatory agent for the treatment of arthritis, wound healing after surgery, and to enhance antibody production, which is claimed to improve the body's immune response against tumors.

There are various land-based methods used to clean cartilage but one novel approach used in Australia is to have the cartilage cleaned by the scavenging habits of sea lice. The cartilage is carefully packed in netting bags, which are taken to sea and lowered to near the bottom where there are known concentrations of free-swimming but carnivorous sea lice, family Cirolanidae. The most efficient species are able to clean out a 30–40 kilogram tope shark in about four hours. After a period of about three days, the nets with clean cartilage are hauled to the surface, drained and taken to a factory where the cartilage is dried

and frozen until processing. High hygiene standards are required to prevent bacterial spoilage. The superfine shark cartilage powder is free of chemicals, coloring, fillers, additives or preservatives.

TEETH AS ARTEFACTS

The use of shark teeth as ornaments has a long history. In the watch-chain and waistcoat era, mounted shark teeth were fashionable as attachments to watch-chains. Fortunately, modern wristwatches do not lend themselves to such adornments!

Even today, mounted whole jaws are popular adornments for the walls of game fishermen's homes and as decorations in places sponsoring marine interests. Mounted jaws of sharks are costly but make good conversation pieces.

Among Pacific Islanders, teeth have been used for both ceremonial and warlike purposes. Swords made from teeth fitted into slots in a wooden strip are fearsome weapons because the serrated edges of the many teeth inflict painful jagged wounds. A shortened version of the same basic design is the double-edged knife.

The teeth of requiem sharks *Carcharhinus* spp. were once in demand for weapons, particularly in Kiribati and Hawaii. The Maoris of New Zealand use the teeth of the broadnose sevengill shark *Notorhynchus cepedianus* to make their war weapons, and the teeth of the mako *Isurus oxyrinchus* are greatly prized as ear ornaments (ngutukao). Traditional Inuit make knives from teeth of the Greenland sleeper shark *Somniosus microcephalus*.

LIVER OILS AND SQUALENE

The liver oils of many sharks have proved a valuable source of Vitamin A, which is essential for the formation of visual purple in the retina of the eye; people whose diet lacks or is deficient in this vitamin are likely to suffer night blindness.

When liver lipids (oils) of bony fishes are treated with alkalis—or saponified—a chemical soap and a free alcohol are formed and only traces of unsaponifiable matter remain. The oils from elasmobranchs are more complex and on saponification not only are soap and alcohols formed but a high concentration of unsaponifiable matter remains as residue. This residue contains the concentrations of long-chain carbon saturated and unsaturated fatty acids and other hydrocarbons present in the oil. Vitamin A occurs in the unsaponifiable fraction of liver oils of fish.

Because of its commercial and therapeutic importance, Vitamin A has been studied intensively to establish its occurrence in the liver oils of different species of teleosts and elasmobranchs and to investigate the effect on its potency of such factors as sex, age, length, maturity, seasonability and geographical distribution. As they do not need Vitamin D for bone growth, elasmobranchs have very low concentrations of this vitamin in their liver oils and correspondingly high levels of the commercially valuable Vitamin A.

The unsaturated terpenic hydrocarbon, squalene is the other major component of the unsaponifiable residue of liver oils. Its presence in liver oils was first recognized in Mediterranean sharks. In 1916, a Japanese chemist isolated this unsaturated hydrocarbon from the livers of sharks and named it squalene. Two years later an English chemist, working independently on liver oils from eastern Atlantic Ocean sharks, also isolated the same hydrocarbon and, not being aware of its previous discovery, named it spinacene. This important constituent of shark livers is now known by its earlier name.

In general, squalene is present in high concentrations of liver oils in those sharks that have low levels of Vitamin A. It is synthesized by the shark, not ingested, and is the precursor of cholesterol. It is also a component of vegetable oils. The concentration of squalene in the liver oils of sharks ranges from 63 to 96 percent in some species, particularly in some deep-sea dogfishes. One deepwater dogfish, the kitefin shark *Dalatias licha*, 1.2 meters long and caught at a depth of 450 meters, had a lipid content of 83 percent, of which 40 percent was squalene. Basking sharks have a squalene content of about 50 percent. Squalene has many commercial applications. It is used in high-technology industries, in cosmetics and also in pharmaceuticals that require a non-oily base.

In recent years attention has been directed to the benefits of controlled diets in combating fatal cardiac arrest. In some ways the incidence of this cardiac condition is associated with increased consumption of dietary fats. Polyunsaturated fatty acids from certain vegetable or marine sources are thought to be beneficial in controlling this disease. The liver oils of deep-sea dogfish have been found not only to have high concentrations

BELOW: Game fishermen are proud of their victories over "fighting" sharks such as great whites, makos and threshers, and often preserve their catches' jaws to commemorate a struggle that may last several hours. Divers also obtain trophies by less honorable means, killing inoffensive species with powerheads.

Weldon Trannies

Neville Coleman

LEFT: Simple butchery, with no justification other than to satisfy the ego, has seen thousands of harmless sharks killed by powerheads. This sand tiger *Carcharias taurus* was killed by trophy hunters, its jaws removed and its valuable flesh and liver (shown here after the carcase was senselessly disemboweled) abandoned.

of squalene but also to be rich in the polyunsaturated fatty acids, docosahexaenoic acid (DHA) and eicosapentaenoic acid (EPA) and low in cholesterol. Both these polyunsaturated long-chain fatty acids are undergoing rigid animal experimentation and results to date show a desirable effect in prolonging blood coagulation time and in lowering cholesterol levels in heart tissue. Inuit have been found to have a longer blood clotting time than Europeans and the reason is believed to be the high level of these polyunsaturated fatty acids in their diet.

SHARKS AS FOOD

Just as sharks cruise in every ocean of the world, so are they a truly international food. Humans have been eating sharks for as long, if not longer, than the fish have been attacking swimmers. In cuisines as different as Serbian and Vietnamese, Jamaican and Javanese, shark has appeared on the menu for centuries. In different cultures, varying preparations give the ubiquitous shark specific local flavor.

A favored Vietnamese preparation calls for lime juice, cilantro and red-hot chillies, giving the dish a distinctive character. In Italian recipes, parsley and Parmesan cheese predominate. But the housewife in Lebanon may use olive oil and capers to give the fish a familiar flavor. The French monks of Chartreuse, famed for their cooking, in medieval times invented a preparation for porbeagle shark that called for the fish to be wrapped in leaves with onions and carrots, then braised. Turkish chefs baked porbeagles with green olives for the edification of the Caliphs. In Melanesia, shark is roasted on hot rocks on the beaches, then eaten with coconut sauce.

The fins of sharks, tough, gristly protuberances with little if any nutritional value, play a unique role in Chinese cuisine. For centuries they have been eagerly sought by gourmets along the coastal provinces as the basis for dishes destined for the table of emperor and mandarin. Today, in such citadels of Chinese gastronomy as Hong Kong and Singapore, wealthy merchants will pay a fortune for specialist dishes, the basis of which is shark fin.

Hong Kong is undoubtedly the biggest world market for shark fins, with 60 or more countries exporting fins to it. Several tonnes of fins from western ports of Mexico are exported annually into the western United States, then re-exported to Hong Kong and other Asian markets. Only the single dorsal, the pectoral fins and the lower lobe of the caudal (tail) fin are acceptable for making soup. The price paid in Hong Kong depends on size, color, species, cut, trim and moisture content of the fins.

In the preparation of shark fins for soup, the skin from both sides is removed and any muscle tissue scraped off to leave clean the inner cartilaginous fin rays and outer horny fibers. Only these horny fibers are used; they are compressed into fibrous mats and added to the stock to provide a glutinous texture to the dish.

Shark has traditionally, although in some secrecy, been a staple food in European, American and Australian food. Disguised under

RIGHT: Sharkfin soup is a traditional and expensive Asian delicacy requiring long hours of careful preparation and cooking.

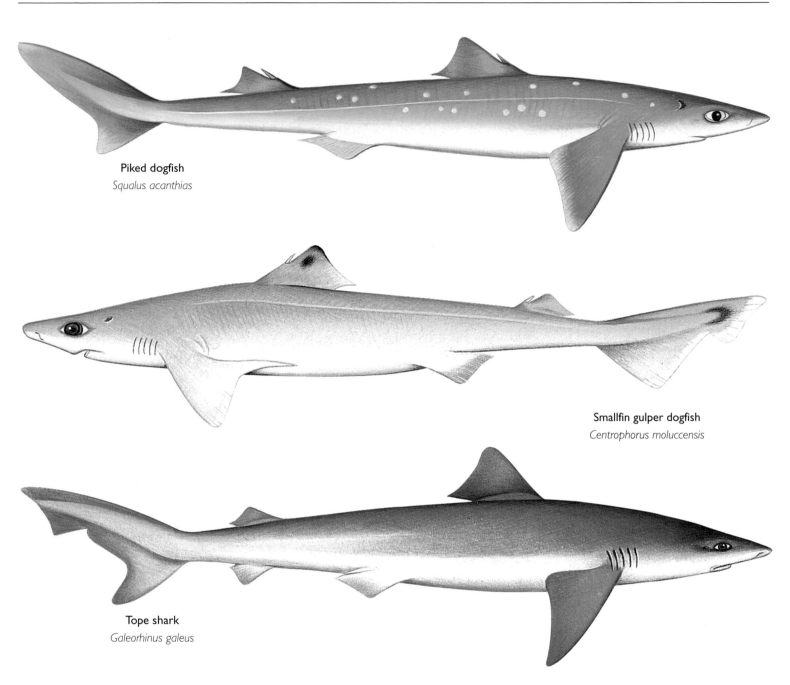

Piked dogfish
Squalus acanthias

Smallfin gulper dogfish
Centrophorus moluccensis

Tope shark
Galeorhinus galeus

such names as dogfish, shark flesh has for centuries been sold in fish markets. The flesh is firm, tasty and nutritious. In the Mediterranean, it is much prized as a delicacy and forms the basis for many a hearty fish stew, simmered with onion and garlic and tomato. In South America, sharks of all varieties are eaten in cuisines from the Yucatan Peninsula of Mexico to the icy shores of the Straits of Magellan. Early explorers wrote in their logs of the wild Indians of frigid Tierra del Fuego roasting shark over fires on the shore.

Greek and Roman gourmets ate shark with enthusiasm and throughout the Mediterranean today, it is a delicacy in many a kitchen. Few places appreciate shark more than Sicily and the island's cooks have a multitude of ways of cooking

the fish. Many of these call for large portions of fish to be casseroled with sharp goat cheese, a preparation which adds a characteristic piquancy to shark.

Why has a fish so universal, so plentiful and so nutritious been regarded for so long by Western diners as distasteful? Presumably because of the fearsome reputation of the shark. No such hesitation exists in most other cultures. Nevertheless, the redemption of the gastronomic reputation of the shark family has occurred in recent years, even in Western cultures. In increasing numbers of trendy restaurants, menu writers are now less coy and label shark dishes by their correct name instead of trying to disguise the dish under a pseudonym.

ABOVE: Although far less impressive than the sharks caught by game fishermen and only 1–2 meters in length, these dogfishes are economically of much greater importance. *Squalus acanthias*, the piked dogfish, is possibly the world's most abundant shark and supports an industry of global significance.

CONSERVING SHARKS

LEONARD J.V. COMPAGNO

*T*here is today wide international recognition of the need to conserve sharks and exploit them rationally, but this attitude is a recent one. Simply put, conserving sharks was not much of an issue before the early 1990s. Here sharks are considered in their broadest sense, to include all cartilaginous fishes: sharks proper; rays or "flat sharks"; and chimaeras, "silver sharks" or "ghost sharks." For every human killed by a shark, 2 million sharks are killed by humans. In other words, 12 million sharks are killed by humans per year compared to six humans by sharks. If we express these statistics as the score of a sports competition it is obvious that the sharks are losing disastrously. And so, in fact, are we humans, because by fishing at this rate we are jeopardizing world populations of apex predators that are essential to the health of marine communities.

Corel Corporation

ABOVE: Nurse sharks are abundant and easy to capture, handle and transport. They therefore have been used as research specimens by biologists. Greater knowledge about sharks is critical to the development of a coherent conservation policy.

LIMITED RESEARCH

Despite early warnings during the 1940s and 1950s of the problems they faced, sharks were overlooked for various reasons by the expanding worldwide conservation movement from the 1960s. The alarm signals stemmed from research in California, Australia and New Zealand on fisheries of tope sharks and elephantfishes, and indicated that the low fecundity of the species being targeted placed a strict limit on their exploitation.

This research was expanded and highlighted by the pioneering work of M. Holden in the United Kingdom in the late 1960s and 1970s. Holden noted that targeted shark fisheries tended to decline rapidly after initial high catches and in some cases collapsed entirely. In many species long maturation times and low fecundity allowed for little reproductive surplus

to compensate for increased mortality through fisheries. Fisheries mortality caused the number of reproductive adults to decline, which in turn caused a decline in recruitment of young to the population, in a cycle that could result in the collapse of fisheries or even extinction of the entire species.

Holden's findings met with limited interest from shark researchers who were often preoccupied with issues such as "shark attack" on people and marine gear, and measures to prevent "attacks." Moreover, a focus developed in some areas on sharks as underutilized resources for human consumption. Sharks were often regarded as "trash fish" of lower value than other fishes or as pests that damaged fishing gear and competed with fisheries for more valuable marine organisms.

The *Jaws* movies in the late 1970s helped to promote an increased and ever-expanding public interest in sharks, at first in the developed world and ultimately worldwide. Ironically, they also resulted in increased capture, killing, utilization and exploitation of sharks in some countries, including the United States. The image of sharks as demonic maneaters did not help the cause of shark conservation during this period, although a few researchers had pointed out in the early 1980s that shark attack was a minuscule issue compared to the vast problem of human attack on sharks in the form of large-scale industrial fisheries.

The negative image of sharks also inhibited shark research, which did not develop the support received by marine vertebrates, such as seabirds and marine mammals, with their positive public images. During the mid 1980s support for shark research hit a trough as funding on issues related to shark attack (including basic research on sensory physiology) dried up. Simply put, sharks were unpopular.

Kevin Deacon

FISHERIES IN DISARRAY

A United States–Japanese workshop on elasmobranchs as living resources was held in Hawaii in 1987, and a volume of its proceedings was published in 1990. This may have been pivotal in focusing on the conservation problems that sharks face from human activities. Detailed information was presented on regional issues of shark fisheries and exploitation, but an attempt was made to focus on conservation issues raised by world shark fisheries utilizing fisheries statistics published by the United Nations Food and Agriculture Organization (FAO) since 1947.

World fisheries catches rose fivefold from the 1940s to the 1990s, but shark fisheries rose only about 3.5 times and the total catch declined about 1 percent in the same period. Although sharks were probably underexploited at the beginning of this period, this was not the case 50 years later as catches declined in many regions and some targeted fisheries collapsed. In the mid 1990s reported catches of sharks and their allies were about 730,000 tonnes worldwide, compared to about 100 million tonnes of all fisheries reported to FAO. Actual catches were estimated as being double the reported catch.

During the past 50 years most of the shark catch was probably taken as bycatch for other marine organisms such as bony fishes, crustaceans and cephalopods. There were also notable increases in targeted shark fisheries during the past two decades that followed the burgeoning

markets for shark products including meat, fins and most recently, cartilage. Some of the shark bycatch was discarded in a minority of maritime countries with limited markets for sharks and by some international high-seas fisheries that targeted far more valuable mackerel-like fishes. However, in most nations and regions sharks are caught, landed, marketed and processed along with other marine organisms and have been so treated for many decades and in some instances for centuries or millennia.

The rising value of shark fins in Asia generated a variety of targeted fisheries and a diffuse but all-pervasive worldwide network to buy, process and distribute fins. More importantly, fins were increasingly harvested as a complementary product of traditional coastal fisheries that utilized sharks for flesh, as well as by offshore international fisheries that had previously discarded sharks but now finned them and disposed of the carcasses.

A major problem with such bycatch fisheries is that they are driven by other, more fecund marine organisms that form the bulk of the catch, and that the sharks affected by such practices could and apparently did decline without affecting catches of the targeted species. Also, some species of sharks were more vulnerable than others: less common, less fecund, and with a longer maturation time. Both targeted shark fisheries and bycatch fisheries could cause the disappearance of those more vulnerable species

ABOVE: A Port Jackson shark and an angelshark caught in a discarded net. Too often, sharks have been killed as unwanted bycatch of commercial fisheries.

ABOVE AND RIGHT: A great white shark is fitted with a tag. Increasingly sophisticated methods of tracing sharks have enabled scientists to study their behavior and migration patterns.

and some rare, restricted or undescribed species have a chance of disappearing before it is recognized that they have problems or even exist.

A DEVELOPING INTEREST

Interest in shark conservation expanded dramatically during the early 1990s in the United States and Europe, and shark conservation increasingly became the subject of symposia, workshops, conferences, newsletters, journals, media articles, and video and movie coverage by filmmakers. The International Union for the Conservation of Nature (IUCN) formed a Shark Specialist Group in the early 1990s, which publishes the newsletter *Shark News*. Dedicated shark conservation journals such as *Chondros* and shark conservation groups such as the SPPA (Shark Preservation and Protection Association) appeared in the early 1990s. In 1977 the Japanese Group (now Society) for Elasmobranch Studies was founded and the American Elasmobranch Society followed in 1985. These professional societies focused on shark research but increasingly addressed conservation issues in the early 1990s. They were joined by the conservation-oriented European Elasmobranch Association in 1996, with several associated organizations including the UK Shark Trust and similar groups in Portugal, Italy, Germany and Switzerland.

The problems of shark conservation caught the interest of other international and national conservation and fisheries organizations. The IUCN Shark Specialist Group began to assess cartilaginous fishes, and is preparing a Red List with IUCN ratings for many species and an action plan for cartilaginous fishes. It also prepared recommendations for the 1997 meeting of CITES, the Convention on International Trade in Endangered Species. Other major organizations became interested in shark conservation, including the World Wide Fund for Nature (WWF), FAO, US National Audubon Society's Ocean Wildlife Campaign, Center for Marine Conservation and the US National Marine Fisheries Service.

In 1995 a paper was published highlighting the vulnerability of freshwater elasmobranchs from overexploitation and habitat destruction, which led to efforts to gain CITES protection for sawfishes and other elasmobranchs that enter fresh water. The World Wide Fund for Nature commissioned its trade monitoring body TRAFFIC to do a global study on the status of world shark fisheries which was published in 1997–98. FAO also began supporting shark conservation and rational utilization, and is currently (1998) preparing its own Action Plan with recommendations to UN nations. National and regional management plans have come into operation in some countries, including the USA, while high-visibility species such as the white

while the more resistant ones persisted and helped to continue the fisheries. Another problem was that the catching process killed, injured or stressed the sharks, adding to their mortality even if they were discarded. Fishermen sometimes killed unwanted sharks if they were still alive.

At least half and possibly over two-thirds of the more than 1,100 species of sharks and their allies figure in fisheries if only as discarded bycatch or low-end products such as fishmeal. These are mostly little studied, in part because they are caught in low numbers and are of little value compared to many commercial bony fishes, cephalopods and crustaceans. Most maritime countries have limited fisheries research organizations and personnel. Facilities and research are generally prioritized to other marine species that generate more value. Fisheries often outstrip knowledge of the biology of the sharks being caught. What is not known is not missed, shark, basking shark, whale shark and sand tiger have been protected in various countries. Regional and national endemics and rare species are now recognized as being vulnerable or endangered and are highlighted for serious conservation efforts.

CURRENT AND FUTURE CONCERNS

Although the global nature of the shark conservation problem is now firmly established and recognized by most nations, the tasks that lie ahead are daunting and difficult. Most nations don't manage their sharks and don't report species-specific data. This will take a major effort to correct and will be difficult to enforce through existing infrastructures and funding bodies, which are often poorly subsidized and overtasked. Most national bycatch and targeted fisheries are essentially out of control, expanding, and driven by increasingly intensive, expensive and sophisticated fisheries that are penetrating new and fragile deepwater habitats for constantly diminishing resources.

Increasing globalization of some shark products is paced by local utilization of others. World fisheries output is apparently flattening out, most major fisheries are overexploited, and fisheries production is being far outstripped by the needs of the burgeoning human population, which has become the ultimate omnivore and threatens all its competitors and all its food sources. With an approximately 28-year doubling time and 5.5 billion population, the hungry mass of humanity portends disaster for world fisheries production, and with it the small fraction that comprises sharks and which is largely stuck in the gears of bycatch fisheries. Other problems sharks face include modification and destruction of habitats, particularly easily accessible rivers, estuaries, coasts and bays that form nursery grounds; reefs; and remote, isolated deepwater habitats such as submarine ridges, seamounts and insular slopes.

Present efforts at shark conservation face a shortfall in expertise. Shark researchers are confronted with an increasing demand for knowledge about all aspects of sharks. However, shark researchers are ridiculously few and are generally overcommitted and poorly subsidized. Many work in inadequate facilities and are deflected by other duties including incessant fundraising and bureaucratic justification of their existence. Many researchers have little opportunity to develop critical mass with research teams at their facilities, and have limited prospects for training new shark researchers.

One dislikes apocalyptic nay-saying, and one can wish that the numerous high-profile efforts in shark conservation are successful, but the problems loom Everest-like and are linked to the ultimate destiny and role of humankind in the world biota. In the modern world of instant information, publicity often equates to reality, but in addition to public relations a vast amount of unglamorous hard work is required to achieve even modest goals in shark conservation. Moreover, our basic biological knowledge of most species is sketchy at best and zero at worst, and a lot of basic research is necessary to address questions of shark conservation.

Shark conservation is in some instances in direct opposition to fisheries interests that have enormous sums invested in doing business as usual, however short-sighted this may be. Well-intentioned conservation measures can be nullified by poor enforcement in the face of growing and ever-lucrative markets for shark products. The value of white shark jaws and teeth has reached levels comparable to elephant tusks and rhino horns, and has raised similar problems with illicit black-market traffic. Large shark fins are not far behind. The rise of shark-based ecotourism and the realization that sharks alive may be more valuable than dead as fisheries products is one hopeful counter to the relentless

BELOW: The whale shark is now protected in some countries. Increasing numbers of divers are experiencing the thrill of diving with these marine giants.

Kevin Deacon

march of the fisheries, as are occasional changing attitudes to sharks in the media that portray them as complex and interesting creatures and not one-dimensional demons.

The most effective approach to shark conservation may come through consumer education and marketing. Although most people know that sharks are fishes, many still do not know that sharks' longevity and rates of reproduction differ from those of other fishes and that consequently sharks cannot be harvested in the same quantities. Since consumers are the ones who generate the demand for a product, an educated consumer might decide that their need for shark products is not great enough to cause the demise of shark populations. Even the bycatch problem could be addressed by consumer boycotts, such as those targeted at driftnet fishing operations in response to the accidental killing of dolphins.

We are presently witnessing a shift in the way people view sharks, from a sinister and expendable resource to a fascinating and ecologically vital inhabitant of our oceans. However, much work remains to be done. It would be tragic if we were responsible for the demise of creatures that have survived so many calamitous upheavals over the past 450 million years.

The alarm has been rung on shark conservation around the world, but future prospects remain uncertain. Are a handful of cartilaginous fishes destined for preservation in reserves and artificial habitats like terrestrial predators? Are many other species doomed to extinction? Have a few species in the Old World tropics become extinct already? Possibly, but hopefully not. Of special concern are the effects of loss of cartilaginous fishes to marine ecosystems. Sharks are varied in their roles in marine environments, and range from plankton feeders to high-level predators. Their decline or loss may have negative repercussions on other marine life far beyond their relatively low biomass. One can hope for and work for the survival of sharks in an increasingly difficult world; the alternative is appalling.

Corel Corporation

ABOVE: A blacktip reef shark cruises in its natural habitat. The protection of sharks is now on the international conservation agenda.

RIGHT: A diver explores a strand of coral in the Red Sea. Increasingly, sharks are being seen as tourist attractions rather than animals to be slaughtered.

Corel Corporation

THREATENED SPECIES

Several species of sharks that gather in coastal waters to feed or breed are regarded as vulnerable. Notably, large, maturing or mature great whites are easily caught when feeding around seal-breeding colonies. The decline in abundance of the great white has led to protection in South Africa, Namibia, the Maldives and several states of the United States and Australia. The sand tiger *Carcharias taurus* is protected in New South Wales and Queensland, Australia.

Dogfishes and chimaeras inhabiting the continental slopes are taken as bycatch in several bottom-trawl fisheries. Much of the catch of these species is either discarded dead, or not recorded. Like many of the bony fishes studied from these deeper and colder waters, the dogfishes are likely to be particularly long-lived and to have relatively few young. Given the limited areas occupied by these species, and the intensity of fishing, some of the species of dogfish and chimaera are at risk of severe depletion in some regions.

Some of the most threatened species of sharks are those occurring in freshwater habitats. These species are more vulnerable than those inhabiting marine waters, partly because the amount of fresh water in rivers and lakes is small compared with the amount of seawater on earth. Moreover, tropical rivers and lakes where freshwater species occur are mostly in developing countries with large and expanding human populations. Such areas are much more vulnerable to exploitation than marine waters. The Ganges shark *Glyphis gangeticus* is known only from the Ganges–Hooghly River system of the Indian subcontinent, although it is possible that more than one species of *Glyphis* occurs in the region of New Guinea, northern Australia and Borneo.

As sharks are being killed for so many reasons, there is no single solution to the decline in their numbers. Governments need to develop and enforce a global approach to shark management, perhaps in the same way the United Nations successfully banned the use of driftnets on the high seas. Other important conservation measures may include developing techniques and fishing gear that reduce the numbers of sharks caught by fisheries targeting other fishes. Unfortunately, any attempt to radically overhaul fishing methods would be likely to encounter stiff resistance from commercial operators.

BELOW: The sand tiger is now protected in two Australian states.

Jeff Rottman

DIVING WITH SHARKS

RICHARD MARTIN

Although sharks are not the ravenous killers so often portrayed in film and literature, they must be respected and not provoked by divers and observers. All those who dive with sharks—or observe them from the safety of a cage— should heed the 10-point advice below.

Understand and respect the environment. Find out what kinds of sharks you are likely to encounter where you are diving and learn what to expect of each species' behavior. Remember that diver safety becomes more difficult with decreasing visibility—at night or in muddy water—and with increasing depth and currents, also with increasing number of sharks and their level of stimulation. Make adequate provision for carrying equipment such as an underwater camera or speargun. The ocean itself is far more dangerous than any shark. Know, and dive within, your own limitations. Be thoroughly familiar with—and practise—logistics and contingency plans before you enter the water. Enter the water quietly, using a controlled seated entry rather than a spectacular and distruptive "giant stride" entry. Sharks may react with great excitement to the commotion created by such splashy entries.

Be a good guest. You are a visitor in the shark's domain. The shark is a wild animal that may defend itself if it feels threatened, although it will probably simply swim away, rather than attack you. Allow any shark you meet to investigate you on its own terms. Do not touch, corner or chase the shark.

Keep still. Remain as motionless as possible, preferably on or near the bottom, where you may be perceived by the shark to be part of the natural seafloor topography. Quick movement may cause the shark to become fearful and thus provoke a defensive attack. Avoid making direct eye contact with the shark. Try to watch it from "the corner of your eyes." Nevertheless, it is important not to lose sight of the shark. Remain vigilant for several minutes after the shark is out of sight, to make sure that it has, in fact, gone.

Reduce your vertical profile. Sharks often seem more unnerved by height than length. Reduce your vertical profile by crouching down on or near the bottom, or orient yourself horizontally in the water column.

Avoid clustering with other divers. Sharks seem to perceive tightly packed groups of divers as a single, large, noisy, unfamiliar and therefore frightening organism. Remain close enough to your buddy to ensure mutual safety, but keep a distance from other divers. Solo diving with sharks should be left to the professionals.

Take advantage of the shark's natural curiosity. Try humming quietly into your regulator, clinking two rocks together or clanging the butt of your dive knife against your scuba tank. These simple techniques can sometimes lure a curious shark closer to investigate. A brightly colored camera housing or reef gloves may also help pique a shark's curiosity—but do not gesture while wearing such gloves as they may look edible to a shark.

Do not use bait or attempt to feed a shark while underwater. Feeding situations radically change the nature of a shark's investigative behavior, and may lure other sharks. Under these conditions, a shark encounter can change from evocative to dangerous in a fraction of a second. Leave shark feeding and working with baited sharks to the professionals.

Observe and respond to the shark's behavior. If a shark appears agitated—with jerky movements, pectoral fins held stiffly downward, abrupt changes in swimming style and an increase in muscular tension—or otherwise begins to swim in an erratic manner, leave the water immediately, following the guidelines outlined below. The shark will then either make good its escape

RIGHT: A diver observes mating Port Jackson sharks. Divers are visitors to the shark's domain, and must understand and respect their environment.

Kevin Deacon

Kevin Deacon

or return to its former, more languid and non-threatening cruising style.

Be aware of the behavior of other marine creatures. If fishes and other creatures in the immediate area suddenly dive for cover or begin to behave erratically, leave the water immediately (following the guidelines outlined below). Trust your instincts—if something doesn't feel right about the situation, head for the surface.

Leave quietly. If you need to surface while a shark is in your immediate vicinity, move slowly and deliberately, never losing sight of the shark. Swim directly to your pre-planned exit site. Avoid a long surface swim, which is tiring and may leave you vulnerable to attack from below. When you arrive at your exit point, leave the water smoothly but efficiently.

ABOVE: Coming face to face with a whale shark can be an exhilarating experience. Care must be taken to avoid accidental injury.

RIGHT: The silky shark is widely distributed in tropical and warm temperate waters.

Corel Corporation

OBSERVING SHARKS

Kevin Deacon
Leighton R. Taylor Jr.

The following pages list 20 places where you may come face to face with a shark in its own marine habitat. Sharks can be found in all the world's oceans, but they can sometimes be hard to locate. In some areas, access to sharks may be fairly easily gained, and little planning is required. Caribbean reef sharks in the Bahamas, for example, can be found there all year round, and day trips provided by local dive centers or dive resorts will virtually guarantee sightings. However, many species are not only unique to the waters of certain countries, but they may gather in an area for only limited seasons. The whale sharks at Ningaloo Reef in Western Australia are an excellent example of this—they congregate there only during late March, April and May. To experience the thrill of diving with them may involve traveling long distances, and proper timing of your trip is critical. Some sharks are found in remote locations. For example, to see the silvertip sharks in Papua New Guinea or the sharks in the Galapagos Islands, you may have to take a trip on a live-aboard dive boat for seven to 10 days to reach the area.

Careful planning is essential to ensure that your encounters with sharks are safe, environmentally sound, exciting and memorable. Some dive operations feature dive-guides that hand feed sharks. In extreme cases, sport-divers are invited to hold or touch smaller sharks. Biologists strongly advise against this interruption of the shark's natural behavior—and not just for the danger it presents to divers. They are more concerned with changing the behavior and ecology of sharks by "training" them to approach divers and to gather at the sound of boat engines. The best course of action is to relax and observe sharks without interacting with them.

BELOW: Hammerheads are widely distributed in the Atlantic and Pacific oceans. Large schools can be seen off the western coast of Mexico.

SAN DIEGO, UNITED STATES OF AMERICA

When to visit Best diving conditions Apr–Sept
Weather Temperate year-round; summer mornings can be foggy, clearing by midday; rain and rough conditions most likely Dec–Feb
Water temperature 15–21° C
Dive logistics Cage diving with scuba gear from day boats or live-aboards for trips of three days; pre-booking essential; shore diving and snorkeling around kelp beds and rocky points
Accommodation A wide selection is available in San Diego, ranging from budget motels to bed and breakfast guesthouses and five-star resorts

KONA COAST, HAWAII, UNITED STATES OF AMERICA

When to visit Fine year-round; humpback whale season Dec–May
Weather Warm days and cool nights; 21–29° C; gentle to brisk northeast trade winds; rainy Dec–Feb
Water temperature 23–28° C
Hazards Venomous animals include medusae and Portuguese man-of-war
Dive logistics Snorkeling from shore; day boats and live-aboards for week-long trips (pre-booking essential) offer access to sites along the Kona Coast
Accommodation A wide range, from beach camping and budget hotels to five-star resorts

Notes Bernice P. Bishop Museum, the archive of Hawaiian culture in Honolulu, has many artefacts relating to sharks. The University of Hawaii has conducted research on sharks for more than 50 years. Selected results are displayed at the University's Waikiki Aquarium in Honolulu, along with a fine collection of living species. The aquarium is a good place to see sharks without getting wet.

SEA OF CORTEZ, MEXICO

When to visit Year-round; preferred diving season June–Dec
Weather Generally temperate to hot; 38° C or more June–Sept; strong winds and tropical storms occur infrequently May–Oct
Water temperature 21–27° C June–Nov; 16–21° C Dec–May
Hazards Variable weather conditions and occasional strong tidal currents
Dive logistics Day boats operate from La Paz and Cabo San Lucas; live-aboards offer 3–10 day excursions to Gulf Islands; pre-booking advised
Accommodation La Paz has a full range, from pensions, comfortable hotels, to high-rise luxury hotels

REVILLAGIGEDO ISLANDS, MEXICO

When to visit Nov–May only, to avoid stormy

Pacific waters and seasonal problems caused by offshore location
Weather Tropically warm; often windy
Water temperature 21–27° C
Hazards Strong currents, rough water, and the remoteness of the location
Dive logistics Large, comfortable live-aboards only; book well in advance; boats depart from San Diego, USA, or Cabo San Lucas, which is closer
Accommodation Cabo San Lucas offers a range of accommodation from lodges to luxury hotels

COCOS ISLAND, COSTA RICA

When to visit Mar–Sept
Weather Cocos Island can be wet; offshore weather can be windy, with rough seas; trust the skipper to make a safe crossing and find the lee
Water temperature Varies with currents; surface can be 27–28° C, with thermoclines dropping to 18–21° C
Hazards Strong currents and deep diving in a remote area
Dive logistics Live-aboards for 11-day trips, offering 7 full days of diving; advance bookings with dive charter operators are necessary
Accommodation Large, comfortable live-aboard vessels are necessary because of the long ocean passage to Cocos Island; they accommodate between 12 and 22 divers

Notes This is a trip for avid and experienced divers only.

THE BAHAMAS

When to visit Year-round; summer is hot, but the sea refreshes
Weather Influenced by trade winds; cooler Nov–Apr, warmest June–Sept; watch forecasts for tropical storms
Water temperature From 21–24° C in Feb to

ABOVE: Reef sharks are a favorite of divers and photographers. The stocky, graceful Caribbean reef sharks abound in the Bahamas.

28–31° C in Sept
Dive logistics Day trips from Grand Bahamas and New Providence; live-aboards also; booking essential
Accommodation A wide range even on remote cays, from camping and comfortable dive lodges to luxury hotels; Walker Cay on Abaco Island has shore-side accommodation near Shark Rodeo

GALAPAGOS ISLANDS, ECUADOR
When to visit Year-round, but best in late Feb–May
Weather Equatorial; warm to hot; cooler season from May–Dec; hotter season Jan–May
Water temperature Variable with location and depth; from 18–27° C
Hazards Blue-water diving with strong currents; this is not for novices
Dive logistics Live-aboards only; book packages through dive operators
Accommodation: Live-aboards only, booking essential; hotels and guesthouses at Puerto Ayora, Santa Cruz Island, but little or no diving support

Notes Be aware of the political climate in Ecuador; check government advisories.

RIGHT: The whitetip reef shark can be found in caves off the Galapagos Islands and Hawaii.

BELOW: Observing a great white close up is the archetypal shark diver's experience.

Corel Corporation

Ron and Valerie Taylor

ISLE OF MAN, UNITED KINGDOM
When to visit June to early Sept
Weather Cool, maritime climate influenced by the warm Gulf Stream; cool summers, 16–20° C
Water temperature 16° C
Hazards Avoid becoming chilled
Dive logistics Day trips on local dive boats and as volunteers with a well-organized research project, the Isle of Man Basking Shark Project; look up its website at http://www.isle-of man.com/interests/shark/index.htm
Accommodation Hotels and guesthouses; special packages can be pre-booked through travel agents and dive operators

RAS MUHAMMAD, EGYPT
When to visit Best diving conditions during warm months, June–Oct; more variable visibility and risk of rough seas during cool season, Nov–Feb; sharks and manta rays more in evidence during the mating season, Dec–Feb
Weather Arid desert climate, hot days, cooler at night; very little rain; cool winds during Nov–Feb make days cool and nights quite cold
Water temperature 21–28° C
Dive logistics Day boats, live-aboards, and shore-based diving from jeeps; pre-booking recommended
Accommodation Excellent range, from budget hotels to five-star resorts

Notes Very cosmopolitan dive travelers; be prepared for many different diving techniques and attitudes. Heed any political advisories for Egypt and neighboring countries.

CAPE TOWN, SOUTH AFRICA
When to visit High season Feb–Sept, almost 100% likelihood of sightings; low season Oct–Jan, about 80% likelihood
Weather Usually pleasant, temperate; sometimes stormy and windy, or still and foggy
Water temperature 14–18° C
Dive logistics Day boats; day trips from Cape Town; overnight trips or 10-day excursions based at Gansbaai; book through dive operators
Accommodation A range of accommodation in Cape Town; guesthouses at Gansbaai, some self-catering

Notes During winter (June–Aug), high shark activity, but weather only permits trips to the island one or two days a week.

SIMILAN AND SURIN ISLANDS, THAILAND
When to visit Best during the dry season, Nov–Apr; sunny, calm seas
Weather Tropical climate, 25–31° C
Water temperature 26–28° C
Hazards Conditions are very wet during the monsoon season in Sept.

Dive logistics Snorkeling or scuba diving from live-aboard boats for trips of 2–12 days; pre-booking recommended

Accommodation A wide range of resorts, hotels and guesthouses is available in Phuket

YAP AND PALAU, MICRONESIA
When to visit Year-round

Weather Good year-round; trade winds May–Nov

Water temperature 28–30° C

Hazards Be extra alert when wreck diving; poisonous spiny trees on Palau, but only encountered if you hike inland to "jellyfish lakes" (highly recommended but no sharks)

Dive logistics Day boats and live-aboards from all islands; a live-aboard amphibious airplane based at Palau visits outer islands, including Yap. Pre-booking before departure essential

Accommodation Palau has luxury hotels; Yap and Truk have comfortable hotels and lodge accommodation

Notes Yap offers best combination of indigenous culture and dive sites. Nitrox and rebreathers, and training in their use, are available on Yap and Truk.

RANGIROA ATOLL, FRENCH POLYNESIA
When to visit Year-round, but best Nov–Apr

Weather Excellent, although trade winds can blow strongly across low-lying atoll; sun protection is always necessary

Water temperature Up to 27° C

Dive logistics Day boats essential to dive the passes; pre-book through local Polynesian dive shops; also live-aboards

Accommodation Packages from Tahiti by air include live-aboards or, more frequently, lodge-like shore accommodation; booking essential

Notes Strong currents make pass diving a challenge for beginning divers, and local guides expect some experience. Plan your trip carefully to permit ample diving between the infrequently scheduled flights.

MAMANUCA ISLANDS, FIJI
When to visit Year-round; best weather in dry season (May–Oct)

Weather Daytime temperatures 20–30° C; mild, dry May–Oct; wetter, warmer Nov–Apr (wet season); highest rainfall and humidity in Jan–Feb; east–southwest trade wind

Water temperature 27–28° C from Nov–Apr; 25–26° C May–Oct

Hazards Stonefish and medusae

Dive logistics Snorkeling and scuba diving from the shore, live-aboards or day boats; booking essential

Accommodation There is a full range of

Kevin Deacon

accommodation, from thatched fales to comfortable lodges and resorts; some resorts cater exclusively to the needs of divers

Notes Fiji is friendly and hospitable and has a rich culture. The region abounds with a variety of sharks, and the reef system for the most part has not been damaged.

VALERIES REEF, PAPUA NEW GUINEA
When to visit All year round

Weather Very warm, tropical; no distinct wet season

Water temperature 26–28° C

Hazards Malaria

Dive logistics Scuba diving from day boats or live-aboards; the snorkeling is excellent, but is not recommended where there are sharks

ABOVE: The zebra shark is a widespread tropical species. These non-threatening sharks allow divers to come very close.

ABOVE: Small sharks are common inhabitants of tropical reefs. Photographing them is challenging but the results can be spectacular.

Accommodation Hotels in Kavieng; excellent live-aboards, booking essential

Notes Heed security advisories, particularly in the capital, Port Moresby. This is the most famous site in the world for silvertip sightings.

NINGALOO REEF, AUSTRALIA
When to visit Late March to early May
Weather Warm, tropical, very sunny; afternoon sea breezes
Water temperature 23–26° C
Hazards Occasional cyclones
Dive logistics Snorkeling or scuba diving from day boats; some live-aboard boats, but not essential for good access
Accommodation Hotels, caravans and camp sites in Exmouth

Notes Avoid operators without spotter planes. Book your dive tours and accommodation before departure. Plan a minimum of five days' diving to guarantee many encounters

NEPTUNE ISLANDS, AUSTRALIA
When to visit Jan–May
Weather Temperate; very changeable from calm and hot to windy and cold; calm to quite rough seas
Water temperature 16–19° C
Hazards Seals can be aggressive when ashore; seek local advice
Dive logistics Cage diving with snorkel or scuba gear from live-aboard dive boats, trips from 3–16 days; pre-booking essential

Notes No guarantees; best shark sightings May–March

GREAT BARRIER REEF, AUSTRALIA
When to visit Good conditions almost year-round; occasional strong winds; cyclone season late Dec–Apr
Weather Warm to very hot, tropical conditions; consistently dry, except during the cyclone, or wet, season
Water temperature 22° C in southern Queensland to 28° C in northern Queensland; cooler June–Aug
Hazards Venomous animals include the lionfish, stonefish, sea snakes, box jellyfish (or sea wasp), cone shell and blue-ring octopus. None is aggressive and accidents are rare, but learn to identify these species and their behavior

Dive logistics Day boats (be prepared for long trips to get out to the reef); live-aboards, trips of 4–8 nights, mostly from Cairns and Townsville, pre-booking recommended as the area is a popular tourist site.

Accommodation From camping to five-star resorts ashore or on coastal islands; also on several islands out on the reef; pre-booking recommended

Notes Shark feeding is not permitted inside the Marine Park.

LEFT: A diver feeds a gray reef shark. one of the most common species of Indo-Pacific coral reefs.

NEW SOUTH WALES, AUSTRALIA
When to visit Year-round
Weather Warm Oct–Mar, cool Apr–Sept; no distinct rainy season; unpredictable
Water temperature 14–21° C
Hazards Rough seas during periods of strong offshore winds
Dive logistics Forster: day boats only; Jervis Bay: live-aboards or day boats, both offering equally good access
Accommodation Good quality hotels, guesthouses, camping, and caravan sites at all locations

Notes An excellent region for self-driving, camping, and exploring a diverse range of dive locations and sighting the plentiful marine species.

LORD HOWE ISLAND, AUSTRALIA
When to visit Nov–May
Weather Cool, tropical summer, Oct–May; occasional unpredictable strong winds and regular rainfall; no distinct wet season
Water temperature 20–24° C
Hazards The banded scalyfin, a very aggressive small fish, has a bite that can draw blood; swim away from its territory
Dive logistics Glass-bottom boats and day boats for snorkeling or scuba diving; pre-book during peak season, Dec–Jan
Accommodation Small resorts and guesthouses, fully catered or self-catering; pre-book Dec–Jan

Notes Only 400 tourists are allowed on the island at one time. Pack a waterproof coat for rainy spells and a warm jacket for cool evenings.

A MATTER OF PERCEPTION

Biological illustration has changed dramatically over the centuries. Today's illustrators are trained to study specimens and understand principles of anatomy. Contemporary scientific illustration contrasts markedly with the often fanciful interpretations of the past.

The craftsman who labored to create the etching of the blue shark, below right, positioned it conveniently on a rock with a suitably appropriate backdrop. A fearsome set of teeth was added for effect. Nevertheless, there are enough similarities with a "real" blue shark to suggest that the artist had actually seen specimens.

BLUE SHARK.
BBC Hulton Picture Library

PHOTOGRAPHING SHARKS

MARTY SNYDERMAN

Most species of sharks make wonderful photographic subjects. To the eyes of underwater photographers, sharks are swift, powerful, sleek, exciting and potentially dangerous predators. It is difficult to imagine a more dramatic subject for a wildlife photographer than a large shark swimming, mouth agape, teeth exposed, as it attacks its prey. Even when it is simply cruising, the shark's hydrodynamic design creates a potential for images that most photographers can only dream about.

And yet, while many sport divers encounter sharks on a regular basis, only a comparative handful of underwater photographers ever aquire top-quality pictures. It may seem that it is the threat of being bitten that keeps photographers from getting close to sharks but, in fact, it is usually the sharks who won't approach divers.

What makes shark photography different and difficult?

Marty Snyderman

Perhaps the most fundamental difference between filming potentially dangerous predators on land and filming sharks is that underwater photographers must be very close to their subjects to achieve the desired results. The best underwater photographers use wide-angle lenses and get as close as possible to their subjects in order to shoot through as little water, and therefore as few suspended particles, as possible. How close is close? Three meters is about as far away as an underwater photographer can ever work unless he or she is shooting silhouettes. And getting closer means even better pictures.

If you examine some photographs of sharks you might question whether the photographer was further than 3 meters from the subject when he or she tripped the shutter. Keep in mind that the perspective created by the use of wide-angle lenses is different from that of your eyes. Even in crystal-clear, shallow, tropical water you can count on the fact that if the image is of good quality and is not a silhouette, the photographer was within 3 meters of the shark. It might help to put the underwater photographer's problem in perspective if you realize that while 60-meter visibility is exceptional when filming underwater, in similar conditions on land, airports are closed because of restricted visibility.

And no matter how much visibility one has, water is a selective filter of the color spectrum. At depth, photographers have a difficult time trying to create visual separation between photographic subjects and backgrounds, regardless of whether the background is water or reef. In addition, many species of sharks are countershaded, being darkly colored on top and lightly colored on the underside, in order to blend in with their surroundings. If you film a shark from above, looking down on to its darkly colored back, the animal will blend in with the dark water or reef below. The opposite is true if your perspective is looking upward. Countershading is an obvious advantage to predators and prey alike. But for underwater photographers, the separation problems created by countershading and the physics of light in the water combine to make it extremely challenging to obtain quality photographs. Shark photographers occasionally work from inside a protective cage that can be lowered and raised. However, most of us who make our living in this field do our best work when filming from the outside, so that is where we prefer to be. This holds true whether we are working with large groups of scalloped hammerheads in Mexico's Sea of Cortez, lemon sharks on the sand flats of the Bahamas, blue sharks in the middle of nowhere at two in the morning and when filming great white sharks in South Australia.

It is not easy to swim face-to-face with a shark, simply because many sharks will not allow a diver to get close. The best way to close the gap is for the photographer to use bait, often called chum. But it is important to understand that chumming come at a cost. Normally sharks are not the proverbial frenzied feeding machines portrayed in Hollywood films. But when aroused, they can become boldly aggressive, and when excited, many species are among the ocean's fastest swimmers. Most sharks swim rather slowly when not feeding in order to conserve energy, but when offered food, their behavior often changes dramatically.

Potentially dangerous situations do exist when hungry sharks become excited, and it is imperative for divers to be fully aware of the exact location of the food source. Sharks almost always approach a bait from the down current side (or downwind side, if wind is causing a boat to drift in mid-ocean, which creates a bait slick downwind from the boat). When swimming in the baited corridor, sharks are stimulated by the presence of food, and it is easy to understand how a diver who is in the corridor close to the bait might be mistaken for the food source. But sharks are not indiscriminate feeders and the difference in being in the odor corridor and being a meter in front of the boat, and being a meter on the upcurrent side is like the difference between night and day. I am convinced that even in baited situations, most shark "attacks" are mistakes. The sharks understandably believe they are biting at a natural food source and, in their excited state, mistakenly bite a diver.

Filming sharks from outside a shark cage while suspended over hundreds of meters of water in the middle of nowhere is a demanding diving situation, to say the least. In mid-ocean there is no apparent bottom to help divers get their bearings. There is only blue-black water below and lighter water and sunshine near the surface. Currents and drifts are difficult to detect, and it is all too easy to become involved in setting up just one more shot only to turn around after you trip the shutter and not be able to see your boat, the shark cage, or your diving buddies, who have been wise enough to remain close to the cage. Being alone in the middle of the ocean surrounded by a large group of baited sharks is about as empty a feeling as one can experience.

Marty Snyderman

The development of the stainless steel Neptunic anti-shark suit has been of real benefit to shark photographers. The suit is made of approximately 400,000 electronically welded stainless steel links backed up by solid Culver plates. While the suit cannot prevent injury from all species of sharks, it does make working with sharks less than 100 kilos and under 3 meters long much safer. Photographers wearing the suit can work suspended almost motionless in the water column outside a cage rather than being bounced around in a cage that is jolted every time a wave passes overhead or the boat rocks with the swell. Cages do not make steady platforms, and even in moderate wind and swell being inside one is rather like being inside a washing machine.

The weight of the Neptunic suit made for a diver 2 meters tall and of average build is nearly 8 kilos. In temperate water divers can simply exchange their weight belt for a shark suit without any significant changes in buoyancy. However, the suit is difficult to swim in because of its bulk and the increased drag. Muscle cramps are common. Divers using the suit must realize that in an emergency they no longer have the option of dropping their weight belt in order to float to the surface. Getting out of the suit

in an underwater emergency would be virtually impossible. But there can be no doubt that all the extra effort is worthwhile the first time a shark chomps down on the suit and you escape without a scratch.

Most underwater photographers use Nikonos cameras and wide-angle lenses to take still photographs of sharks. Nikonos 15 mm, 20 mm or 28 mm lenses are popular. Nikonos cameras are rangefinder cameras, not single lens reflex (SLR) systems. Prefocused point-and-shoot cameras are much easier to use than SLRs, especially when filming from outside a cage. Trying to keep your focusing eye glued to the viewfinder of an SLR system without flinching while the viewfinder fills up with the face of a great white shark is a task that requires an incredible amount of discipline and courage. When looking through the viewfinder, photographers can easily lose their perspective of size and distance, and experienced shark photographers know how dangerous the viewfinder illusion can be. Even large sharks swimming only a few meters away can look deceptively small and rather far away through a viewfinder. But when you look over the camera instead of through the lens, reality hits hard.

CHECKLIST OF LIVING SHARKS

Leonard J. V. Compagno

ORDER HEXANCHIFORMES
SIXGILL, SEVENGILL AND FRILLED SHARKS

FAMILY CHLAMYDOSELACHIDAE—FRILLED SHARKS

Chlamydoselachus anguineus . . . . Frilled shark

FAMILY HEXANCHIDAE—SIXGILL AND SEVENGILL SHARKS

Heptranchias perlo . . . . Sharpnose sevengill shark
Hexanchus griseus . . . . Bluntnose sixgill shark
Hexanchus nakamurai . . . . Bigeye sixgill shark
Notorynchus cepedianus . . . . Broadnose or spotted sevengill shark

ORDER SQUALIFORMES
DOGFISH SHARKS

FAMILY ECHINORHINIDAE—BRAMBLE SHARKS

Echinorhinus brucus . . . . Bramble shark
Echinorhinus cookei . . . . Prickly shark

FAMILY SQUALIDAE—DOGFISH SHARKS

Cirrhigaleus asper . . . . Roughskin spurdog
Cirrhigaleus barbifer . . . . Mandarin dogfish
Squalus acanthias . . . . Piked dogfish
Squalus blainvillei . . . . Longnose spurdog
Squalus brevirostris . . . . Japanese shortnose spurdog
Squalus cubensis . . . . Cuban dogfish
Squalus japonicus . . . . Japanese spurdog
Squalus megalops . . . . Shortnose spurdog
Squalus melanurus . . . . Blacktail spurdog
Squalus mitsukurii . . . . Shortspine spurdog
Squalus rancureli . . . . Cyrano spurdog

FAMILY CENTROPHORIDAE—GULPER DOGFISH

Centrophorus acus . . . . Needle dogfish
Centrophorus atromarginatus . . . . Blackfin gulper dogfish
Centrophorus granulosus . . . . Gulper dogfish
Centrophorus harrissoni . . . . Dumb gulper dogfish
Centrophorus isodon . . . . Dark gulper dogfish
Centrophorus lusitanicus . . . . Lowfin gulper dogfish
Centrophorus moluccensis . . . . Smallfin gulper dogfish
Centrophorus niaukang . . . . Taiwan or giant gulper dogfish
Centrophorus squamosus . . . . Leafscale gulper dogfish
Centrophorus tesselatus . . . . Mosaic gulper dogfish
Deania calcea . . . . Birdbeak dogfish
Deania hystricosum . . . . Rough longnose dogfish
Deania profundorum . . . . Arrowhead dogfish
Deania quadrispinosum . . . . Longsnout dogfish

FAMILY ETMOPTERIDAE—LANTERNSHARKS

Aculeola nigra . . . . Hooktooth dogfish
Centroscyllium excelsum . . . . Highfin dogfish
Centroscyllium fabricii . . . . Black dogfish
Centroscyllium granulatum . . . . Granular dogfish
Centroscyllium kamoharai . . . . Bareskin dogfish
Centroscyllium nigrum . . . . Combtooth dogfish
Centroscyllium ornatum . . . . Ornate dogfish
Centroscyllium ritteri . . . . Whitefin dogfish
Etmopterus baxteri . . . . New Zealand lanternshark
Etmopterus bigelowi . . . . Blurred smooth lanternshark
Etmopterus brachyurus . . . . Shorttail lanternshark
Etmopterus bullisi . . . . Lined lanternshark
Etmopterus carteri . . . . Cylindrical lanternshark
Etmopterus compagnoi . . . . Brown lanternshark
Etmopterus decacuspidatus . . . . Combtooth lanternshark
Etmopterus gracilispinis . . . . Broadband lanternshark
Etmopterus granulosus . . . . Southern lanternshark
Etmopterus hillianus . . . . Caribbean lanternshark
Etmopterus litvinovi . . . . Smalleye lanternshark
Etmopterus lucifer . . . . Blackbelly lanternshark
Etmopterus molleri . . . . Slendertail lanternshark
Etmopterus perryi . . . . Dwarf lanternshark

Etmopterus polli . . . . African lanternshark
Etmopterus princeps . . . . Great lanternshark
Etmopterus pusillus . . . . Smooth lanternshark
Etmopterus pycnolepis . . . . Densescale lanternshark
Etmopterus schultzi . . . . Fringefin lanternshark
Etmopterus sentosus . . . . Thorny lanternshark
Etmopterus spinax . . . . Velvet belly
Etmopterus splendidus . . . . Splendid lanternshark
Etmopterus tasmaniensis . . . . Tasmanian lanternshark
Etmopterus unicolor . . . . Brown lanternshark
Etmopterus villosus . . . . Hawaiian lanternshark
Etmopterus virens . . . . Green lanternshark
Miroscyllium sheikoi . . . . Rasptooth dogfish
Trigonognathus kabeyai . . . . Viper dogfish

FAMILY SOMNIOSIDAE—SLEEPER SHARKS

Centroscymnus coelolepis . . . . Portuguese dogfish
Centroscymnus crepidater . . . . Longnose velvet dogfish
Centroscymnus cryptacanthus . . . . Shortnose velvet dogfish
Centroscymnus macracanthus . . . . Largespine velvet dogfish
Centroscymnus owstoni . . . . Roughskin velvet dogfish
Centroscymnus plunketi . . . . Plunket shark
Scymnodalatias albicauda . . . . Whitetail dogfish
Scymnodalatias garricki . . . . Azores dogfish
Scymnodalatias oligodon . . . . Sparsetooth dogfish
Scymnodalatias sherwoodi . . . . Sherwood dogfish
Scymnodon ichiharai . . . . Japanese velvet dogfish
Scymnodon ringens . . . . Knifetooth dogfish
Scymnodon squamulosus . . . . Velvet dogfish
Somniosus microcephalus . . . . Greenland sleeper shark
Somniosus pacificus . . . . Pacific sleeper shark
Somniosus rostratus . . . . Little sleeper shark

FAMILY OXYNOTIDAE—ROUGHSHARKS

Oxynotus bruniensis . . . . Prickly dogfish
Oxynotus caribbaeus . . . . Caribbean roughshark
Oxynotus centrina . . . . Angular roughshark
Oxynotus japonicus . . . . Japanese roughshark
Oxynotus paradoxus . . . . Sailfin roughshark

FAMILY DALATIIDAE—KITEFIN SHARKS

Dalatias licha . . . . Kitefin shark
Euprotomicroides zantedeschia . . . . Taillight shark
Euprotomicrus bispinatus . . . . Pygmy shark
Heteroscymnoides marleyi . . . . Longnose pygmy shark
Isistius brasiliensis . . . . Cookiecutter or cigar shark
Isistius labialis . . . . China Sea cookiecutter shark
Isistius plutodus . . . . Largetooth cookiecutter shark
Mollisquama parini . . . . Softskin dogfish
Squaliolus aliae . . . . Smalleye pygmy shark
Squaliolus laticaudus . . . . Spined pygmy shark

ORDER PRISTIOPHORIFORMES
SAWSHARKS

FAMILY PRISTIOPHORIDAE—SAWSHARKS

Pliotrema warreni . . . . Sixgill sawshark
Pristiophorus cirratus . . . . Longnose sawshark
Pristiophorus japonicus . . . . Japanese sawshark
Pristiophorus nudipinnis . . . . Shortnose sawshark
Pristiophorus schroederi . . . . Bahamas sawshark

ORDER SQUATINIFORMES
ANGELSHARKS

FAMILY SQUATINIDAE—ANGELSHARKS

Squatina aculeata . . . . Sawback angelshark
Squatina africana . . . . African angelshark
Squatina argentina . . . . Argentine angelshark
Squatina australis . . . . Australian angelshark
Squatina californica . . . . Pacific angelshark

Squatina dumeril . . . . Sand devil
Squatina formosa . . . . Taiwan angelshark
Squatina guggenheim . . . . Angular angelshark
Squatina japonica . . . . Japanese angelshark
Squatina nebulosa . . . . Clouded angelshark
Squatina occulta . . . . Hidden angelshark
Squatina oculata . . . . Smoothback angelshark
Squatina squatina . . . . Angelshark
Squatina tergocellata . . . . Ornate Angelshark
Squatina tergocellatoides . . . . Ocellated angelshark

ORDER HETERODONTIFORMES
BULLHEAD SHARKS

FAMILY HETERODONTIDAE—BULLHEAD SHARKS

Heterodontus francisci . . . . Hornshark
Heterodontus galeatus . . . . Crested bullhead shark
Heterodontus japonicus . . . . Japanese bullhead shark
Heterodontus mexicanus . . . . Mexican hornshark
Heterodontus portusjacksoni . . . . Port Jackson shark
Heterodontus quoyi . . . . Galapagos bullhead shark
Heterodontus ramalheira . . . . Whitespotted bullhead shark
Heterodontus zebra . . . . Zebra bullhead shark

ORDER ORECTOLOBIFORMES
CARPETSHARKS

FAMILY PARASCYLLIIDAE—COLLARED CARPETSHARKS

Cirrhoscyllium expolitum . . . . Barbelthroat carpetshark
Cirrhoscyllium formosanum . . . . Taiwan saddled carpetshark
Cirrhoscyllium japonicum . . . . Saddled carpetshark
Parascyllium collare . . . . Collared carpetshark
Parascyllium ferrugineum . . . . Rusty carpetshark
Parascyllium variolatum . . . . Necklace carpetshark

FAMILY BRACHAELURIDAE—BLIND SHARKS

Brachaelurus waddi . . . . Blind shark
Heteroscyllium colcloughi . . . . Bluegray carpetshark

FAMILY ORECTOLOBIDAE—WOBBEGONGS

Eucrossorhinus dasypogon . . . . Tasselled wobbegong
Orectolobus japonicus . . . . Japanese wobbegong
Orectolobus maculatus . . . . Spotted wobbegong
Orectolobus ornatus . . . . Ornate wobbegong
Orectolobus wardi . . . . Northern wobbegong
Sutorectus tentaculatus . . . . Cobbler wobbegong

FAMILY HEMISCYLLIIDAE—LONGTAILED CARPETSHARKS

Chiloscyllium arabicum . . . . Arabian carpetshark
Chiloscyllium burmensis . . . . Burmese bambooshark

Chiloscyllium griseum . . . . Gray bambooshark
Chiloscyllium hasselti . . . . Indonesian bambooshark
Chiloscyllium indicum . . . . Slender bambooshark
Chiloscyllium plagiosum . . . . Whitespotted bambooshark
Chiloscyllium punctatum . . . . Brownbanded bambooshark
Hemiscyllium freycineti . . . . Indonesian speckled carpetshark
Hemiscyllium hallstromi . . . . Papuan epaulette shark
Hemiscyllium ocellatum . . . . Epaulette shark
Hemiscyllium strahani . . . . Hooded carpetshark
Hemiscyllium trispeculare . . . . Speckled carpetshark

FAMILY GINGLYMOSTOMATIDAE—NURSE SHARKS

Pseudoginglymostoma brevicaudatum . . . . Shorttail nurse shark
Ginglymostoma cirratum . . . . Nurse shark
Nebrius ferrugineus . . . . Tawny nurse or giant sleepy shark

FAMILY STEGOSTOMATIDAE—ZEBRA SHARKS

Stegostoma fasciatum . . . . Zebra shark

FAMILY RHINCODONTIDAE—WHALE SHARKS

Rhincodon typus . . . . Whale shark

ORDER LAMNIFORMES
MACKEREL SHARKS

FAMILY ODONTASPIDIDAE—SAND TIGER SHARKS

Carcharias taurus . . . . . . Sand tiger, spotted raggedtooth or gray nurse shark
Carcharias tricuspidatus . . . . Indian sand tiger
Odontaspis ferox . . . . Smalltooth sand tiger or bumpytail raggedtooth
Odontaspis noronhai . . . . Bigeye sand tiger

FAMILY PSEUDOCARCHARIIDAE—CROCODILE SHARKS

Pseudocarcharias kamoharai . . . . Crocodile shark

FAMILY MITSUKURINIDAE—GOBLIN SHARKS

Mitsukurina owstoni . . . . Goblin shark

FAMILY MEGACHASMIDAE—MEGAMOUTH SHARKS

Megachasma pelagios . . . . Megamouth shark

FAMILY ALOPIIDAE—THRESHER SHARKS

Alopias pelagicus . . . . Pelagic thresher
Alopias superciliosus . . . . Bigeye thresher
Alopias vulpinus . . . . Thresher shark

FAMILY CETORHINIDAE—BASKING SHARKS

Cetorhinus maximus . . . . Basking shark

1. The Fox Shark. 2 The Picked Dog Fish.

FAMILY LAMNIDAE—MACKEREL SHARKS

Carcharodon carcharias . . . . Great white shark
Isurus oxyrinchus . . . . Shortfin mako
Isurus paucus . . . . Longfin mako
Lamna ditropis . . . . Salmon shark
Lamna nasus . . . . Porbeagle shark

ORDER CARCHARHINIFORME
GROUND SHARKS

FAMILY SCYLIORHINIDAE—CATSHARKS

Apristurus acanutus . . . . Flatnose catshark
Apristurus atlanticus . . . . Atlantic ghost catshark
Apristurus brunneus . . . . Brown catshark
Apristurus canutus . . . . Hoary catshark
Apristurus fedorovi . . . . Federovís catshark
Apristurus gibbosus . . . . Humpback catshark
Apristurus herklotsi . . . . Longfin catshark
Apristurus indicus . . . . Smallbelly catshark
Apristurus investigatoris . . . . Broadnose catshark
Apristurus japonicus . . . . Japanese catshark
Apristurus kampae . . . . Longnose catshark
Apristurus laurussoni . . . . Iceland catshark
Apristurus longicephalus . . . . Longhead catshark
Apristurus macrorhynchus . . . . Flathead catshark
Apristurus macrostomus . . . . Broadmouth catshark
Apristurus maderensis . . . . Madeira catshark
Apristurus manis . . . . Ghost catshark
Apristurus microps . . . . Smalleye catshark
Apristurus micropterygeus . . . . Smalldorsal catshark
Apristurus nasutus . . . . Largenose catshark
Apristurus parvipinnis . . . . Smallfin catshark
Apristurus pinguis . . . . Fat catshark
Apristurus platyrhynchus . . . . Spatulasnout catshark
Apristurus profundorum . . . . Deepwater catshark
Apristurus riveri . . . . Broadgill catshark
Apristurus saldanha . . . . Saldanha catshark
Apristurus sibogae . . . . Pale catshark
Apristurus sinensis . . . . South China catshark
Apristurus spongiceps . . . . Spongehead catshark
Apristurus stenseni . . . . Panama ghost catshark
Apristurus verweyi . . . . Borneo catshark
Asymbolus analis . . . . Gray spotted catshark
Asymbolus vincenti . . . . Gulf catshark
Atelomycterus fasciatus . . . . Banded sand catshark
Atelomycterus macleayi . . . . Australian marbled catshark
Atelomycterus marmoratus . . . . Coral catshark
Aulohalaelurus kanakorum . . . . New Caledonia catshark
Aulohalaelurus labiosus . . . . Blackspotted catshark
Bythaelurus alcocki . . . . Arabian catshark
Bythaelurus canescens . . . . Dusky catshark
Bythaelurus clevai . . . . Broadhead catshark
Bythaelurus dawsoni . . . . New Zealand catshark
Bythaelurus hispidus . . . . Bristly catshark
Bythaelurus immaculatus . . . . Spotless catshark
Bythaelurus lutarius . . . . Mud catshark
Cephaloscyllium fasciatum . . . . Reticulated swellshark
Cephaloscyllium isabellum . . . . Draughtsboard shark
Cephaloscyllium laticeps . . . . Australian swellshark
Cephaloscyllium silasi . . . . Indian swellshark
Cephaloscyllium sufflans . . . . Balloon shark
Cephaloscyllium umbratile . . . . Japanese swellshark
Cephaloscyllium ventriosum . . . . Swellshark
Cephalurus cephalus . . . . Lollipop catshark
Galeus arae . . . . Roughtail catshark
Galeus atlanticus . . . . Atlantic sawtail catshark
Galeus boardmani . . . . Australian sawtail catshark
Galeus eastmani . . . . Gecko catshark
Galeus gracilis . . . . Slender sawtail catshark
Galeus longirostris . . . . Longnose sawtail catshark
Galeus melastomus . . . . Blackmouth catshark
Galeus murinus . . . . Mouse catshark

Galeus nipponensis . . . . Broadfin sawtail catshark
Galeus piperatus . . . . Peppered catshark
Galeus polli . . . . African sawtail catshark
Galeus sauteri . . . . Blacktip sawtail catshark
Galeus schultzi . . . . Dwarf sawtail catshark
Galeus springeri . . . . Springer's catshark
Halaelurus boesemani . . . . Speckled catshark
Halaelurus buergeri . . . . Blackspotted catshark
Halaelurus lineatus . . . . Lined catshark
Halaelurus natalensis . . . . Tiger catshark
Halaelurus quagga . . . . Quagga catshark
Haploblepharus edwardsii . . . . Puffadder shyshark
Haploblepharus fuscus . . . . Brown shyshark
Haploblepharus pictus . . . . Dark shyshark
Holohalaelurus punctatus . . . . African spotted catshark
Holohalaelurus regani . . . . Izak catshark
Parmaturus campechiensis . . . . Campeche catshark
Parmaturus macmillani . . . . New Zealand filetail
Parmaturus melanobranchius . . . . Blackgill catshark
Parmaturus pilosus . . . . Salamander shark
Parmaturus xaniurus . . . . Filetail catshark
Pentanchus profundicolus . . . . Onefin catshark
Poroderma africanum . . . . Striped catshark or pyjama shark
Poroderma pantherinum . . . . Leopard catshark
Schroederichthys bivius . . . . Narrowmouth catshark
Schroederichthys chilensis . . . . Redspotted catshark
Schroederichthys maculatus . . . . Narrowtail catshark
Schroederichthys tenuis . . . . Slender catshark
Scyliorhinus besnardi . . . . Polkadot catshark
Scyliorhinus boa . . . . Boa catshark
Scyliorhinus canicula . . . . Smallspotted catshark
Scyliorhinus capensis . . . . Yellowspotted catshark
Scyliorhinus cervigoni . . . . West African catshark
Scyliorhinus comoroensis . . . . Comoro catshark
Scyliorhinus garmani . . . . Brownspotted catshark
Scyliorhinus haeckelii . . . . Freckled catshark
Scyliorhinus hesperius . . . . Whitesaddled catshark
Scyliorhinus meadi . . . . Blotched catshark
Scyliorhinus retifer . . . . Chain catshark
Scyliorhinus stellaris . . . . Nursehound
Scyliorhinus tokubee . . . . Izu catshark
Scyliorhinus torazame . . . . Cloudy catshark
Scyliorhinus torrei . . . . Dwarf catshark

FAMILY PROSCYLLIIDAE—FINBACK CATSHARKS

Ctenacis fehlmanni . . . . Harlequin catshark
Eridacnis barbouri . . . . Cuban ribbontail catshark
Eridacnis radcliffei . . . . Pygmy ribbontail catshark
Eridacnis sinuans . . . . African ribbontail catshark
Proscyllium habereri . . . . Graceful catshark

FAMILY PSEUDOTRIAKIDAE—FALSE CATSHARKS

Gollum attenuatus . . . . Slender smoothhound
Pseudotriakis microdon . . . . False catshark

FAMILY LEPTOCHARIIDAE—BARBELED HOUNDSHARKS

Leptocharias smithii . . . . Barbeled houndshark

FAMILY TRIAKIDAE—HOUNDSHARKS

Furgaleus macki . . . . Whiskery shark
Galeorhinus galeus . . . . Tope shark, soupfin, school shark or vitamin shark
Gogolia filewoodi . . . . Sailback houndshark
Hemitriakis abdita . . . . Deepwater sicklefin houndshark
Hemitriakis japanica . . . . Japanese topeshark
Hemitriakis falcata . . . . Sicklefin houndshark
Hemitriakis leucoperiptera . . . . Whitefin topeshark
Hypogaleus hyugaensis . . . . Blacktip topeshark
Iago garricki . . . . Longnose houndshark
Iago omanensis . . . . Bigeye houndshark
Mustelus antarcticus . . . . Gummy shark
Mustelus asterias . . . . Starry smoothhound
Mustelus californicus . . . . Gray smoothhound

Mustelus canis	Dusky smoothhound	
Mustelus dorsalis	Sharpnose smoothhound	
Mustelus fasciatus	Striped smoothhound	
Mustelus griseus	Spotless smoothhound	
Mustelus henlei	Brown smoothhound	
Mustelus higmani	Smalleye smoothhound	
Mustelus lenticulatus	Rig or spotted estuary smoothhound	
Mustelus lunulatus	Sicklefin smoothhound	
Mustelus manazo	Starspotted smoothhound	
Mustelus mento	Speckled smoothhound	
Mustelus minicanis	Dwarf smoothhound	
Mustelus mosis	Arabian, hardnose or Moses smoothhound	
Mustelus mustelus	Smoothhound	
Mustelus norrisi	Narrowfin or Florida smoothhound	
Mustelus palumbes	Whitespot smoothhound	
Mustelus punctulatus	Blackspot smoothhound	
Mustelus schmitti	Narrownose smoothhound	
Mustelus sinusmexicanus	Gulf smoothhound	
Mustelus whitneyi	Humpback smoothhound	
Scylliogaleus quecketti	Flapnose houndshark	
Triakis acutipinna	Sharpfin houndshark	
Triakis maculata	Spotted houndshark	
Triakis megalopterus	Spotted gully shark or sharptooth houndshark	
Triakis scyllium	Banded houndshark	
Triakis semifasciata	Leopard shark	

FAMILY HEMIGALEIDAE—WEASEL SHARKS

Chaenogaleus macrostoma	Hooktooth shark
Hemigaleus microstoma	Sicklefin weasel shark
Hemipristis elongatus	Snaggletooth shark
Paragaleus leucolomatus	Whitetip weasel shark
Paragaleus pectoralis	Atlantic weasel shark
Paragaleus randalli	Slender weasel shark
Paragaleus tengi	Straighttooth weasel shark

FAMILY CARCHARHINIDAE—REQUIEM SHARKS

Carcharhinus acronotus	Blacknose shark
Carcharhinus albimarginatus	Silvertip shark
Carcharhinus altimus	Bignose shark
Carcharhinus amblyrhynchoides	Graceful shark
Carcharhinus amblyrhynchos	Gray reef shark
Carcharhinus amboinensis	Pigeye or Java shark
Carcharhinus borneensis	Borneo shark
Carcharhinus brachyurus	Bronze whaler or copper shark
Carcharhinus brevipinna	Spinner shark
Carcharhinus cautus	Nervous shark
Carcharhinus dussumieri	Whitecheek shark
Carcharhinus falciformis	Silky shark

Carcharhinus fitzroyensis	Creek whaler
Carcharhinus galapagensis	Galapagos shark
Carcharhinus hemiodon	Pondicherry shark
Carcharhinus isodon	Finetooth shark
Carcharhinus leiodon	Smoothtooth blacktip
Carcharhinus leucas	Bull or Zambezi shark
Carcharhinus limbatus	Blacktip shark
Carcharhinus longimanus	Oceanic whitetip shark
Carcharhinus macloti	Hardnose shark
Carcharhinus melanopterus	Blacktip reef shark
Carcharhinus obscurus	Dusky shark
Carcharhinus perezi	Caribbean reef shark
Carcharhinus plumbeus	Sandbar shark
Carcharhinus porosus	Smalltail shark
Carcharhinus sealei	Blackspot shark
Carcharhinus signatus	Night shark
Carcharhinus sorrah	Spottail shark
Carcharhinus tilstoni	Australian blacktip shark
Carcharhinus wheeleri	Blacktail reef shark
Galeocerdo cuvier	Tiger shark
Glyphis gangeticus	Ganges shark
Glyphis glyphis	Speartooth shark
Isogomphodon oxyrhynchus	Daggernose shark
Lamiopsis temmincki	Broadfin shark
Loxodon macrorhinus	Sliteye shark
Nasolamia velox	Whitenose shark
Negaprion acutidens	Sharptooth lemon shark
Negaprion brevirostris	Lemon shark
Prionace glauca	Blue shark
Rhizoprionodon acutus	Milk shark
Rhizoprionodon lalandei	Brazilian sharpnose shark
Rhizoprionodon longurio	Pacific sharpnose shark
Rhizoprionodon oligolinx	Gray sharpnose shark
Rhizoprionodon porosus	Caribbean sharpnose shark
Rhizoprionodon taylori	Australian sharpnose shark
Rhizoprionodon terraenovae	Atlantic sharpnose shark
Scoliodon laticaudus	Spadenose shark
Triaenodon obesus	Whitetip reef shark

FAMILY SPHYRNIDAE—HAMMERHEAD SHARKS

Eusphyra blochii	Winghead shark
Sphyrna corona	Mallethead shark
Sphyrna lewini	Scalloped hammerhead
Sphyrna media	Scoophead shark
Sphyrna mokarran	Great hammerhead
Sphyrna tiburo	Bonnethead shark
Sphyrna tudes	Smalleye hammerhead
Sphyrna zygaena	Smooth hammerhead

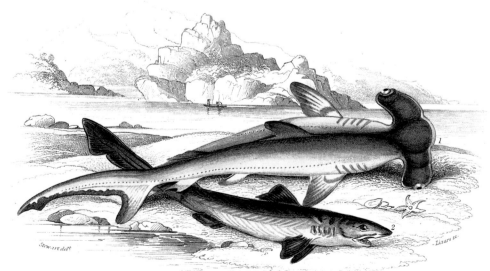

BBC Hulton Picture Library

1. The Hammer Headed Shark. 2 Common Tope.

RESOURCE GUIDE

BOOKS

Adventures in Scuba Diving: A Text for the Beginning Diver, by National Association of Underwater Instructors (NAUI) Staff (Mosby–Year Book, 1994).

Aqua Expeditions: A Global Travel Guide for the Scuba Diver and Snorkeler, by Wendy C. Church (Heathcoat Publishing, 1994).

Cousteau's Great White Shark, by Jean-Michel Cousteau and Mose Richards (Abradale Books, 1992).

FAO Species Catalogue. *Sharks of the World: An Annotated and Illustrated Catalogue of Shark Species Known to Date*, Fisheries Synopsis No. 125, Vol. 4, Pt 1 & 2, by L. J. V. Compagno (Food & Agriculture Organization of the United Nations, 1984).

Fossil Sharks of the Chesapeake Bay Region, by Bretton W. Kent (Egan Rees & Boyer, 1994).

Great White Shark, by Richard Ellis and John McCosker (Harper Collins/Stanford University Press, 1991).

Great White Sharks: The Biology of Carcharodon Carcharias, by Peter Klimley and David G. Ainley, eds (Academic Press, 1996).

Guide to the Sharks and Rays of Southern Africa, by L. J. V. Compagno, D. A. Ebert, and M. J. Smale (New Holland Publishers, London, 1989).

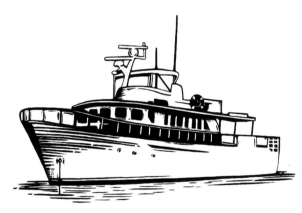

Half Mile Down, by William Beebe (Harcourt, Brace and Co., New York, 1934). Documents Beebe's early deepwater explorations of the world's oceans.

Reef Sharks & Rays of the World: A Guide to Their Identification, Behavior, and Ecology, by Scott W. Michael (Sea Challengers, Monterey, 1993). Descriptions and identifying photos of sharks and rays that dwell on the world's reefs.

Scuba Diving, by Dennis K. Graver (Human Kinetics Books, 1993).

Scuba Diving Explained: Questions and Answers on Physiology and Medical Aspects of Scuba Diving, by Lawrence Martin (Lakeside Press, 1995).

Sea Change: A Message of the Oceans, by Sylvia A. Earle (G. P. Putnam's Sons, New York, 1995).

Shadows in the Sea: The Sharks, Skates and Rays, by Harold W. McCormick, Thomas Allen, and William E. Young (Lyons & Burford, 1996).

Shark: A Photographer's Story, by Jeremy Stafford-Deitsch (Headline, London, 1987).

Shark Attack: How, Why, When and Where Sharks Attack Humans, by V. Coppleson and P. Goadby (Angus & Robertson, London, 1988). Evaluates the relative dangers and patterns of attacks by various shark species.

Shark: Endangered Predator of the Sea, by Marty Snyderman (Key Porter Book, Toronto, 1995). An exploration of sharks and their threatened world, accompanied by underwater photographer Marty Snyderman's images.

Shark! Nature's Masterpiece, by R. D. Lawrence (Chapter's Publishing, 1994). From the Curious Naturalist Series.

Sharks, by Leonard Compagno, Colin Simpfendorfer, John E. McCosker and others (Reader's Digest, 1998). Attractive and highly illustrated survey of sharks.

Sharks and Rays, edited by Leighton Taylor (Time Life, Alexandria, 1997). Well-illustrated, multi-authored book featuring an informative field guide and information about where and how to observe sharks and rays.

Sharks and Rays of Australia. by P. R. Last and J. D. Stevens (CSIRO, Australia, 1994). A reference work containing descriptions and illustrations of the shark and ray species that inhabit Australian waters.

Sharks and Rays of the Pacific Coast, by Ava Ferguson and Gregor Caillet (Monterey Bay Aquarium, 1990).

Sharks in Question—The Smithsonian Answer Book, by V. Springer and J. P. Gold (Smithsonian Institution Press, 1989).

Sharks: Myth and Reality, by Gaetano Cafiero and Maddelena Jahoda (Thomasson-Grant, 1994).

Sharks of Arabia, by John E. Randall (Immel Publishing, 1990).

Sharks of Hawaii, their Biology and Cultural Significance, by Leighton Taylor (University of Hawaii Press, 1993). A well-illustrated account of the sharks found in Hawaiian waters, including material depicting the important role that sharks played in Hawaiian religion and culture.

Sharks of the World, by R. Steel (Blanchford, London, 1992).

Sharks of Tropical and Temperate Seas, by R. H. Johnson (Gulf Publishing Co., 1995).

Sharks: Silent Hunters of the Deep, by Reader's Digest (Reader's Digest, Sydney, 1986). A brief overview of shark biology and ecology.

Sharks! The Mysterious Killers, by Discovery Editors (Crown Publishers/Random House, 1996).

The Book of Sharks, by Richard Ellis (Grosset & Dunlap, New York, 1989). A revised edition, including Richard Ellis's illustrations.

The Diver's Handbook, by Alan Mountain (New Holland, London, UK, 1996).

The Encyclopedia of Recreational Diving, by Alex Brylske, Karl Shreeves, and Harry Averill (PADI, USA, 1988). 560-page encyclopedic coverage of diving, with illustrations.

The Lady and the Sharks, by Eugenie Clark (Harper & Row, New York, 1969). Details the work of Professor Eugenie Clark, a pioneer shark researcher.

The Natural History of Sharks, by Thomas H. Lineaweaver III and Richard H. Backus (Schocken Books/Lyons & Burford, USA, 1986). An illustrated introduction.

The Scuba Diving Handbook: A Complete Guide to Salt and Fresh Water Diving, by Paul McCallum (Betterway Books, USA, 1991).

The Shark: Splendid Savage of the Sea, by Jacques-Yves Cousteau (Cassell, London, 1989).

The Sharks of North American Waters, by José I. Castro (Texas A. & M. University Press, College Station, 1983).

The Sea Around Us, by Rachel Carson (Oxford University Press, New York, 1951). A classic conservation book.

WEBSITES

American Elasmobranch Society,
   http://www.elasmo.org
   Research news from shark and ray scholars.

International Shark Attack File,
   http://www.flmnh.ufl.edu/natsci/ichthyology/shark.htm
   Information about the attack file, with a summary of worldwide attack data.

Isle of Man Basking Shark Project,
   http://www.isle-of-man.com/interests/shark/index.httm
   Details about a basking shark research project in the Irish Sea, with opportunities for volunteers.

Natal Sharks Board,
   http://goofy.iafrica.com/~carch/
   Information about South Africa's major beach-netting service and its research activities and public programs.

Mote Marine Library,
   http://www.mote.org
   Information about the research and public programs of a major center for shark research in Florida.

Project Aware (Aquatic World Awareness, Responsibility and Education),
   http://www/padi.com/
   Details of environmental and educational programs of a PADI umbrella organization, to help preserve and protect the underwater environment.

Shark Links Galore,
   http://www.oceanstar.com/shark/links.htm
   A comprehensive and frequently updated listing of many websites on sharks, including research, public displays and diving tours.

Sonny Gruber,
   http://www.wattcom.com/sharks/
   Information and shark research updates.

US State Department Travel Warnings and Consular Information Sheets,
   http://www.stolaf.edu/network/travel-advisories.html
   Information about medical and political security matters.

VIDEO CASSETTES AND CD–ROMs

Great White!, Discovery Channel, 1992. The great white shark filmed in four oceans around the world.

Great White Shark, BBC/ National Geographic, 1995.

Jaws, the True Story, BBC/Nova, 1984.

Ocean Planet, CD–ROM, Discovery Channel, 1995. Explores the world's oceans, aquatic life, and issues related to ecological balance.

Shark Attack Files, Discovery Channel, 1994. Scientists, conservationists, and shark hunters look at shark attacks.

The Ultimate Guide to Sharks, Discovery Channel, 1996. Examines the most dangerous sharks and their killing cycles.

AQUARIUMS, MUSEUMS AND UNIVERSITIES

The following institutions hold excellent study collections or exhibits of sharks:

Africa Marine World USA, Vallejo, California, USA

Aquarium of the Americas, New Orleans, Louisiana, USA

Australian Museum, Sydney, Australia

Bernice P. Bishop Museum, Honolulu, Hawaii, USA

California Academy of Sciences, San Francisco, California, USA

Living Seas Exhibit, Disneyworld, Florida, USA

Monterey Bay Aquarium, California, USA

National Aquarium, Baltimore, Maryland, USA

Okinawa Expo Aquarium, Okinawa, Japan

Osaka Aquarium, Osaka, Japan

Point Defiance Zoo and Aquarium, Tacoma, Washington, USA

Scripps Institution of Oceanography, University of California, San Diego, California, USA

Sea World, Florida, USA

Sea World, San Diego, California, USA

Smithsonian Museum of Natural History, Washington, DC, USA

South African Museum, Cape Town, South Africa

Waikiki Aquarium, Hawaii, USA

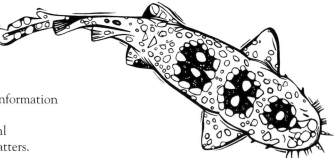

INDEX

ACKNOWLEDGMENTS

The extract from Peter Benchley's Jaws is reproduced by permission of Doubleday & Company Inc. and International Creative Management; the extract from Ernest Hemingway's The Old Man and the Sea is reproduced by permission of Jonathan Cape. The extract from Art of the Pacific (Brake, McNeish and Simmonds) is reproduced by permission of Oxford University Press.

The following publications have been cited in the summary of shark attack records in the Pacific on page 158.

Bagnis, R. 1968. A propos de 10 cas de blessures par requins chez des pêcheurs sousmarins en Polynésie Française. Médecine Tropicale 28, 3, 368–73.
Balazs, G. and Kam, A. 1981. A review of shark attacks in the Hawaiian Islands. Elepaio 41, 10, 97–106.
Baldridge, H.D. 1973. Shark Attack Against Man. Mote Marine Laboratory, Sarasota, Florida.
Cook, C. 1985. Shark "wipes out" surfers at Pakala. Garden Isle (Kaui) 27 May.
Fellows, D.P. and Murchison, A.E. 1967. A non-injurious attack by a small shark. Pacific Science 21, 1, 150–51.
Fouques, M. and others. 1972. Traumatismes et blessures par les poissons en Polynésie Française. La nouvelle Presse Médicale 1, 47, 3175–9.
Jones, R.S. 1971. Two nonfatal shark attacks in the Truk district, eastern Caroline islands. Micronesia 7, 230–3.

Lagraulet, J. and others. 1972. Les morsures par requins en Polynésie Française (à propos de 14 cas). Bulletin de la Société de Pathologie Exotique 4, 592–605
Lipman, V. 1983. When shark meets man. Honolulu Magazine April, 58–94.
Randall, J.E. 1977. Contribution to the biology of the whitetip reef shark (Triaenodon obesus). Pacific Science 27, 3, 226–38.
Read, K.R.H. 1971. Nonfatal shark attack, Palau Islands. Micronesia 7, 233–4.
Schulz, L.P. and Malin, M.H. 1963. A list of shark attacks for the world. In:P.W. Gilbert (ed). Sharks and Survival, D.C. Heath & Co, Boston.
Schweitzer, D. 1982. Shark attack defense. Wind Surf Magazine, November, 71.

Illustrations are by Martin Camm: 38, 46; Chris Forsey: 60–61; Ray Grinaway: 20 (all shark illustrations), 21, 22 b, 23, 24 t, 25 t, 26 (c and b), 27, 28 b, 32 (t and b), 33 (t and c), 35 (tl and tr) 41 (tl, tr, cl, cr, br), 87, 128(ac, bc and b), 136 bl, 150 c, 151 bc, 159 c, 165 c, 213, 225; Gino Hasler: 26, 49, 50, 77, 81, 83, 85, 99, 206; Frank Knight: 15, 55; Kylie Mulquin: 20 (chart only), 122;Tony Pyrzakowski: 22 (t and c), 24 b, 25 b, 26 tl, 28 t, 29, 30, 31 c, 32 c, 33 b, 34, 35 (bl and br), 128 t, 129, 133, 142, 150 t, 165 (t, ac, bc, b); Ngaire Sales: 41 bl; Genevieve Wallace: 234–235

Maps are by Greg Campbell: 62, 63, 67, 70, 71, 72, 73 and Lorenzo Lucia: 106–107, 109–111, 113, 114, 117–118, 127, 147, 148, 152.

Graphic layout by CAT efx, Sydney, Australia